The end of Irish history?

Critical reflections on the Celtic Tiger

edited by Colin Coulter
and Steve Coleman

Manchester University Press
Manchester and New York

distributed exclusively in the USA by Palgrave

Published by Manchester University Press
Oxford Road, Manchester M13 9NR, UK
and Room 400, 175 Fifth Avenue, New York, NY 10010, USA
www.manchesteruniversitypress.co.uk

Distributed exclusively in the USA by
Palgrave, 175 Fifth Avenue, New York,
NY 10010, USA

Distributed exclusively in Canada by
UBC Press, University of British Columbia, 2029 West Mall,
Vancouver, BC, Canada V6T 1Z2

British Library Cataloguing-in-Publication Data
A catalogue record for this book is available from the British Library

Library of Congress Cataloging-in-Publication Data applied for

ISBN   0 7190 6230 6   *hardback*
       0 7190 6231 4   *paperback*

First published 2003

11 10 09 08 07 06 05 04 03   10 9 8 7 6 5 4 3 2 1

Typeset by Ralph J. Footring, Derby

Printed in Great Britain
by Biddles Ltd, Guildford and King's Lynn

This book is dedicated
to the memory of
Joe Strummer, 1952–2002
With love and admiration
and endless gratitude

Contents

List of tables and figures   *page* ix
Notes on contributors   x
Acknowledgements   xii

1 The end of Irish history? An introduction to the book   1
   Colin Coulter

2 Macroeconomic policy in the Celtic Tiger:
   a critical reassessment   34
   Denis O'Hearn

3 Neither Boston nor Berlin: class polarisation and
   neo-liberalism in the Irish Republic   56
   Kieran Allen

4 Welcome to the Celtic Tiger: racism, immigration
   and the state   74
   Steve Loyal

5 Irish women and the Celtic Tiger economy   95
   Sinéad Kennedy

6 Globalised Ireland, or, contemporary transformations
   of national identity?   110
   G. Honor Fagan

7 Millenarianism and utopianism in the new Ireland:
   the tragedy (and comedy) of accelerated modernisation   122
   Kieran Keohane and Carmen Kuhling

8 Fear and loathing in lost ages: journeys through
   postmodern Dublin   139
   David Slattery

9   Contemporary discourses of working, earning and spending:
    acceptance, critique and the bigger picture   155
    Anne B. Ryan

10 The centralised government of liquidity: community,
    language and culture under the Celtic Tiger   175
    Steve Coleman

11 Northern Ireland: a reminder from the present   192
    Pete Shirlow

    Index   208

List of tables and figures

Tables

2.1 Percentage real economic growth rates in the 1990s in the Republic of Ireland   36
2.2 Fixed industrial investments in the Republic of Ireland, by country of origin, 1990–98   39
2.3 Employment and percentage employment change during the 1990s   42
2.4 Changing composition of GDP during the Celtic Tiger period 46
3.1 Declining economic dynamism: average annual percentage change in gross domestic product   63
3.2 Adjusted wage share of the total economy in Ireland and the EU   67
11.1 Community attitudes to peace building and reconciliation, 1999 and 2002   203

Figure

4.1 Annual numbers of asylum applications in Ireland, 1992–2001   77

Notes on contributors

Kieran Allen lectures in the Department of Sociology, University College Dublin. His most recent book is *The Celtic Tiger: The Myth of Social Partnership in Ireland* (Manchester: Manchester University Press, 2000).

Steve Coleman lectures in the Department of Anthropology, the National University of Ireland, Maynooth. He is an associate of the Humanities Institute of Ireland. At present he is working on a book about the Irish language and culture.

Colin Coulter lectures in the Department of Sociology, the National University of Ireland, Maynooth. He is the author of *Contemporary Northern Irish Society: An Introduction* (London: Pluto, 1999).

G. Honor Fagan lectures in the Department of Sociology, the National University of Ireland, Maynooth. She is the author of *Cultural Politics and Irish Early School Leavers: Constructing Political Identities* (Westport, CT: Bergin and Garvey, 1995) and is presently working on a book on culture and globalisation.

Sinéad Kennedy is a doctoral student in the Department of English, the National University of Ireland, Maynooth. She is working on a forthcoming book dealing with the issue of abortion in Ireland.

Kieran Keohane lectures in the Department of Sociology, University College Cork. He is the author of *Symptoms of Canada: An Essay on the Canadian Identity* (Toronto: University of Toronto Press, 1997) and has written on environmentalism and popular culture in an Irish context.

Carmen Kuhling lectures in the Department of Government and Society, University of Limerick. She has written a number of articles on the New

Age movement in Ireland and is the co-author of a forthcoming book on the 'collision culture' in contemporary Ireland.

Steve Loyal lectures in the Department of Sociology, University College Dublin. He is the author of a forthcoming book on the social theory of Anthony Giddens.

Denis O'Hearn lectures at the School of Sociology and Social Policy at Queen's University, Belfast. He is the author of a number of books, including *Inside the Celtic Tiger: The Irish Economy and the Asian Model* (London: Pluto, 1998). His latest book, *The Atlantic Economy: Britain, the US and Ireland* (Manchester: Manchester University Press, 2002) won the American Sociological Association's PEWS award for outstanding book in 2002.

Anne B. Ryan is a researcher based at the Department of Adult and Community Education, the National University of Ireland, Maynooth. She is the author of *Feminist Ways of Knowing: Towards Theorising the Person for Radical Adult Education* (Leicester: National Institute of Adult and Continuing Education, 2001) and *Balancing Your Life: A Practical Guide to Work, Time, Money and Happiness* (Dublin: Liffey Press, 2002).

Pete Shirlow lectures in the Department of Geography, the University of Ulster at Coleraine. He has written widely on issues of identity and division within Northern Ireland and is the co-editor of *Who Are 'the People'? Unionism, Protestantism and Loyalism in Northern Ireland* (London: Pluto, 1997).

David Slattery is Dean of Arts at Dublin Business School. His recent publications include 'Paradigms of British social anthropology', in *European Paradigms of the Humanities*, edited by Thomas Keutner (Hagen: Fernuniversity, 2000). His books include *The End of the Anthropological Self: Foucault in the Trobriand Islands* (Poznan: Adam Mickiewicz University Press, 1993).

Acknowledgements

We would like to express our gratitude to everyone at Manchester University Press for their assistance in the production of this book. In particular, we would like to thank Tony Mason for his commitment and patience. We are grateful to Andy Storey for his invaluable assistance. Apologies to the countless individuals who were neglected while the book was being completed.

The authors wish to acknowledge the generous support of the National University of Ireland in the form of a Grant in Aid of Publication.

1

The end of Irish history?
An introduction to the book

COLIN COULTER

During the Easter vacation of 2001, I happened to be travelling through the United States and picked up a copy of a renowned popular music magazine to pass the time on a short internal flight. While leafing through the publication, I stumbled across a feature that struck me as having no little cultural significance. It was a single-frame, full-page advertisement for some commodity or other set in a stylish contemporary bathroom that could have been located in more or less any major city in the western world. The central focus of the feature in question falls upon a young attractive heterosexual couple dressed solely in bath towels and caught in what might perhaps be best described as an implausibly gymnastic pre-coital clinch. The woman who appears in the frame seems blissfully unaware of the presence of the camera as she longingly addresses her partner. He does not, however, return her gaze. Rather, the reflection in the bathroom mirror shows the male subject looking squarely into the eye of the reader/viewer. Eyebrows arched suggestively beneath a fulsome mane of fashionably spiked hair, his expression is that of a sublime sexual self-confidence that demands our prurient admiration.

The general tone and form of the promotion outlined above could scarcely, of course, be considered innovative or daring. Sexual images and innuendo have, after all, become so commonplace in contemporary advertising that they often fail to register in any meaningful way with the audience. The advertisement under examination here does, however, contain one remarkable detail that makes it distinctly worthy of our attention. The young man, who is in effect the central figure of the promotion, almost inevitably exhibits an appetite for the current vogue of elaborate body art. Across his broad back there appears an enormous tattoo that comprises a single word mapped out in a decidedly baroque and ersatz version of traditional Celtic script. The text that the young suitor has chosen to bear offers a simple but unmistakable declaration of his pride in being 'Irish'.

1

The ethnic designation of our amorous hero ensures that a simple advertisement that might otherwise be considered entirely unworthy of comment actually comes to exercise a distinct cultural resonance. That the attractive swain who appears in the promotion should happen – or perhaps even aspire – to be Irish might perhaps be considered as emblematic of a rather broader and more profound change in the meaning(s) of that particular term. In historical terms, the dominant constructions of 'Irishness' have, of course, been distinctly uncomplimentary. Traditionally, the Irish have been regarded – not least in the circles of imperial authority – as feckless, inebriated and violent. Elements of these deeply unflattering representations of Irishness have persisted into the present day. It comes as little surprise when watching *The Simpsons* – to take a fairly innocuous example – that we discover that the amiably boorish drunk Barney Gumble hails from Irish stock.

In recent times, however, the essentially racist stereotypes through which Irish people have conventionally been regarded have been increasingly challenged and even displaced perhaps by a sequence of rather more complimentary perspectives. The specific advertisement sketched earlier might be read as illustrative of this rather wider and more critical shift in cultural meaning. In the single frame of the promotion, the term 'Irish' comes to assume solely positive connotations. To be Irish is to be young, fun, fashionable and, above all perhaps, belligerently sexual. Irishness has, in other words, become shorthand for 'cool'.

The brazen tattoo etched across the shoulder blades of one particular male model selected by a single advertising agency might be taken, then, as suggestive of a radical recent transformation of the manner in which Irishness is perceived, signified and imagined. Over the last decade or so, it has become commonplace for cultural commentators to pronounce that it has never been more fashionable to be Irish. There is certainly no shortage of evidence that could be used to bear out this particular estimation. In the last few years, numerous filmmakers, artists, actors and musicians from the Republic of Ireland have secured commercial success and even critical acclaim abroad. The phenomenal popularity of *Riverdance* has, moreover, encouraged the view that versions of traditional Irish culture – albeit highly hybridised ones – have the potential to reach a global audience.

The burgeoning cultural appeal of the Irish Republic has been underlined further by the changing fortunes of the national capital. If we were to go back fifteen years or so, the reputation that Dublin held among foreigners was essentially that of a fairly drab and unsophisticated place. In the course the 1990s, the image of the city would, however, be transformed almost beyond recognition. Consequently, the view that outsiders have of Dublin today is invariably that of a thriving and cosmopolitan place to visit. The decision of the Music Television (MTV) Corporation to host its prestigious European awards in the city in the winter of 1999 suggested that Dublin has possibly become one of that select band of urban centres that constitutes the principal network for the circulation of cultural capital.

The impressive cultural revival that has overtaken the Irish Republic over the last decade has, of course, fed off and into an even more remarkable turnaround in the economic fortunes of the state. In the late 1980s, the twenty-six counties were mired in an economic depression from which there appeared no possibility of escape. When political commentators at the time posed the question of whether the Republic of Ireland could be considered a 'third world country', they did so with no discernible trace of irony.[1] In terms of all the principal indices of economic performance, southern Ireland lagged disastrously far behind most of the other member states of the European Union (EU).[2] The return of mass unemployment ensured that the annual haemorrhage of young people emigrating in pursuit of a better life elsewhere reached levels that had not been seen since the dark days of the 1950s. The national debt per capita was for a time greater than that of any other state on the face of the planet.

When viewed against this singularly miserable backdrop, the subsequent economic performance of the Irish Republic seems almost incomprehensible. Throughout the 1990s, it registered levels of economic growth that soon became the envy of every other western state. Over the decade as a whole, gross domestic product (GDP) per capita grew on average by seven per cent each year. In 1996, an important psychological barrier was breached when the economy of the twenty-six counties overtook that of the United Kingdom for the first time ever. In the following year, GDP per capita in the Irish Republic was recorded as being larger than that of the EU average. The unprecedented and unanticipated performance of the economy was inevitably greeted with delight within the twenty-six counties. In the words of one influential historian, the recent change in economic fortune marked the transformation of the Irish Republic from the status of a 'carthorse' to that of a 'thoroughbred'.[3]

As the evidence of a nascent economic boom began to accumulate in the mid-1990s, numerous analysts sought to characterise the nature of the changes underway. While various terms were coined to capture the transformation of the southern Irish economy, there was, of course, one that would become indelibly inscribed upon the process and the period. In the summer of 1994, Kevin Gardiner of the Morgan Stanley investment bank in London sought to draw a comparison between the performance of the Irish Republic and that of the 'tiger' economies of south-east Asia.[4] The resemblance was sufficiently close, Gardiner suggested, to justify the description of the twenty-six counties as the 'Celtic Tiger'. Rarely can a metaphor spun by a financial analyst have had such a dramatic impact upon popular discourse. In the years since it was invented, the term 'Celtic Tiger' has become a common feature of every-day speech in the Irish Republic. Indeed, the phrase has been issued with such regularity that it has become a bane for a great many Irish people. This understandable irritation has done little, however, to diminish the ubiquity or authority of the metaphor.

Originally, then, the phrase 'Celtic Tiger' was turned in order to capture the newfound dynamism of the southern Irish economy. It would not be long, however, before the metaphor would slip its moorings and begin to move through a range of other debates on the nature of culture and politics within the twenty-six counties. In a remarkably short space of time, the notion of the 'Celtic Tiger' would come to operate as a widely recognised and understood master signifier for a very particular and essentially hegemonic reading of the nature of contemporary Irish society. The precise substance of this ideological programme will be examined in detail later in this chapter. In part, the ideas and concerns that circulate within the figure of the Celtic Tiger articulate the interests and experiences of certain sections of southern Irish society. The distinctive ideological enterprise that has come to hold sway within the twenty-six counties in recent times also draws upon a set of perspectives that are rather more universal. In particular, the readings of southern Irish society that are encoded within the conceit of the Celtic Tiger clearly draw from specific understandings of 'the modern' that have enjoyed a renaissance over the last dozen years or so. It is to these distinctive constructions of modernity that we turn our attention next.

The new world order of things

The decades that immediately followed the Second World War offered witness to a fierce and prolonged ideological contest as to which path of development humanity should follow. During the Cold War, the presumed political interests and inclinations of western societies were articulated in part by a diverse band of social scientists whose work is conventionally designated under the umbrella term of 'modernisation theory'.[5] The writings of modernisation theorists evidently plundered the concerns and terms of certain strands of classical social theory and reworked them to suit and serve the particular ideological climate of the times. At the heart of their outlook was a distinctive and specific under-standing of the nature of the good or 'modern' society. Modernisation theorists insisted that the mode of social organisation to which all peoples should aspire was that of the liberal democracies of the west. The specific society identified and celebrated as the acme of modernity was inevitably that of the United States. The tenets of modernisation theory held that the social forms characteristic of western states were not merely desirable but attainable. Every society could, in principle, follow the path towards liberal democracy and mass consumption that had been pioneered by the United States and its allies.

The quest for modernity would, however, place enormous demands upon societies regarded as existing at a rather more primitive stage of development. Modernisation would inevitably entail the installation of those institutions and processes deemed conducive to capitalist accumulation. In particular, existing forms of social interaction and regulation would have to be replaced with those of the free market. The drive to modernity would require not only systematic structural reform but radical cultural change as well. Modernisation theorists contested that if underdeveloped states were ever to evolve to the level of the west, they would have to dispense with customary ways of thinking and being. In more specific terms, people living in these societies would have to nurture those narrowly rational approaches to work and consumption that one figure within the modernisation school famously characterised as the 'need to achieve'.[6] The acquisition of these instrumentalist and entrepreneurial dispositions was deemed essential if the poorer nations of the world were to access the path to development that western societies had followed much earlier. At some stage in this particular journey, there would come a fundamental moment of rupture when underdeveloped states would finally free themselves of the burdens of tradition and take their place in the exalted company of the genuinely 'modern'.

In the quarter century or so that followed the Second World War, the modernisation school enjoyed considerable currency and influence. Various modernisation theorists were, of course, intimately and personally connected to the conduct of US foreign policy during this period. In the late 1960s, however, the previously hegemonic status of modernisation theory began to wane. In part this was due to the growing body of withering critiques advanced by radical writers operating out of the dependency school. The decline in the fortunes of the modernisation theorists probably owed a great deal more, though, to certain events in a 'real world' that they had helped to shape. The assertion that the free market was an innately rational mechanism that promised ultimately to bestow affluence upon all seemed risible as global capitalism slumped from one crisis to another. Equally, the conviction that the United States was essentially a force for progress in the world seemed rather less than persuasive as the US military visited mass slaughter on Vietnam and its neighbours.

The seemingly terminal demise of the modernisation approach coincided with a significant change in intellectual fashion in the west. The 1970s marked the genesis of certain postmodern forms of thought that would gradually come to exercise enormous influence within western academies.[7] The postmodernist perspective insists that the universalist discourse that defines various other prominent philosophical traditions

renders them inherently objectionable. Those 'grand narratives' that promise
a faithful and total understanding of the world in fact offer only a partial
and distorted version of it that ultimately serves the interests of power.
As the popularity of postmodernism grew throughout the 1980s, the
classical bourgeois ideals of the modernisation theorists appeared out of
date. The notion of a philosophical programme with an absolute vision
of how the social world could – and should – operate struck many people
as not only implausible but thoroughly reactionary as well.

Regarded against this backdrop, the subsequent turn in the course of
intellectual affairs might be considered especially surprising. Over the
last dozen years or so, there has been a remarkable revival of versions of
social theory concerned to examine and ultimately celebrate the nature
of 'modernity'. While contemporary readings of 'the modern' assume a
range of guises, there are two that are relevant to our purposes and will
therefore be considered at length.

The first of these finds its clearest expression, perhaps, in the hugely
influential writings of the political scientist Francis Fukuyama. In a famous
polemic published in the summer of 1989, Fukuyama appeared to foretell the imminent demise of the Soviet Union.[8] The central premise of his
argument was that the particular form of modernity that was actualised
in the west had proved itself superior to any other mode of social organisation. While the institutions of liberal democracy had offered western
citizens optimal security and freedom, the operation of the capitalist free
market had proved able to sate their desires as consumers. The ideological victory of liberal capitalism – Fukuyama insisted – ensured that
the future course of human development was essentially preordained. In
order to progress, people living outside the west would simply have to
mimic that particular version of modernity at work in the United States
and countries like it.

What is often overlooked is that Fukuyama explicitly acknowledges
that the process of modernisation will inevitably entail losses and reversals.[9]
In common with many other commentators on the subject, Fukuyama
notes that the transition to modernity entails the displacement of feeling
by calculation. Living in the modern world involves its own particular
sadness. Fukuyama also observes that there are a great many people
who will seek to frustrate and reverse the drift towards modernity. In a
recent reiteration of his views, for instance, he explains the slaughter in
the United States on 11 September 2001 in precisely these terms.[10] All
such attempts to stem the tide of the modernity will ultimately, however,
amount to nothing. In the absence of any meaningful alternative, there
is no option other than to embrace the free market and the liberal democratic state. While the paths that individual societies will follow may
differ, we all face essentially the same destination. We are therefore –
Fukuyama famously declares – living at 'the end of history'.

The second recent approach to the notion of modernity that we shall consider is the one that appears in the writings of the eminent sociologist Anthony Giddens over the last dozen years or so. An axiom of Giddens' recent work is that there is a need to accept the reality that capitalism represents the form of social organisation under which we will live for the foreseeable future.[11] In the absence of any meaningful alternative – he asserts – the concern of those who regard themselves as progressive must be to ameliorate some of the more harmful ways in which capitalist practice affects people and their environment. The political strategy that Giddens seeks to construct is essentially that of a revived social democracy. The policies to which he lends his name are intended to wed the presumed dynamism of capital to the supposed benevolence of civil society and the state.[12] It is this particular desire to reconcile the private and the public, apparently in the interests of all, that underlies the politics of the 'third way'.

Although he is willing to acknowledge its failings, it becomes readily apparent that Giddens regards capitalism as having rather more strengths than weaknesses.[13] In his recent writings, the various ways in which forms of capitalist practice operate to connect people who live large distances apart – what is often termed 'globalisation' – are depicted as essentially benign. In particular, Giddens tends to praise the ability and tendency of advances in communications to emancipate social actors from the physical and cultural settings in which they reside.[14] The speed and scope of recent developments in global capitalism are sufficient to persuade Giddens to contend that we have entered a new era, which he chooses to term 'late modernity'. The essential attribute of the late modern age is held to be 'biographical autonomy'.[15] Individuals are no longer constrained by those traditional forms of identity that arise out of the likes of nation, religion or class. Rather than adhere to the dictates of custom, social actors are increasingly willing and able to assemble their own biographies out of the manifold resources of everyday life. In the eyes of Anthony Giddens, then, the principal subject of late modernity is the reflexive individual constantly revising and reinventing her notion of herself throughout the entire course of her life.

The two distinctive conceptions of modernity circulating within contemporary public discourse that we have examined here would appear – at least at first glance – to be radically different. In his ruminations, Francis Fukuyama emerges as the principal heir to the classical tradition of modernisation theory. The metaphor of the 'end of history' entails the most unabashed declaration imaginable of the superiority of the values and institutions of western bourgeois society. The radical prescriptions that Fukuyama has advanced have, of course, proved profoundly persuasive to those agencies and individuals that exercise power at a global level. Since the fall of the Berlin Wall, the world has been radically reconfigured upon the presumption that the operation of the free market will ultimately confer universal benefit. The devastating reforms imposed upon large swathes of the planet have been guided by the imperative that goods, services and finance – but not people – should be allowed to flow freely across international boundaries.

At first glance, the disposition of Anthony Giddens would seem to have little in common with the neo-liberal intellectual tradition recently revived in the writings of Francis Fukuyama. The vision of the good society that Giddens seeks to advance is, after all, one in which capital is not given free rein but rather is harnessed in the interests of a rather broader public good. The philosophical inclinations that animate Giddens, moreover, are not those of the original modernisation theorists but rather those of the classical social theorists, whom the former sought to appropriate in often highly questionable ways. The reflexive social agency that he identifies and admires as the hallmark of our times, for instance, has clear echoes of the 'ethic of responsibility' that Max Weber proposed as a counterweight to the dislocations of modernity.[16]

While the disposition of Anthony Giddens may initially appear radically different from that of the modernisation school, the shared source of certain of their philosophical suppositions suggests that they may have rather more in common than might first meet the eye. A series of moments of convergence may be identified here. First, it would appear that Giddens broadly shares with the neo-liberals a belief in the essential benevolence of capital. While he issues demands for greater regulation by national and global institutions, it is particularly evident in his most recent writings that Giddens regards capital as being overwhelmingly a force for good in the world. Second, the particular values and practices that Giddens highlights as admirable and desirable in the late modern age would draw few quibbles from orthodox modernisation theorists. While the tone and scope of his discourse are singularly global, it quickly becomes apparent that Giddens' understanding of how the world works – or rather of how the world *should* work – is premised upon the actions and interests of a rather small section of western society. What runs through the recent social theory of Anthony Giddens is a clear presumption – one that is mirrored in classical modernisation theory – that things would be very much better if only the rest of the planet could bring themselves to behave in a manner similar to people like himself. Third, the course of social development that Giddens charts and envisages entails a radical moment of departure. In his examination of the late modern age, Giddens insists that social actors have come increasingly to discard the strictures of custom in order to assemble their own understandings of themselves as individuals. At the heart of the supposedly sophisticated and contemporary theoretical reflections of Anthony Giddens, then, is that crude distinction between the 'traditional' and the 'modern' that was originally at the height of intellectual fashion during the Cold War.

The multiple resemblances that obtain between the outlook of Anthony Giddens and that of more orthodox modernisation theorists allude to the existence of substantial common ground between social democracy and neo-liberalism. The complementary nature of these allegedly antagonistic doctrines becomes apparent when we turn to examine the specific political programmes to which they have given rise in practice. The course that New Labour has pursued since assuming office in the United Kingdom offers an especially telling illustration of the processes and interests with which we are concerned. It is often remarked that Anthony Giddens has exercised a palpable influence upon the outlook and conduct of Tony Blair. Indeed, the terms and concerns that embroider the discourse of the British Prime Minister are evidently those that arise out of 'third way' politics.[17] One of the principal areas in which New Labour has sought to implement this particular ideological agenda is the provision of public services. Since coming to office, Blair has attempted to establish the conditions under which the likes of health and education would be financed jointly by government and business. In principle, the Private Finance Initiative is conceived as an admirable social democratic measure that promises to enhance a range of public and private interests. Those who support the scheme contend that it promises both improved services to every citizen and legitimate opportunities for profit to enterprising corporations. In practice, however, the benefits of the third way marriage of capital and the state have been rather less than universal.

In his remarkable book *Captive State*, George Monbiot[18] illustrates the various ways in which New Labour has employed the language and forms of social democracy to serve and advance a narrow range of corporate interests. The various case studies that Monbiot presents reveal that the Private Finance Initiative has had the perverse effect of increasing public expenditure while at the same time reducing standards of public provision. Hospitals that have been built under the scheme have cost vastly more than it would have taken to refurbish existing facilities. Health workers employed in privately funded institutions face low wages and little security, and the patients whom they tend have to wait longer for a poorer standard of treatment.[19] While the wedding of the public and the private in the provision of essential services may have done little to enhance the lives of ordinary people in the United Kingdom, it has done a great deal to improve the balance sheets of a range of large corporations. It is hardly surprising, then, that Monbiot feels compelled to conclude that the formal social democratic rhetoric of the 'third way' is simply a convenient ruse that facilitates and conceals the transfer of resources from the poor to the wealthy.[20]

The specific forms of political practice that are chronicled between the covers of *Captive State* suggest that we need to adopt a more critical stance than is often the case when approaching the rather more abstract affairs that define the sphere of human ideas. The two distinctive understandings of modernity that we have examined here would appear to advocate starkly different political agendas. In the more significant realm of actual social practice, however, it soon becomes apparent that these seemingly divergent readings of 'the modern' frequently give rise to remarkably similar ideological enterprises. Social democrats may well be sincere in their belief that they inhabit a late modern age in which a historic dialogue and compromise between the private and public is possible. It remains the case, though, that the language and logic of social democracy are engaged with numbing regularity to produce outcomes that are as conducive to the interests of capital as even the most ardent neo-liberal could wish for.

Hagiographies of the Celtic Tiger

The period since the demise of Stalinism has, therefore, seen the rise of two rather different – though perhaps ultimately compatible – conceptions of 'modernity'. The distinctive understandings of the nature of 'the modern' – of the identity of the good society – that Fukuyama and Giddens have sought to advance have had an important bearing upon the manner in which the recent transformation of the Irish Republic has been interpreted. This is not to suggest, of course, that notions of the 'end of history' or the 'late modern age' have become pervasive elements of public debate or indeed everyday speech within the twenty-six counties. The channels that connect ideological production and popular discourse are invariably rather less direct and rather more subtle than that. It remains reasonable, nonetheless, to suggest that the distinctions, ambitions and prognoses that arise out of the constructions of modernity scrutinised above have been strongly echoed in the pronouncements of those who have thus far been considered to have provided the most persuasive accounts of the radical changes that have overtaken the twenty-six counties in the last generation.[21] It is these orthodox explanations of the 'Celtic Tiger' that we shall consider next.

The voices that have dominated public debate upon the nature of the seismic social changes that have overtaken the Irish Republic over the last decade have been overwhelmingly positive. In the main, social commentators have traced the origins of the 'Celtic Tiger' to developments within rather than without the twenty-six counties. The dramatic progress assumed to have been made during the 1990s has typically been attributed to a series of astute policy decisions implemented in earlier decades.[22] In most orthodox accounts, the move towards fiscal prudence in the late 1980s is considered to have been essential in creating the conditions for the possibility of an economic boom. The enormous cuts in public expenditure that marked this period are held to have established a desirable, stable macroeconomic environment that, in time, induced investment by some of the largest and most dynamic multinational corporations in the world. The introduction of formally free schooling in the late 1960s is also often identified as a measure that would ultimately serve to alter the economic fortunes of the Irish Republic.[23] It has become a common assertion within certain influential strands of public commentary that multinational capital would not have been drawn to the twenty-six counties were it not for the existence of an especially highly educated workforce.

While conventional interpretations highlight a range of policies as having nurtured the Celtic Tiger, there is one in particular that is considered to have been absolutely crucial to the revival of the southern Irish economy. In principle, the recent books written by Paul Sweeney,[24] on the one hand, and Ray MacSharry and Padraic White,[25] on the other, articulate viewpoints drawn from radically different points of the ideological spectrum. The analyses that are advanced within the texts transpire, however, to be remarkably similar. An argument that features prominently in both insists that the apparent economic progress of the 1990s would have been simply impossible had it not been for the institution of neo-corporatist social relations in the previous decade. In 1987, the first of a series of 'social partnership' agreements was signed, principally between the Irish government and the representatives of organised labour. At a superficial level, at least, the advent of the scheme appeared to mark the dawning of a more harmonious era in labour relations. In return for placing limits on wage demands, the trade unions were offered certain assurances about the future conduct of government policy. The many prominent admirers of social partnership contend that it is the development that, more than any other, secured the recent economic prosperity of the twenty-six counties. It is held that the voluntary restraints that have been placed upon wages have been essential in creating the conditions that have allowed indigenous and foreign businesses to flourish. In the eyes of MacSharry and White,[26] for instance, the significance of social partnership is so great that it should be acknowledged as the 'crowning achievement' of the Celtic Tiger era.

The interpretations of the boom that have exercised perhaps greatest influence over the popular imagination suggest that the turnaround in the economic performance of the Irish Republic hinged upon not only the allegedly 'daring' measures adopted at senior levels of the state but also a wider shift in the values and practices of the population as a whole. The dynamic between structure and culture considered to have driven the Celtic Tiger is regarded as having found expression in the guise of social partnership.[27] In the minds of its advocates, the new social relations of corporatism entail not merely a series of legally recognised agreements and agencies but also a distinctive network of moral values. The era of social partnership has attended a great deal of cultural change within the Republic of Ireland. In order to negotiate the rather more demanding environs of the 1990s, many people in the twenty-six counties were compelled to dispense with customary ways of being and acting and to adopt more flexible and energetic approaches to life and work. The orthodox reading of the period suggests that the Irish people have proved to be more than equal to the challenges that modernisation has offered. The formally leftist commentator Paul Sweeney, for instance, has spoken with evident pride of the ability of employees in the Irish Republic to adapt to the new demands made upon them within the branch plants of multinational corporations. Irish employees have – he argues – not merely survived the new regime of more flexible working practices but actually flourished under it.[28]

The orthodox reading suggests, then, that the modernisation of the twenty-six counties has demanded and articulated important changes in the ways in which Irish people think and act. While the cultural values deemed to be admirable are regarded as having become increasingly widespread throughout the general population, they are perceived to be articulated most clearly in the lives of certain sections of southern Irish society. The principal heroes of the dominant narrative of the Celtic Tiger are a small number of state functionaries celebrated for their imagination, as well as a somewhat larger body of capitalists lionised for their enterprise. The elevation of the entrepreneur within contemporary Irish culture finds especially telling illustration in a recent book entitled *Driving the Tiger*. Drawing upon a series of interviews, John Travers seeks to identify the talent and zeal of those who have accumulated personal fortunes in a time of boom in a country that, until recently, was scarcely associated with business acumen.[29] The tone of this sequence of hagiographies strives, predictably, to translate the elementary pursuit of profit into a rather higher moral calling.

The perspectives that social commentators have advanced most frequently have sought, then, to attribute the recent transformation of southern Irish society to a series of astute structural adjustments on the part of the state and the acquisition of values regarded as consistent with the 'modern world' on the part of the people. The explanation of the origins of the Celtic Tiger that has assumed almost hegemonic status within the twenty-six counties emerges, therefore, as one that is entirely consistent with the distinctive readings of modernity discussed at length earlier. The resemblance to the modernisation school becomes more pronounced still when mainstream commentators move beyond explanations of the important social changes at work within the Irish Republic and begin to evaluate these particular developments.

In most orthodox approaches to the Celtic Tiger, the evidence that would seem to point to an economic miracle in the Republic of Ireland is typically regarded as transparent and unproblematic. The annual data that indicate rapid and unpunctuated expansion of the national economy are read simply as a faithful reflection of what is actually going on. We must be living through an economic golden age. After all, the people who collect and decipher the relevant data have told us time and again that it is so. And, in any case, the recurrent pronouncements of a buoyant economy would seem to be borne out amply in those various trends and indices that register at the more immediate level of everyday experience. The official contention that the 1990s saw the most successful programme of job creation in the history of the state seems more credible when one constantly passes the windows of retail outlets carrying advertisements for new staff. The declaration that the former scourge of mass emigration has been vanquished, moreover, appears persuasive when friends and family are no longer compelled to leave the country and when some of those who left in previous times begin to return. In light of these experiences, it is far from surprising that a great many people have come to assume with astonishment and delight that the Irish Republic has become the site of an economic miracle. MacSharry and White reiterate a widely held view when they remark ostentatiously that the twenty-six counties have ceased to be an economic casualty and have become instead 'a shining light and a beacon to the world'.[30]

The burgeoning levels of wealth generated within the Irish Republic over the last dozen years have, of course, found increasingly stark expression in radically altered patterns of consumption. While the conceit of the Celtic Tiger connotes a great many social processes, it articulates with singular ease a particular image of how young Ireland shops, dines and plays. The accounts that appear most regularly in media portrayals of contemporary southern Irish society seek not merely to document current modes of consumption but to celebrate them.[31] The ways in which the individual who resides in the twenty-six counties chooses to spend his time and money have come to be viewed as part of an ongoing attempt to arrive at an understanding of himself and others. In effect, the seemingly straightforward act of consumption has come to be regarded as a rather grander ontological enterprise. The popularity of the seemingly endless sequence of fashionable restaurants that have opened in most Irish cities is read as indicative of a desire for cultural refinement. The phenomenal growth in the sales of new high-performance cars as the millennium turned is seen as expressive of a longing for exhilaration and mobility. The sudden ubiquity of the mobile phone is interpreted as feeding into a wish to be autonomous and connected simultaneously. In the distinctly changeful context of contemporary southern Irish society, it would appear that the reflexive social agent so beloved of Anthony Giddens may transmute with telling ease into the sovereign consumer who constitutes the principal hero of late capitalism.

The acceleration of consumption in the twenty-six counties is invariably taken as indicative of the wider cultural changes that have defined the Irish Republic over the past generation. The social psychologist Michael O'Connell[32] has set out to chart the manner in which the era of the Celtic Tiger has altered the ways in which Irish people regard and represent themselves. The substantial body of opinion poll evidence that appears in the text broadly accords with the rather more impressionistic accounts of cultural change in southern Ireland published in countless Sunday supplements and features articles. Inevitably, O'Connell argues that younger people living in the twenty-six counties are altogether less constrained by customary norms and practices than were their predecessors. The teachings of the Catholic Church have come to exercise relatively little moral influence. The younger generation in the Irish Republic conceive of themselves less as members of collectivities than as individuals. This sense of individuality is articulated principally through material possessions rather than spiritual dispositions. The cultural changes that have emerged under the Celtic Tiger are – O'Connell suggests – expressed most keenly in relation to issues of sexual morality.[33] The statistical evidence that he presents indicates that young Irish people have rather more tolerant views than their parents on issues such as premarital sex, abortion and homosexuality. In the last decade, then, the sexual morals and practices prevalent within the twenty-six counties have begun to converge towards the liberal norms of continental Europe.

The particular moral trajectory that O'Connell maps out is, of course, the familiar one predicted and prescribed by the theorists of modernity to whom we have returned many times in this chapter. To be fair, the account of social change that O'Connell provides is rather more nuanced and critical than that advanced by the modernisation school.[34] While the cultural developments of the last decade are considered to be largely progressive, it is explicitly acknowledged that they have been secured at substantial cost to the moral fabric of the Irish Republic. In the final instance, however, O'Connell chooses to dispense with the dialectical model of social change that he seems to recommend and opts instead for a characterisation of the Celtic Tiger era that even the most orthodox modernisation theorist would find acceptable. The cultural evolution of the twenty-six counties over the last generation is conceived as having entailed a radical departure at some unspecified moment in the 1990s. It is this that prompts and enables O'Connell to insist that, in the recent past, an 'old Irish psyche' was replaced with a new one.[35] For 'old' and 'new' we should, of course, read 'traditional' and 'modern'. The cultural narrative that O'Connell outlines is, therefore, one in which the people of southern Ireland awoke one morning to discover that their previously cherished beliefs and practices had been displaced with a set more suitable to the rigours of modernity. It is this perennially seductive tenet of modernisation theory that draws O'Connell to declare – in the title of his book – that the Irish Republic has 'changed utterly'.

In most orthodox analyses, contemporary Irish society is depicted as the home not only of people who have changed but also of a changed people.[36] The advent of the Celtic Tiger is held to have marked an era in which the Irish Republic emerged from its former underdevelopment in order to take its rightful place as an equal among the nations of the world. Commentators examining the recent changes at work within the twenty-six counties can often barely conceal their pride in how far the state has come in such a short time. The excellence of Irish athletes and artists is interpreted as symptomatic of a deeper and growing sense of self-belief. The supposed ease with which politicians from the twenty-six counties operate on a European and global stage is considered to mark a certain coming of age.[37] The regularity with which conventional statistics record that the Irish Republic is economically more advanced than the United Kingdom is a recurrent source of satisfaction. A view that is heard with some regularity suggests that the burgeoning cultural self-confidence that defines contemporary southern Ireland has nurtured a version of nationalism that is rather more palatable than is often the case. The current of self-belief that energises younger Irish people is said to have encouraged them not be introspective and chauvinistic but rather to be cosmopolitan and inclusive. The mode of nationalism assumed to have been kindled under the Celtic Tiger is, in a sense then, post-nationalist.[38]

Deliberations upon the nature of Irish nationalism are an inevitably heated and recurrent element of public debate on an island with a long and bloody history of political division. For most of the period since partition, the political distinctions that are evident in Ireland have had a clear material subtext. As recently as the early 1990s, it was the case that people living in Northern Ireland generally enjoyed a substantially better standard of living than their counterparts south of the border. The arrival of the Celtic Tiger has, of course, changed all that. In some quarters, the recent transformation of the economic life of the twenty-six counties is regarded as having served to transform the political context of the entire island.[39] The changing cultural values and traits of people living in the Irish Republic are considered to be conducive to the cause of political reconciliation. The rather softer and more inclusive version of nationalism regarded as increasingly prevalent south of the border is conceived as one rather better equipped than its predecessors to accommodate the interests and anxieties of northern unionists.

In addition, the enormous material advances that the Irish Republic has secured over the last decade are held to have the potential to heal the political divisions that persist on the island.[40] One of the traditional taunts of Ulster unionism has been that Dublin could simply never afford to maintain Northern Irish people in the manner to which they have become accustomed.[41] The phenomenal expansion of the southern Irish economy during the 1990s swiftly eliminated that particular rationale for partition. As a consequence, nationalist commentators have come to argue forcefully that the conditions for the unification of Ireland are now firmly in place.[42]

In sum, then, the various developments that are signified within the figure of the Celtic Tiger might be considered to have radically altered the field of political possibility in Ireland. The multiple changes at work over the last decade have, in principle, established cultural and material conditions that might enable and allow the peoples living on the island to transcend their differences within the context of a unitary state. It is in this sense not least, perhaps, that we might be considered to be living at 'the end of Irish history'.[43]

Dislocations and distortions

Over the last decade, popular debate within the twenty-six counties has been dominated by the contention that the path the Irish Republic has followed in the last generation has been essentially benign. While it has enjoyed substantial currency both at home and abroad, this distinctly optimistic take on where southern Irish society is going must be acknowledged as deeply problematic. The orthodox reading of the Celtic Tiger era exhibits shortcomings that are the hallmark of the particular ideological tradition upon which it draws. The specific construction of modernity that has exercised a palpable influence over public commentary within the twenty-six counties adheres to a model of social change that proves entirely inadequate. The evolution of human societies is held to centre upon that fundamental moment of progress in which the traditional is displaced by the modern. This particular opposition has – as Tovey and Share[44] point out – exercised a perennial appeal for social scientists and others within the twenty-six counties. It has been entirely predictable, therefore, that the advent of the Celtic Tiger should have moved a range of commentators to declare and delineate the demise of traditional Ireland. In recent times, it has become commonplace to portray the Irish Republic as a thoroughly modern society that has changed utterly and for the better.

The particular conception of social development that emerges out of the hegemonic reading of Celtic Tiger Ireland is, of course, distinctly threadbare.[45] The actual ways in which real human societies evolve tend to be rather more complicated than those betrothed to a certain notion of the modern are willing to allow. The assertion that the process of modernisation in effect entails the obliteration of those inclinations and practices conventionally understood as 'traditional' simply flies in the face of historical evidence. It is the experience of most developed societies that the onset of modernity allows for the persistence and even the revival of certain forms of tradition. The musings of modernisation theorists and those within their orbit are also questionable in that they fail to grasp the genuinely contradictory nature of social development. In the course of their evolution, human societies tend to get both better and worse more or less at the same time.[46] In the outlook of those who advocate a particular version of modernity there appears, however, to be little or no appreciation of the dialectics of social change. The present course of development is interpreted as singularly and uniformly progressive. The dislocations and casualties of the modernisation process are understated or even airbrushed out of the picture altogether.[47]

In the absence of an adequate understanding of the dialectical nature of social change, it is inevitable that the orthodox perspective should tender a vision of the recent course of southern Irish society that turns out to be deeply distorted. Over the last decade, the voices that have been raised with greatest frequency and clarity have sought to depict the era of the Celtic Tiger as a time of unprecedented and unanticipated progress in which we should all simply rejoice. This familiar interpretation is, of course, one that is not entirely without justification. In certain respects, the last decade has marked a period of progress within the twenty-six counties. The fact, for instance, that huge numbers of young Irish men and women are no longer compelled to emigrate involuntarily in pursuit of a better life overseas constitutes a genuinely welcome development. The advances that have undoubtedly been made since the dark days of the 1980s should not, however, be allowed to cloud our critical judgement. While the era of the Celtic Tiger has evidently been a golden age for some Irish people, it has also marked a time of disadvantage and disruption for a great many others. It is the tales of the latter that are all but absent from the official narratives of the recent social history of the Irish Republic.

The omissions that define orthodox readings of contemporary southern Irish society merely serve to disclose the particular ideological interests they are intended to serve. Individuals operating out of a modernisation perspective have often sought to contend that the mode of social organisation to which they lend their name would best serve the interests of all. The advent of the genuinely modern society would offer everyone the multiple advantages that only liberal democracy and the market can bestow. In reality, of course, the admirably universal rhetoric of the modernisation school has been employed to advance a very particular set of interests. Liberal capitalism is, after all, a social form that in its marrow seeks to elevate the concerns of the few over those of the many. The ideological interests that animate modernisation theorists and their ilk find their echo in a great deal of mainstream commentary on the nature of contemporary southern Irish society. Those versions of Celtic Tiger Ireland that have assumed almost hegemonic status have offered a rather less than faithful account of the period. While the achievements of the last decade or so are repeatedly underlined, the 'dark side' of contemporary social life in the twenty-six counties has been consistently concealed. In striving to advance a systematically distorted vision of the era of the Celtic Tiger, mainstream commentators have conspired to conceal and defend the interests of that small body of individuals who have been the principal beneficiaries of the boom years. The orthodox reading of the turn that the Irish Republic has taken over the last generation should be regarded, therefore, as not merely intellectually feeble but politically reactionary as well.

An alternative biography of the Celtic Tiger

The shortcomings that characterise most mainstream analyses of the Celtic Tiger era become readily apparent when we turn to consider the conventional interpretation of the origins of the economic boom. In the eyes of many commentators, the apparent economic miracle of the 1990s should be attributed principally to the energies and ingenuity of the Irish people. Special mention is afforded to those politicians and civil servants who are regarded as having had the vision and courage to alter public policy.[48] The reform of the education system and the reform of labour relations are frequently identified as measures that created the conditions that made economic prosperity possible and sustainable. The tone of the accounts of those associated with these supposedly critical changes in public policy verges, at times, on hubris. This is hardly surprising, though. The discourse of those who rule tends habitually, after all, towards an 'uninterrupted monologue of self-praise'.[49]

While the notion that the origins of the Celtic Tiger are to be found within the twenty-six counties has exercised considerable influence, it scarcely stands up to even the most cursory analysis. The dramatic recent reversal of the economic fortunes of the Irish Republic owes rather less to the visionary status of Irish politicians than to convenient changes in the operation of global capitalism.[50] The decisions that led to the seeming economic miracle of the 1990s were taken not in the corridors of Leinster House but in the boardrooms of a handful of multinational corporations. As the 1980s came to a close, the flows of foreign direct investment crossing international boundaries began to expand enormously. The principally US multinationals that were keen to produce in and for the EU were drawn disproportionately to the Irish Republic. The motives that informed these decisions to establish branch plants in the twenty-six counties bore little resemblance to the formal explanations offered at press conferences to mark their announcement. The routine assurances of senior executives that their corporations were attracted to the Irish Republic principally by the prospect of dealing with a highly educated workforce have rarely managed to convince. The education system in the twenty-six counties remains, after all, hugely under-funded and emerges poorly out of international comparisons.[51] The simple truth is that those multinational corporations that flocked to the Irish Republic in the early 1990s were attracted first and foremost by its status as an exceptionally good place to turn a profit.

The rate of corporation tax charged in the Irish Republic has for some time been by far the lowest in the EU.[52] This state of affairs has encouraged multinationals not only to invest in the twenty-six counties but also to engage in some distinctive creative accountancy practices as well. The relatively lenient fiscal regime that faces multinational corporations operating in the Irish Republic offers an enormous incentive to maximise the profits they declare within the state. Through the manipulation of their internal accounts – by selling on components to the branch plant in Ireland at a relatively cheap price and selling on the finished product at a relatively high price – multinationals can register profits in the twenty-six counties rather than in another region with a higher rate of corporation tax. The suspicion that this strategy of 'transfer pricing' is a routine practice of transnational corporations with subsidiaries in the Irish Republic would seem to be borne out by the astronomical profits that they declare in the state.[53] Those powerful corporations that have invested in the Irish Republic in recent times have come to enjoy rates of profit that are well in excess of what might be ordinarily anticipated on the basis of their output and productivity. One illustrative tale that is often recounted is that of the Coca Cola plant in Drogheda, which, in a single year, announced profits of IR£400 million, even though it had a workforce of only 200 people.[54]

The cunning accountancy practices of multinational capital suggest that we need to approach the recent performance of the southern Irish economy in a rather more cautious and indeed critical spirit than has often been the case. As the standard indicators turned consistently favourable a decade or so ago, most mainstream commentators hastened to identify the Irish Republic as the author of an economic miracle. Statistics such as those that chart movements in GDP were routinely offered as compelling evidence of this economic transformation. Consideration of the conduct of multinational corporations would seem to

suggest, however, that the faith that its hagiographers have invested in
the southern Irish economy might not have been entirely well placed. It
is undoubtedly true that the economic capacity of the Irish Republic has
expanded remarkably. Throughout the 1990s the amount of wealth
generated within the southern Irish economy grew at unanticipated rates.
A great deal of that money never made it, however, into the wallet or
the bank account of an Irish man or woman. In recent times, an increasingly enormous gulf has opened up between the amount of wealth
that is created within the Irish Republic and the amount of wealth that
is retained within the state. The disparity between the two owes a great
deal to the conduct of multinational capital. Perhaps as much as one-
fifth of the value generated within the southern Irish economy each year
is spirited out of the country, principally in the guise of the repatriated
profits of transnational corporations.[55]

The accountancy scams that are operated within multinational enterprises mean that evaluating the economic performance of the Irish Republic
represents a rather more arduous task than might first meet the eye. The
enormous sums that multinationals routinely repatriate from the twenty-
six counties and deposit in tax havens across the globe ensure that official
statistics hugely overstate the speed at which – and the scale to which –
the southern Irish economy has grown. In simple terms, there is rather
less wealth circulating within the Republic of Ireland than appears to be
the case on paper. The growing weight of evidence to suggest that official
measures exaggerate the performance of the southern Irish economy has
done little, however, to dampen the enthusiasm of many mainstream
analysts. At times, the pronouncements of politicians and other establishment figures have shaded into unabashed boosterism. The performance
and potential of the southern Irish economy have, on occasion, been
overstated. Conventional and convenient statistics have been dropped into
discussion in a manner that suggests they are straightforward and faithful measures of what is actually going on the economic life of the state.

Although admittedly impressive, the performance of the southern
Irish economy since the early 1990s has been consistently exaggerated
in a great deal of mainstream analysis. It should also be noted that the
foundations of the economic renaissance are somewhat less secure than
many commentators would have us believe. After partition, the twenty-
six counties followed a path of development that was profoundly dependent. For most of the twentieth century, the southern Irish economy
relied heavily upon revenues from exports, principally of live animals,
to the United Kingdom. Over the last few decades, however, the importance of British markets has waned considerably. The growing proportion
of exports destined for elsewhere has prompted the view that the southern
Irish economy has come to assume a rather more healthy and autonomous form than hitherto. In reality, however, the economic course that

the Irish Republic has taken over the last generation has – as Denis O'Hearn illustrates in his contribution to this volume – merely entailed swapping one version of dependency for another.

The bullish rhetoric that has attended the era of the Celtic Tiger conspires to conceal the actual fragility of the southern Irish economy. The record rates of economic growth that were registered throughout the 1990s were attributable, in the main, to the activities of a remarkably small number of multinational corporations operating within a remarkably narrow range of economic sectors.[56] In the course of the decade, a handful of principally US computer companies came to assume a pivotal importance within the southern Irish economy. This marked reliance upon certain sections of multinational capital has rendered the Irish Republic exceptionally vulnerable to the increasingly rapid changes that characterise the global economy and corporate strategy. The fragility of the southern Irish economy becomes especially apparent if we turn to consider the potential ramifications if, for instance, the Intel Corporation were to close its flagship branch plant in County Kildare. The impact of this single corporate decision would, in all probability, be sufficiently grave to undermine conventional estimations of the vitality and prospects of the Celtic Tiger. It would at least suggest that those commentators who hold to the view that the Irish Republic has now entered an era of sustained and genuinely autonomous development have been seriously misled.[57]

At the heart of optimistic accounts of the Celtic Tiger era is the assumption that the period has bestowed considerable benefit upon every section of southern Irish society. The contention that the boom years have served the interests of all is reflected in part in the rash of collective (pro)nouns that litter public discourse. Politicians and journalists are wont to reflect that '*we* have never had it so good' or that '*the Irish* are living through a golden age'. The assumption that there exist collective interests within the twenty-six counties finds institutional expression in the various corporatist schemes that have been devised since the late 1980s. The formal rationale of 'social partnership' is, of course, that it facilitates restraint from, and cooperation between, the various sections of southern Irish society, to the advantage of all.

The notion that the economic boom has conferred benefit upon all Irish people represents, perhaps, the most pernicious of the myths that have bloomed during the Celtic Tiger era. The Republic of Ireland exhibits, of course, all those class distinctions and inequalities that are the hallmark of a capitalist society.[58] As a consequence, it has been entirely inevitable that the distribution of the advantages of economic growth should have been neither even nor universal.[59] The principal beneficiaries of the advent of the Celtic Tiger have been those elements of southern Irish society that already enjoyed considerable affluence.[60] Irish business men and women have come to receive growing profits and dividends, which they have often lodged, on the recommendation of their banks, in offshore accounts that avoid the necessity of paying tax. Speculators in a position to invest in several properties have reaped the benefits of ever spiralling rents and house prices. The owners of the numerous stud farms scattered throughout the twenty-six counties have amassed enormous personal fortunes, unmolested by the state's revenue commissioners.

The era of the Celtic Tiger has, therefore, constituted a time of considerable opportunity for the more affluent elements of southern Irish society. The same could hardly be said, however, for most working-class people living in the twenty-six counties. In principle, the corporatist structures at work within the Irish Republic are intended to operate to the advantage of everyone. In practice, however, social partnership represents a ruse that acts to conceal and advance the interests of the most privileged sections of southern Irish society[61] – a point that Kieran Allen develops more fully in chapter 3. During the boom years the salaries, rents, profits and dividends that accrue to the wealthy have not been restrained and have grown exponentially. Over the same period, however, the wages that are paid to ordinary folk have been subject to strict controls and have grown only marginally. It should scarcely come as a surprise, therefore, to discover that the era of the Celtic Tiger has witnessed an acceleration of the polarisation of wealth.[62] Indeed, international statistics have shown consistently in recent years that the Irish Republic has come to represent the second most unequal society in the western world.[63]

The operation of social partnership agreements in the context of an economic boom has worked to the considerable disadvantage of the southern Irish working classes. Modest wage increases have simply been insufficient to keep pace with spiralling rents and house prices in particular. While many working-class people have struggled to make ends meet, especial hardship has often been faced by those who have entered the new forms of employment that have emerged since the birth of the Celtic Tiger. Over the last decade, more jobs have been created than at any other time in the history of the state. In the main, these posts have been filled by the record numbers of women entering the labour force for the first time – a trend that Sinéad Kennedy maps out in her chapter. The new modes of employment that define the Celtic Tiger era are often poorly paid and protected.[64] In addition, these positions tend to entail working practices that are rather less than enviable. Some commentators – as we saw earlier – have sought to argue that Irish people have actually flourished under these new ways of working. Those observers who celebrate 'flexible' labour practices might, of course, adopt a rather different perspective if they personally were facing a future that consisted of twelve-hour shifts, the endless repetition of a standardised spiel to randomly selected phone owners or delving into their own pockets to buy the materials required to perform the tasks involved in a contract cleaning position.

The creation of a large body of badly paid jobs – coupled with the often overlooked persistence of long-term unemployment – has ensured that the recent period of economic boom has been accompanied by growing levels of poverty within the twenty-six counties. While this particular trait of the Celtic Tiger might appear to be an aberration, it is in fact entirely in keeping with wider international trends.[65] The coincidence of burgeoning wealth and growing poverty features in the course of development that all western societies have followed in the last generation. The number of poor people in the twenty-six counties would, however, seem to be exceptionally high. Indeed, recent statistics would suggest that the Irish Republic now has the second greatest concentration of poverty in the western world. Among the developed states, only that supposed paragon of modernity, the United States, has a larger proportion of people who are poor.[66]

The disadvantages that the southern Irish working classes face could, of course, be ameliorated to some extent were the state to provide adequate levels of certain essential services. The era of the Celtic Tiger has provided a golden opportunity to bring public provision in the Irish Republic up to scratch. In spite of the fact that the fortunes amassed by multinational capital and a few private citizens go largely untaxed, the Irish state acquired a healthy fiscal surplus during the 1990s. While these funds offered the chance to improve essential public services dramatically, the opportunity was all but spurned. Indeed, over the period since the phrase 'Celtic Tiger' was coined, the proportion of national income devoted to state spending has in fact declined.[67] The underdevelopment of public services in the Irish Republic is illustrated most keenly in the context of the health system. In the last few years, gnawing dissatisfaction with pay and working conditions has prompted doctors and nurses to increasingly militant industrial action. The success of a sequence of independent candidates campaigning on health issues in the general election held in the early summer of 2002 suggests that the grievances of those working in hospitals have found a resonance with the wider Irish public.

In most mainstream commentaries, the advent of the Celtic Tiger is held to have signalled an era of widespread affluence and contentment. The years of sustained economic growth are held to have enabled people in the Irish Republic to banish the austerity of previous times in order to become sophisticated consumers, akin to their neighbours in other western European states. The euphoria that has exemplified the era of the Celtic Tiger has often failed to square with the everyday realities of the lives of actual flesh-and-blood southern Irish people. While the incomes of professionals as well as many other workers living in the twenty-six counties have increased substantially, it is debatable whether the quality of their lives has in fact improved. In the last decade or so, the culture of work in a range of occupations has changed dramatically. It is the experience of many professionals that the pace and length of their working day have increased considerably. The stresses that arise out of these new work cultures have been among the factors that have led to spiralling levels of drug and alcohol abuse in the twenty-six counties.[68]

While many of the salaries that are available within the Irish Republic are impressive, they are often insufficient to enable people to live in comfort, let alone luxury. The increasingly exorbitant cost of property has meant that even individuals earning ostensibly substantial incomes have been compelled to live in cramped but expensive rented accommodation in one of the many complexes that jerry-builders have thrown up in southern Irish cities since the beginning of the boom. The quest for somewhere larger in which to breathe or raise children has persuaded many people working in Irish cities to migrate to dormitory towns or even further afield.[69] An increasingly lengthy and arduous commute to work has become a recurrent bane of many of those who are supposedly living the good life in Celtic Tiger Ireland.[70]

The lives of people who reside in the twenty-six counties – as Anne Ryan illustrates in chapter 9 – exhibit all the pressures and dislocations that are the hallmark of the modern world. The course that it has taken over the last generation has begun to gnaw at the very fabric of southern Irish society. Increasingly, there are signs of atomisation among people who were formerly renowned for their sense of connectedness. As individuals in the twenty-six counties have grown less attached to one another, they have inevitably grown more attached to things. After all, if we are truly living at the end of human history, then what else is there to do but shop?

As we noted in passing earlier, the conceit of the Celtic Tiger has a particular facility to connote the changing patterns of consumption that have marked life in the twenty-six counties over the last generation. In countless features devoted to the period, journalists have sought to celebrate the practices of Irish consumers. The ways in which younger Irish people in particular choose to spend their leisure time has been considered emblematic of a population that has become increasingly confident, imaginative and sophisticated. The hagiographies of the southern Irish consumer that appear in orthodox accounts of the Celtic Tiger period ultimately fail to convince, however. The ways in which people living in the twenty-six counties dress and play are often taken as expressive of a reflexive agency through which individuals seek to create an authentic and original notion of self. It is perplexing, then, that contemporary southern Irish society should be characterised not by diversity and individuality but rather by a baleful blandness. While we may well live at a time when there has never been greater choice, it is remarkable how few choices are actually being made.[71] It is extremely difficult to judge the claims of features writers that everyone looks better nowadays, simply because everyone sort of looks the same. It was this corrosive uniformity that recently prompted one journalist – in a curious though compelling phrase – to berate the 'homogeneous sartorial communism' of contemporary southern Irish society.[72]

The materialism that has overtaken the twenty-six counties in the era of the Celtic Tiger articulates a spiritual emptiness that invariably attends the process of modernisation[73] – a theme that recurs throughout the chapter by Kieran Keohane and Carmen Kuhling. Over the last generation, the Republic of Ireland has, like all other western societies, become a place that elevates having over being. It would seem, increasingly, that the principal way in which most southern Irish people are willing or able to express their sense of who they are is through the commodity form. The rampant consumption that has come to define the period of the Celtic Tiger has inevitably nurtured a culture of narcissism.[74] As the devotion to self has escalated, consideration for others would appear to have waned. In recent times, a certain arrogance and callousness have appeared within southern Irish society that did not seem to exist before.[75] An increasingly substantial body of people seem entirely oblivious to the courtesies that can render everyday social interactions vaguely bearable. Possession of a mobile phone would seem to have come to be regarded as a licence to behave in whatever way you please. Unprovoked random assaults under the influence of excess alcohol have become a lamentably common occurrence in all southern Irish cities.[76]

Irish people are, of course, not merely the subjects of the process of commodification that defines contemporary bourgeois society but its objects as well. The course that late capitalism has taken entails a collapse of the distinctions between the cultural and the economic.[77] Western societies have increasingly become sites less of production than of consumption. The modes of cultural practice and the details of historical triumph and catastrophe have been rendered into the commodity form. This relentless process that leads to the commodification of everything – to the advent of the society of the spectacle – is as apparent in the context of Ireland as in that of other developed societies. In the twenty-six counties, various social practices that were once simply ways of being have been distorted into ways of making money. It is difficult, at times, when walking around Dublin to shake the conviction that the entire city has been transformed into a cultural theme park for the entertainment and distraction of natives and visitors alike. The process of the commodification of Irishness is among the most important forces shaping the contemporary social life of the twenty-six counties. The theme is, therefore, one that is afforded considerable attention in the book and is taken up in rather different ways in the chapters written by Steve Coleman, Honor Fagan and David Slattery.

There is, perhaps, one final consideration that should receive our attention before we proceed. Among the multiple ideas that emerge out of the deceptively simple conceit of the Celtic Tiger are those that centre upon what it now means to be Irish. It has become commonplace to suggest that recent generations growing up in the twenty-six counties have come to define themselves in ways that are increasingly similar to those of their counterparts in other regions of the EU. Although explicitly proud of where they are from, younger southern Irish people are held to subscribe to a version of Irishness that is outward looking and inclusive. The enmities and injustices that so preoccupied previous generations are considered to be of little concern or interest. The rather gentler mode of nationalism assumed to have gained ground within the twenty-six counties in recent times would appear to be one that promises to heal the divisions that have blighted the island as a whole.

In the minds of some, the prospects of national reconciliation have been heightened further by the economic strides that the Irish Republic has made. The phenomenal rates of growth registered throughout the 1990s have ensured that the economic conditions that might enable the creation of a single polity on the island are now in place. The common-sense association often made between economic prosperity and political progress has, of course, been encouraged by a particular historical co-incidence.[78] The years in which the phrase 'Celtic Tiger' became a recurrent motif of everyday speech also happened to be those in which the peace process in Northern Ireland finally got off the ground.[79] While the relationship between economic development and political reconciliation remains implicit in the minds of many people living in the twenty-six counties, nationalist politicians have at times sought to make the connection more explicit.

Although comforting, the notion that the advent of the Celtic Tiger will ultimately pave the way to reconciliation among the peoples of Ireland remains a fiction nonetheless. The associations between prosperity and peace that are drawn implicitly in mainstream accounts of contemporary Irish society betray a fundamental weakness of the ideological tradition from which they derive. Among modernisation theorists, there tends to be a belief that, as societies evolve towards the nirvana of high mass consumption, individuals become increasingly disinterested in those practices and beliefs considered to be 'primitive' or 'traditional'. Why would you bother with being a unionist or a nationalist when you can always just go to the mall instead? The essential difficulty with these bourgeois readings of the development process arises out of the fact that they misunderstand the nature of the relationship between what are arbitrarily designated as 'tradition' and 'modernity' respectively. In reality, of course, those rites and practices that are conventionally understood as 'traditional' are not impediments to modernisation but rather products of it. There are few things as modern as tradition. It is important to remember this when considering the prospects of a place with a history like that of Ireland.

While the economic boom has undoubtedly had some benign effects, it has inevitably served little to diminish the divisions that blight relations among Irish people. The prejudices and preoccupations that define old-school nationalism continue to have a certain currency south of the border. The origins of many of those who have offered their services to the cause of dissident republicanism are merely the most explicit expression of this. While 'traditional' concerns and beliefs persist often under the surface of everyday life in the twenty-six counties, they tend – as Pete Shirlow shows in his contribution to the book – to find rather more vehement articulation north of the border. Over the last decade, a great deal of political progress has, of course, been made in Northern Ireland. The number of young working-class men murdering one another in the name of equally worthless causes has declined enormously. The sense of prejudice and grievance that in part drove 'the troubles' remains obstinately in place, however. Indeed, according to one major survey published in the early summer of 2002, levels of sectarian animosity have in fact heightened within the six counties over the period of the peace process.[80] The growth of ethnoreligious hatred in Northern Ireland finds particularly chilling expression in the routine violence and intimidation that remain an everyday reality in many parts of the region. If we are really living through the end of Irish history then it would appear that no one has bothered to inform the residents of north and east Belfast.

The contention that contemporary Irish society has become an essentially inclusive and cosmopolitan place, which appears in many orthodox accounts of the Celtic Tiger era, should be denied on at least one further ground. Over the last decade, the Irish Republic has suddenly and unexpectedly become a net importer of people. The experiences of those who have come to these shores from elsewhere are necessarily complex and diverse. While some recent immigrants have encountered warmth and opportunity, a great many others have been met by suspicion and hostility. Those who have arrived from a range of African states in pursuit of a better life have been treated especially badly. The racism that appears increasingly endemic within the twenty-six counties has, predictably, been fomented by those in positions of authority. The institutions and agents of the state seem unable – as Steve Loyal argues in his chapter – to conceive of those seeking asylum in the Irish Republic as being other than a burden. Elements of the media have issued disgraceful misrepresentations of the new immigrants that clearly chime with established racial stereotypes. In this chill climate, it is hardly surprising that members of ethnic minorities within the twenty-six counties recount that they are often the victims of verbal and physical violence. There are many deplorable facets of the way in which southern Irish society has evolved over the last generation. The manner in which refugees and asylum seekers have been mistreated – especially by the forces of the state – leaps out, though, as the most shameful of all.

How soon is now?

The radical changes that have overtaken the Irish Republic in the course of the last generation have, in the main, been read and refracted through a very particular ideological perspective. In most contemporary accounts, people living in the twenty-six counties are represented as newly and uniformly affluent and contented. While mainstream accounts of the Celtic Tiger do, of course, possess at least a kernel of truth, they offer a vision of southern Irish society that is nonetheless systematically distorted. In particular, orthodox readings tend to understate or overlook entirely those dislocations and injustices that have marked the process of social change in the recent period of economic boom. The purpose of this book is to illuminate and contest the numerous dubious assumptions that inform the hitherto hegemonic readings of the nature of contemporary southern Irish society. It is the conviction of the authors who have contributed to the text that most orthodox analyses have conspired to misrepresent the transformations that have attended the era of the Celtic Tiger. The intention of the book is, then, to add to existing critical voices that are essential if we are ever to arrive at a more faithful appreciation of what the Irish Republic is like and where it might be going.

While the contributors to the text share a conviction that there needs to be a more critical understanding of the nature of contemporary Irish society, their points of view are, of course, far from uniform. The authors who appear in the pages that follow are drawn from a wide range of academic perspectives. The disciplines of adult education, anthropology, English literature, geography, sociology and women's studies are all represented between the covers. The individuals who have contributed to the text also come from a broad arc of ideological viewpoints. In a certain sense, the book represents an endeavour to see whether it is possible to have a fruitful critical dialogue between Marxism and postmodernism. It is hoped and anticipated that the variety of voices that are raised within the text will represent one of its fundamental strengths.

The finishing touches were put to the book in the late summer of 2002. Over the previous year, there had been increasingly dire warnings from authoritative figures that the southern Irish economy had begun to slow down and that a full-blown recession might be just around the corner.[81] In the last few weeks, there has been a fresh round of expressions of concern for the health of the Celtic Tiger.[82] Of greatest significance, perhaps, has been the alarm within the International Monetary Fund that has been prompted by the ever more perilous state of the public finances in the Irish Republic. It would appear that the seemingly golden age of the Celtic Tiger might be drawing to a close. This is probably an especially opportune moment, then, to reflect upon the remarkable developments of the last dozen years or so.

The faltering of the southern Irish economy should, of course, be seen as emblematic of a rather more universal trend. In the 1990s, liberal capitalism appeared to be in especially rude health. The rates of growth and profit registered in the lodestar economy of the United States were read in many quarters as heralds of an era of expansion and prosperity.[83] This confidence in the performance and potential of global capitalism found its ideological echo, of course, in the contention that the political disputes of the past were over and that we now lived at the end of history. As the millennium turned, however, the difficulties that were already apparent in the world economy began to become rather more pronounced. The horrendous slaughter in New York and elsewhere on 11 September 2001 threatened to accelerate a nascent global recession. The sequence of corporate scandals that have rocked the United States in the months after have merely served to compound the nagging suspicion that all is not well with global capitalism.

Ironically, the essential fragility of global capitalism is encrypted within the very metaphor that was coined to convey its presumed invincibility. While the declaration that we live at the end of history clearly articulates a sense of the ultimate triumph of capital, it produces an echo that suggests a radically different outcome. It would seem that the sole cultural commentator who has been sufficiently astute to have appreciated this has, predictably, been the literary critic Fredric Jameson.[84] It is his view that, although the metaphor of 'the end of history' might appear to be about time, it is in fact about space.[85] In the era of globalisation, capital has been able to expand into new and lucrative markets. While the opportunities for profit have been substantial, they remain strictly finite, nonetheless. Jameson suggests that an acknowledgment of the spatial limits of capital is latent within the conceit that most famously celebrates the globalisation process. The notion of the end of history – he contends – articulates a sense not only of the majesty of capitalism but of its mortality as well. It expresses, in other words, not only a belief that the reign of capital represents the culmination of human civilisation, but also a terror that capitalism will inevitably be replaced at some point in the future by a form of society that is genuinely human and sustainable. Speed the day.

Notes

1 T. Caherty, A. Storey, M. Gavin, M. Molloy and C. Ruane (eds), *Is Ireland a Third World Country?* (Belfast: Beyond the Pale, 1992).

2 D. O'Hearn, *Inside the Celtic Tiger: The Irish Economy and the Asian Model* (London: Pluto, 1998), p. 2.

3 J. J. Lee, 'Ireland's magnificent 7 per cent growth rate stuns the begrudgers', *Irish Times*, 4 January 1996.

4 R. MacSharry and P. White, *The Making of the Celtic Tiger: The Inside Story of Ireland's Boom Economy* (Cork: Mercier Press, 2000), p. 360.

5 A. So, *Social Change and Development: Modernization, Dependency and World System Perspectives* (London: Sage, 1990).

6 D. McClelland, *The Achieving Society* (London: Van Nostrand, 1961).

7 For a full account see P. Anderson, *The Origins of Postmodernity* (London: Verso, 1998), especially chapter 2.

8 F. Fukuyama, 'The end of history?', *National Interest* (summer 1989).

9 *Ibid.*, p. 18.

10 F. Fukuyama, 'The West has won', *Guardian*, 11 November 2001. See also F. Fukuyama, 'History and September 11', in K. Booth and T. Dunne (eds), *Worlds in Collision: Terror and the Future of the Global Order* (Houndmills: Palgrave, 2002).

11 A. Giddens, *The Third Way: The Renewal of Social Democracy* (Cambridge: Polity, 1998), pp. 24, 43; W. Hutton and A. Giddens (eds), *On the Edge: Living With Global Capitalism* (London: Jonathan Cape, 2000), pp. vii, 11–12, 214–16.

12 Giddens, *The Third Way*, pp. 74, 99–100.

13 Hutton and Giddens, *On the Edge*, p. 42.

14 Giddens, *The Third Way*, p. 31.

15 A. Giddens, *The Consequences of Modernity* (Cambridge: Polity, 1990); A. Giddens, *Modernity and Self-Identity: Self and Society in the Late Modern Age* (Cambridge: Polity, 1991); Giddens, *The Third Way*, pp. 36–7.

16 M. Weber, 'Politics as a vocation', in H. H. Gerth and C. W. Mills (eds), *From Max Weber: Essays in Sociology* (London: Routledge and Kegan Paul, 1948).

17 The most systematic critique of the 'third way' politics to which Giddens has lent his name is to be found in the work of Alex Callinicos. See A. Callinicos, 'Social theory put to the test of politics: Pierre Bourdieu and Anthony Giddens', *New Left Review*, 1:236 (July–August 1999); and A. Callinicos, *Against the Third Way: An Anti-capitalist Critique* (London: Blackwell, 2001).

18 G. Monbiot, *Captive State: The Corporate Takeover of Britain* (London: Macmillan, 2000).

19 *Ibid.*, pp. 59–92.

20 Although initiatives between the state and business are less common in Ireland than in the United Kingdom, they are beginning to gather pace. For a critique of the operation of these schemes, see W. Kingston, 'Public–private partnership plan is a recipe for ripoffs', *Irish Times*, 12 August 2002, p. 14.

21 An important critique of the importation of hegemonic bourgeois ideals to Ireland – a process astutely designated as 'ideological franchising' – appears in P. Kirby, L. Gibbons and M. Cronin (eds), *Reinventing Ireland: Culture, Society and the Global Economy* (London: Pluto, 2002).

22 See, for example, MacSharry and White, *The Making of the Celtic Tiger*, pp. 366–7. A rather more nuanced, but nonetheless overwhelmingly compli-

mentary, account of the role of the Irish state in the Celtic Tiger boom appears in the work of Sean Ó Riain and Philip O'Connell. See, for instance, S. Ó Riain, 'Soft solutions to hard times', in E. Slater and M. Peillon (eds), *Memories of the Present: A Sociological Chronicle of Ireland, 1997–1998* (Dublin: Institute of Public Administration, 2000), and S. Ó Riain and P. O'Connell, 'The role of the state in growth and welfare', in B. Nolan, P. O'Connell and C. Whelan (eds), *From Bust to Boom? The Irish Experience of Growth and Inequality* (Dublin: Institute of Public Administration, 2000).

23 J. FitzGerald, 'The story of Ireland's failure – and belated success', in Nolan *et al.* (eds), *From Bust to Boom?*

24 P. Sweeney, *The Celtic Tiger: Ireland's Continuing Economic Miracle* (Dublin: Oak Tree Press, 1999).

25 MacSharry and White, *The Making of the Celtic Tiger.*

26 *Ibid.*, p. 144.

27 N. Hardiman, 'Social partnership, wage bargaining and growth', in Nolan *et al.* (eds), *From Bust to Boom?*, p. 307.

28 Sweeney, *The Celtic Tiger*, pp. 149–68.

29 J. Travers, *Driving the Tiger: Irish Enterprise Spirit* (Dublin: Gill and Macmillan, 2001).

30 MacSharry and White, *The Making of the Celtic Tiger*, p. 360.

31 E. Ferguson, 'Celtic Tiger is burning bright', *Observer*, 4 July 1999.

32 M. O'Connell, *Changed Utterly* (Dublin: Liffey Press, 2001).

33 *Ibid.*, pp. 75–91.

34 *Ibid.*, pp. 1–11.

35 *Ibid.*, 13–26.

36 FitzGerald, 'The story of Ireland's failure', p. 55; Sweeney, *The Celtic Tiger*, pp. 12, 227.

37 MacSharry and White, *The Making of the Celtic Tiger*, p. 148.

38 R. Kearney, *Postnationalist Ireland: Politics, Culture, Philosophy* (London: Routledge, 1997); R. O'Donnell, 'Reinventing Ireland: from sovereignty to partnership', Jean Monnet inaugural lecture, University College Dublin, 29 April 1999.

39 The economist John Bradley, for instance, has drawn close connections between the advent of the Celtic Tiger and the advance of the Northern Irish peace process. See J. Bradley, 'The island economy: past, present and future', in J. Bradley and E. Birnie, *Can the Celtic Tiger Cross the Irish Border?* (Cork: Cork University Press, 2001), pp. 1, 8, 36, 38, 43.

40 B. O'Leary, 'Comparative political science and the British–Irish Agreement', in J. McGarry (ed.), *Northern Ireland and the Divided World: Post-agreement Northern Ireland in Comparative Perspective* (Oxford: Oxford University Press, 2001), p. 62; S. Smooha, 'The tenability of partition as a mode of conflict regulation: comparing Ireland with Palestine – land of Israel', in McGarry (ed.), *Northern Ireland and the Divided World.*

41 C. Coulter, '"A miserable failure of a state": unionist intellectuals and the Irish Republic', in R. Ryan (ed.), *Writing in the Irish Republic: Literature, Culture, Politics 1949–1999* (Houndmills: Macmillan, 2000).

42 See, for instance, the comments of Seamus Mallon, who was at the time leader of the Social Democratic and Labour Party (SDLP), reported in S. Mallon, 'Build trust with the agreement', press release 28 May 2001, available at www.sdlp.ie/prmallon%2dbuild%20trust.htm.

43 J. Ruane, 'The end of (Irish) history? Three readings of the current conjuncture', in J. Ruane and J. Todd (eds), *After the Good Friday Agreement:*

Analysing Political Change in Northern Ireland (Dublin: University College Dublin Press, 1999).

44 H. Tovey and P. Share, *A Sociology of Ireland* (Dublin: Gill and Macmillan, 2000), p. 50.

45 For a useful discussion of the baleful influence that modernisation theory has exercised over Irish cultural commentary see J. Cleary, 'Modernization and aesthetic ideology in contemporary Irish culture', in Ryan (ed.), *Writing in the Irish Republic*.

46 M. Berman, *All That Is Solid Melts Into Air: The Experience of Modernity* (London: Verso, 1982); M. Horkheimer and T. Adorno, *Dialectic of Enlightenment* (New York: Continuum, 1993 [1944]).

47 P. Kirby, 'Contested pedigrees of the Celtic Tiger', in Kirby *et al.* (eds), *Reinventing Ireland*.

48 MacSharry and White, *The Making of the Celtic Tiger*, p. 331.

49 G. Debord, *The Society of the Spectacle* (New York: Zone Books, 1995), p. 24.

50 Kirby, 'Contested pedigrees of the Celtic Tiger'.

51 K. Allen, *The Celtic Tiger: The Myth of Social Partnership in Ireland* (Manchester: Manchester University Press, 2000), pp. 90–3.

52 *Ibid.*, pp. 24–5.

53 O'Hearn, *Inside the Celtic Tiger*, pp. 78–87.

54 Sweeney, *The Celtic Tiger*, p. 51.

55 P. Kirby, L. Gibbons and M. Cronin, 'Conclusions and transformations', in Kirby *et al.* (eds), *Reinventing Ireland*, p. 205.

56 O'Hearn, *Inside the Celtic Tiger*, pp. 68–74.

57 *Ibid.*, pp. 147–70.

58 B. Nolan, 'Income inequality in Ireland', *Administration*, 47:2 (summer 1999), pp. 78–90.

59 P. Kirby, *The Celtic Tiger in Distress: Growth with Inequality in Ireland* (Basingstoke: Palgrave, 2002).

60 Allen, *The Celtic Tiger*, pp. 59–66.

61 K. Allen, 'The Celtic Tiger, inequality and social partnership', *Administration*, 47:2 (summer 1999), pp. 31–55; Kirby, 'Contested pedigrees of the Celtic Tiger', pp. 31–3.

62 N. Haughey, 'Report by ESRI says rich–poor divide is widening', *Irish Times*, 17 July 2001; O'Hearn, *Inside the Celtic Tiger*, pp. 131–3; M. Wren, 'Rich get the breaks, poor get little', *Irish Times*, 17 April 2002.

63 P. Cullen, 'Ireland a society of poverty, inequality, UN study finds', *Irish Times*, 24 July 2002, p. 1; F. O'Toole, 'Pretending we're on top of the world', *Irish Times*, 13 August 2002, p. 12.

64 Allen, *The Celtic Tiger*, pp. 70–7; O'Hearn, *Inside the Celtic Tiger*, pp. 96–108.

65 D. Harvey, *Spaces of Hope* (Edinburgh: Edinburgh University Press, 2000), chapter 8.

66 P. Cullen, 'Statistical snapshot of a world divided by poverty', *Irish Times*, 24 July 2002, p. 7.

67 Ó Riain and O'Connell, 'The role of the state in growth and welfare', p. 331; P. Sweeney, 'Public spending level shows Ireland moves towards Manila as an economic model', *Irish Times*, 16 April 2000, p. 14.

68 G. Moane, 'Colonialism and the Celtic Tiger: legacies of history and the quest for vision', in Kirby *et al.* (eds), *Reinventing Ireland*, p. 110, 117–18.

69 E. Morgan, 'Former yuppies count cost of success', *Irish Times*, 30 August 2002.

70 M. Cronin, 'Speed limits: Ireland, globalisation and the war against time', in Kirby *et al.* (eds), *Reinventing Ireland*, pp. 63–5.

71 The most lucid examination of the bogus nature of consumer choice under capitalism remains that of Adorno. See, for example, the essays entitled 'The schema of mass culture' and 'Culture industry reconsidered', in T. W. Adorno, *The Culture Industry: Selected Essays on Mass Culture* (London: Routledge, 1991).

72 P. Murphy, 'Radical adults', *Hot Press*, 26:15 (14 August 2002), p. 38.

73 T. Moore, 'In the eye of the Tyger', *Irish Times Weekend Review*, 28 July 2001.

74 For a critique of the culture of narcissism that pervades contemporary Ireland – and elsewhere – see Kirby *et al.* (eds), *Reinventing Ireland*, p. 8.

75 Kirby *et al.*, 'Conclusions and transformations', p. 207; F. O'Toole, 'A new nation of beggars on horseback', *Irish Times*, 6 August 2002, p. 12.

76 K. Cronin, 'A sociological analysis of the recent rise in assaults on young men in Irish society', unpublished MA thesis, National University of Ireland, Maynooth, 2000.

77 F. Jameson, 'Postmodernism: the cultural logic of late capitalism', *New Left Review*, 176 (July–August 1984).

78 Cleary, 'Modernization and aesthetic ideology', p. 107.

79 B. Ó Seaghda, 'The Celtic Tiger's media pundits', in Kirby *et al.* (eds), *Reinventing Ireland*, p. 143.

80 P. Connolly, A. Smith and B. Kelly, *Too Young to Notice? The Cultural and Political Awareness of 3–6 Year Olds in Northern Ireland* (Belfast: Community Relations Council, 2002).

81 J. MacManus, 'The Tiger: asleep or extinct, that is the question', *Irish Times*, 10 November 2001, p. 9; F. Islam, 'Will euro give new life to the old Tiger?', *Observer*, 23 December 2001, p. 13.

82 S. Molony and P. Boyle, 'Gloomsday files warn economy is on slide', *Irish Independent*, 8 August 2002.

83 For a critical reading of the euphoria that often attended the US economy in the 1990s see R. Brenner, 'The boom and the bubble', *New Left Review*, 2:6 (November–December 2000).

84 F. Jameson, 'The "end of art" or the "end of history"?', in F. Jameson, *The Cultural Turn: Selected Writings on the Postmodern, 1984–1998* (London: Verso, 1998), p. 90.

85 For a discussion of the tendency within social theory – and particularly Marxist social theory – to privilege time over space, see D. Harvey, *Spaces of Hope* (Edinburgh: Edinburgh University Press, 2000), especially chapters 2 and 3.

2

Macroeconomic policy in the Celtic Tiger: a critical reassessment

DENIS O'HEARN

The miraculous turnaround in the fortunes of the southern Irish economy during the 1990s fooled most experts. The upturn began in the early 1990s, following one of the worst economic periods in the history of the Irish state. The economy then 'took off' in 1994 for seven years of sustained high growth that earned the Irish Republic the popular name of the 'Celtic Tiger'.

The Celtic Tiger emerged from a historic expansion in the United States that was centred on the information technology (IT) industry. After the restructuring of the 1980s and a decade of speculation that Japan would overtake the United States as world economic leader, the turnaround in US fortunes was as unexpected as the subsequent associated boom in Ireland. During every quarter of every year since the US expansion began, respected economists predicted its demise. In early 2001, the expansion finally ended and the US economy was in recession by the end of the year. Soon after the US slowdown began, Irish growth also began to wane and turned negative in the second half of 2001. Experts began to pronounce the death of the Celtic Tiger, as suddenly as they had discovered its birth some seven years before.

In the light of this downturn, perhaps we can now step back and assess what this period of growth was all about, and specify how the southern Irish economy and society have changed, particularly from a macroeconomic perspective. Such a broad look at the experience of the 1990s, I believe, shows that the correlation most economists make between macroeconomic stability and economic growth is spurious. Irish economic growth was due to a unique set of (mostly exogenous) circumstances, centred on a massive inflow of US corporate subsidiaries, which cannot be replicated in other countries and possibly cannot be sustained in Ireland. Without those special circumstances, all the macroeconomic stability in the world could not have achieved economic growth rapid enough to promote convergence with the wealthier economies of the European Union

(EU) or of the Organisation for Economic Cooperation and Development (OECD). Moreover, an assessment of Ireland's decade of growth indicates that the objective of maintaining growth actually impeded the achievement of many important social goals, for two reasons. First, since the southern Irish state correctly realised that the main incentive to attract transnational corporations (TNCs) was low corporate taxes, it pursued a neo-liberal growth model that matched low taxes and fiscal restraint with minimal government interference in business. Second, for several reasons, including a spurious association of fiscal restraint with economic success, the state abjectly failed to mobilise the fiscal resources that were created by rapid growth in order to reduce inequality and improve social welfare. Instead, it turned these resources back, through tax reductions that favoured the wealthier members of Irish society.

Some initial observations

At the end of the 1980s, the Irish people suffered a twenty per cent *official* rate of unemployment[1] and the state had one of the highest ratios of debt to national income in the world. The 1980s had been a difficult period of restructuring in the world economy. The southern Irish economy, whose indigenous industrial sector had been in rapid decline since Ireland's accession to the European Economic Community in 1972, already relied heavily on investments by TNCs. One of the features of global restructuring was large-scale disinvestment and relocation of TNC activities. Irish growth rates declined and unemployment rates soared as TNC disinvestments and the failure of new TNCs to invest in adequate numbers complemented indigenous industrial decline. No one knew at the time how a subsequent upturn of foreign investments would affect specific regions like Ireland. Some experts feared that peripheral regions like Ireland would lose out, since the 'new investment' of the 1990s appeared to be based on flexible relations, such as subcontracting, instead of the older practice of sinking big amounts of capital in foreign subsidiaries.

By 1994, however, it was already clear that the southern Irish economy was going to be an important site for the new expansion in the world economy, which was led by economic growth in the United States and, particularly, by expansion of 'modern' sectors like IT. As a result of a huge increase in Irish exports produced by foreign-owned subsidiaries in manufacturing and services, Irish gross domestic product (GDP) growth rates rose to 5.8 per cent in 1994 and remained at least as high thereafter (Table 2.1). Southern Irish per capita national income, which had been barely sixty per cent of the EU average in 1988, reached the EU average by the late 1990s. The Irish economy, now popularly known as the 'Celtic

Table 2.1 Percentage real economic growth rates in the 1990s in the Republic of Ireland

Year	Gross domestic product	Gross national product
1991	1.9	2.3
1992	3.3	2.3
1993	2.7	3.4
1994	5.8	6.3
1995	9.7	8.2
1996	7.7	7.4
1997	10.7	9.3
1998	8.6	7.8
1999	9.8	7.8
2000	11.5	10.4

Source: *National Income and Expenditure* (Cork: Central Statistics Office, various years).

Tiger', was widely regarded as a model to be followed by other countries seeking 'economic success'.

What was the basis of this turnaround? For most experts, the answer seems to be that Ireland had finally achieved rapid economic growth because of several policy factors. Successive Irish governments had persisted with a policy of educating workers in IT skills, even during the bleak years when the local economy had insufficient need for them.[2] In time this strategy paid off, because Ireland had a surplus of trained IT experts when capital came a-calling to employ them (and it was also serendipitous that capital wanted English-speaking experts). Social partnership agreements assured pay restraint and flexible labour, which were important to the TNCs but even more important to low-profit service companies. And, most importantly for orthodox economists, southern Ireland achieved a generally stable macroeconomic environment through restrictive fiscal policy, stable exchange rates and so on.[3]

On this basis, economists cite the Irish case to support the orthodoxy of the International Monetary Fund (IMF), the OECD and other international bodies that favour macroeconomic stability over all other social and economic policy variables. The new orthodoxy as the EU enters into a phase of enlargement is to convince the accession countries that they *will* converge if they maximise the openness of their trade, get the macroeconomics right and encourage labour flexibility. Mainstream analysts point to Ireland, the only country that has recently achieved convergence with the EU average, as proof positive of the beneficence of such policies. But is it really true that macroeconomic stability played such a central role in Irish growth and convergence? And at what price was such stability achieved and maintained?

Foreign investment and the Celtic Tiger

Mainstream macroeconomic analyses aside, the single overriding factor in the 'success' of the Celtic Tiger was the arrival of huge clusters of foreign subsidiaries in a few sectors, and predominantly from the United States. The Celtic Tiger has been extremely dependent on foreign activities, particularly on rising exports from Ireland by US computer and pharmaceutical companies. Irish economic growth in the 1990s was dominated by the country's ability to attract investments by TNCs in a changing global environment. If macroeconomic stability played an important role in the creation and maintenance of the Celtic Tiger, it was primarily because a stable environment was more attractive to TNCs. Low corporate taxes were the most important attraction, although they were hardly an innovation, since they had been introduced in the 1950s and extended in the 1970s. Of secondary importance were targeted education policies that created a pool of IT experts (and a small pool, at that, relative to the broad Irish labour market), again a policy feature since the 1960s and 1970s. Finally, the extension of previous corporatist wage agreements into broader 'social partnership' agreements suppressed wages and increased labour flexibility, although the first factor is of relatively minor importance to most TNCs, because their wage bill is extremely low relative to other costs.[4] None of these policies, however, would have turned around the Irish economy was it not for a single factor: the 1990s was a period of unprecedented boom for the US economy, particularly in computers and health-related technologies. The boom sent US corporations looking for access to new markets (of which the EU was most important) and tax shelters where they could shift unprecedented profits.

After a period of worldwide restructuring in the 1980s and an economic threat from Japan, the United States reasserted its global leadership in high-tech sectors during the 1990s, particularly in IT. US TNCs expanded their IT production and searched for new markets, often by setting up regional hubs to service key markets like the EU. This caused a revival of foreign direct investment, but in new patterns. Investment was more concentrated than in previous decades, with groups of TNCs agglomerated in a key country or region. In this way, they could supply each other as well as supplying the target markets. Cheap labour and government subsidies were less important than labour flexibility and the ability to move commodities and profits freely.

The attraction of the EU as a market for US high-tech products increased further after 1992 with the coming of the single European market. US investments in the EU rose rapidly and they agglomerated in Ireland primarily because of its extremely low tax rates on corporate profits – ten per cent compared with thirty to forty per cent elsewhere in Europe. Low tax rates not only meant that TNCs could retain more of the profits they received from their activities in Ireland – they also enabled them to shift profits into Ireland by manipulating transfer prices (prices for intra-firm sales), so that they could reduce their overall global tax liability.[5] While low taxes were the primary attraction, TNCs were also drawn by Ireland's cheap, educated, English-speaking labour force; by its low bureaucratic restrictions on foreign investors; and by a history of close relations with the Irish Industrial Development Authority (IDA).

If a single event can point to the birth of the Celtic Tiger, it was the Irish state's success in attracting Intel to the country in 1990, at a historic-ally high cost to the Irish state. A significant number of IT companies had already located in Ireland during the 1970s and 1980s. But after Intel located its European site for the production of computer chips near Dublin, nearly every major player in the computer industry followed. By the late 1990s, Ireland was home to Gateway, Dell, AST, Apple, Hewlett-Packard and Siemens-Nixdorff in PCs; Intel, Fujitsu, Xilinx and Analog Devices in integrated circuits; Seagate and Quantum in disk drives; and Microsoft, Lotus and Oracle in software. Telesales and teleservicing for these large firms followed, along with hundreds of less well known pro-ducers of boards, power supplies, cables, connectors, data storage, printers, networking and everything else that goes into or around computers, as well as services that are connected to or use computers. The Republic of Ireland's share of foreign investment inflows into the EU tripled between 1991 and 1994, as it attracted forty per cent of US electronics invest-ments in Europe. A similar agglomeration of foreign pharmaceutical companies also located in Ireland.

Fixed investments by US firms, which had fallen rapidly during the 1980s, rose dramatically in the 1990s (Table 2.2), while investments by other TNCs and Irish firms declined. As a result, the share of US-based firms in total fixed industrial investment rose from a third at the begin-ning of the 1990s to two-thirds at the end of the decade.

Because of Ireland's small size, this level of activity directly caused rapid economic growth. TNCs were directly responsible for forty-five per cent of southern Irish economic growth during the first half of the 1990s and were indirectly responsible for additional growth in con-struction and services. Moreover, the impact of TNCs was rising fast. Between 1995 and 1999, TNCs directly accounted for eighty-five per cent of economic growth in terms of their value added (the difference between their incomes for the commodities they produced and their non-wage costs of producing them). Their rising profits alone accounted for fifty-three per cent of economic growth! Where TNCs' value added was equivalent to fourteen per cent of GDP in 1990, it rose above fifty per cent in 1999.

The effect of TNCs on economic growth was concentrated in exports within three manufacturing sectors that were dominated by US firms:

Table 2.2 Fixed industrial investments in the Republic of Ireland, by country of origin (IR£millions at constant 1990 prices), 1990–98

Year	US TNCs	Other TNCs	Irish firms	US share of total (%)	Irish share of total (%)
1990	68.4	52.0	90.0	32.5	42.7
1991	109.8	114.6	71.6	37.1	24.2
1992	126.7	81.6	60.5	47.1	22.5
1993	175.5	62.2	49.1	61.2	17.1
1994	137.1	48.3	52.8	57.6	22.2
1995	157.9	44.2	56.7	61.0	21.9
1996	252.8	49.9	97.1	63.2	24.3
1997	259.0	51.6	70.3	68.0	18.5
1998	256.0	71.3	62.2	65.7	16.0

Source: Central Statistics Office.

chemicals, computers and electrical engineering. These three sectors alone (and not including software and teleservices) accounted for forty per cent of Irish economic (GDP) growth during the 1990s, including fifty-one per cent in 1998, fifty per cent in 1999 and forty-six per cent in 2000. They accounted for seventy-eight per cent of industrial growth (including construction) in 1998, eighty-five per cent in 1999 and eighty-four per cent in 2000. They were the only economic sectors that exceeded the average GDP growth rate of 6.3 per cent during the 1990s, together growing annually by about fifteen per cent. Even a single product could have a large effect on Irish economic growth, as was the case in 1997/98 when Pfizer introduced its Irish-produced drug Viagra onto the world market and 'Irish output' of organic chemical products rose by seventy per cent.[6]

The other side of this heavily concentrated growth was that stagnation could also come quickly and in a concentrated form. This appears to have been the case from the middle of 2001 on, after the US IT-based economy went into recession. Within months, there were reverberations within the Irish economy as IT companies began to close or cut back their operations in record numbers. Despite a relatively healthy beginning, the year ended with the IDA announcing record job losses in foreign-owned companies. Due to closures and cutbacks, the numbers employed in the IT sector fell by eleven per cent in 2001, with job losses of 10,792. Some of these were in the most high-profile US companies of the sector, such as Motorola, Gateway and General Semiconductors.[7]

These sector-specific job losses quickly began to translate into a general economic contraction, as the main sources of economic growth dried up. From this point on, the medium-term trajectory of the Irish economy, including the duration of stagnation and whether stagnation would turn into severe contraction, depended on two things. First, the duration of the US recession would have obvious effects on the duration and depth of Irish recession. And second, the depth of Irish recession would depend on the degree to which the downturn in manufacturing worked its way through other sectors, particularly services and construction. If the 1990s was a period of economic growth, with lagged effects on employment growth and possibly on investment growth, the present decade could easily become one of economic decline, with lagged negative effects on employment and investment.

The extreme relationship between Irish economic growth and the expansion of foreign activity created a number of unique characteristics that set off the Irish economy from others within the EU, including others on the EU periphery. Most distinctly, a gap opened up between GDP and gross national product (GNP).[8] Ireland is unique in Europe in the degree that its gross *domestic* product exceeds its gross *national* product, because of the profits that are removed by TNCs. In 1983, foreign profit repatriations made up just three per cent of GDP. By 1995, they were nearly nineteen per cent of GDP. In 1999, they had risen to an astounding forty per cent of GDP – forty-eight per cent if incomes from royalties and licences are included! The proportion of TNC profits in GDP began to rise to an astonishing extent after 1997. In 1998, growth of foreign profits was equivalent to eighty per cent of economic growth! During the two years of 1997 and 1999, the rise of TNC profits was equivalent to two-thirds of economic growth. As a result, the gap between GDP and GNP widened. In 1980, southern Irish GDP and GNP were practically equal. In 1990, GDP was eleven per cent higher than GNP. By the turn of the century, GDP exceeded GNP by about twenty per cent. In simple language, GDP overstates by a fifth how much of the material wealth created by the economic activities of the Irish people is available for their own use within Ireland.

Arguably, Ireland's most important function today is as a site where US companies can shift their products into Europe, while accumulating profits in order to avoid taxation. TNCs buy (import) their inputs cheap from other subsidiaries and sell (export) them dear, mainly to Europe but also back to the United States (especially in the case of pharmaceuticals). Significant profit shifting through transfer pricing is indicated by the extraordinarily high TNC profit rates cited above, along with unrealistic output growth and rises of labour productivity in the sectors most prone to profit shifting. According to the US Department of Commerce's *Survey of Current Business*, in the Republic of Ireland US-based TNCs maintained profit rates in the 1990s that were five times greater than those achieved elsewhere in the world (up from two and a half times higher in the 1970s). These uncommonly high profit rates were accompanied by rapid output growth, beyond what would have been expected from the TNCs' rates of investment.

Growth and employment

Greater optimism about Ireland's economic prospects emerged in the early 1990s. But this optimism was initially restrained by the fact that economic growth and convergence were so disconnected from other policy variables. The main policy target was employment, as the country had continued to endure high unemployment rates even into the mid-1990s. Some observers were concerned at the lack of employment growth that was associated with early output growth. Essentially, the economy appeared to be growing during the first half of the 1990s without employing more people. The unemployment rate actually rose during parts of the early 1990s and this led to a concern that the economy was experiencing growth without gains in employment.[9]

The economy finally began to generate substantial numbers of new jobs after 1994. The growth of employment in the second half of the 1990s was remarkable. Depending on the source of the estimate, unemployment rates still exceeded fifteen per cent and possibly approached twenty per cent in 1994. Yet, by 2000, the number of jobs in the southern Irish economy had risen by nearly a half compared with 1990, with total employment rising by more than half a million during the decade. As a result, official unemployment rates fell to around four per cent at the end of the decade.

As suggested above, however, employment growth was not directly associated with output growth. During the 1990s, output growth was heavily concentrated in manufacturing and, more precisely, in the three US-dominated manufacturing sectors of computers, electronic engineering and pharmaceuticals. Employment growth, however, was clearly concentrated in services (Table 2.3), which accounted for seventy-eight per cent of the net new jobs in the southern Irish economy. There was a clear lag in the employment effect of growth during the 1990s because the companies that were responsible for output growth, US TNCs, did not employ very many people, relative to their economic size. Gains in employment were mostly within the construction and service sectors, which expanded as some of the effects of manufacturing growth finally filtered through to the rest of the economy.

A structural result of the Celtic Tiger growth period, then, was that the southern Irish economy became even more dependent on services for employment, while it became more dependent on manufacturing as a source of growth. In 1990, services made up fifty-seven per cent of total employment. By 1999, they accounted for sixty-four per cent. This also

Table 2.3 Employment (thousands of employees) and percentage employment change during the 1990s

	Services	Industry	Total[a]
1990 employment	643	321	1,133
Changes			
1991	13	2	1
1992	15	−5	9
1993	18	−7	4
1994	18	20	36
1995	41	15	57
1996	46	5	45
1997	62	19	80
1998	72	58	130
1999	72	23	96
2000	60	25	80
2000 employment	1,064	476	1,671
Change, 1990–2000	*421*	*155*	*538*

[a]Employment totals in industry and services do not add up to the totals for the economy because of employment in agriculture, which is not included here.
Source: Central Statistics Office.

meant that employment was concentrated in a low-wage sector, although certain of the new services included high-wage jobs. There was also a steady transformation from full-time to part-time employment, as the Irish labour market became increasingly flexible. Seven of every twenty new jobs created in the 1990s were part-time. Where less than eight per cent of jobs were part-time in 1990, seventeen per cent were part-time by 2000. Other forms of casualisation of work, such as fixed-term, temporary and 'self-employed' contracting, also increased rapidly. Wage restraint *and* flexibility were enhanced as a feature of the southern Irish economy by social partnership agreements, where labour moderated its demands over wages and job security in return for concessions on income taxes. Thus, rising employment in the 1990s came at the cost of Ireland having one of the most flexible labour regimes in Europe, with low job security, substantially more workers on low wages and fewer workers' rights.[10]

While it took some years for growth to translate into jobs, it also appeared during the early 1990s that growth was taking place without much investment, from either indigenous or foreign sources (TNC-based exports from Ireland grew *much* more rapidly than TNC investments).

The investment share of Irish national income, already low by EU standards, plummeted during the first half of the 1990s. The investment rate (gross capital formation divided by GDP) fell from about twenty per cent in 1990 to fourteen per cent in 1994, which was substantially below the EU average of about twenty per cent. This was considered to be such a problem that the National Economic and Social Council (NESC) carried out a major study into 'investmentless growth' during the mid-1990s. It was only after a lag of a few years that economic growth became associated with rising investment, which recovered during the second half of the 1990s (see Table 2.4, below).

The indigenous economy: following the European path?

Has the rapid growth of the foreign sector spun off into indigenous sectors? Some experts have argued that the 1990s were different from earlier periods because TNC activities encouraged a greater expansion of indigenous companies. O'Malley[11] argued that a dynamic indigenous manufacturing sector grew alongside the foreign sector. Others contend that the TNC investments of the 1990s were more strongly linked to indigenous industry than during previous expansions.[12]

Ó Riain[13] makes a more indirect argument about the effects of the foreign-owned sector on indigenous activity. He argues that there were 'two globalisations' in Ireland in the 1990s. One was the outward movement of US capital through Ireland and into Europe. The other was the development of a dynamic and globally oriented Irish indigenous sector, led by Irish entrepreneurs who were 'globalised' by their connections with TNCs in IT in places like California's Silicon Valley. Ó Riain credits this Irish success to the *flexible* developmental policies of the Irish state, which combined a neo-liberal macroeconomic environment with everyday micro-intervention to identify opportunities for local entrepreneurs.

Accounts of a recent indigenous revival are overstated, however. The Irish state limited its pressure on TNCs to link locally because stronger intervention would have undermined the basic attractiveness of Ireland as a deregulated, hands-off state. In 1996, out of 2,667 indigenous firms that employed ten or more people, only 174 were sub-suppliers to TNCs, mostly providing routine supplies like packaging and printed materials.[14] The proportion of raw materials that were purchased locally by TNCs hardly rose at all during the 1990s, from 18.8 per cent in 1990 to 19.1 per cent in 1996. If we account for the fact that two-thirds of 'local purchases' in the electronics sector actually consisted of one TNC subsidiary buying from another,[15] then TNCs were buying a substantially *smaller* share of their material supplies from Irish firms as the Celtic Tiger developed. While the absolute amount of material purchases by foreign firms certainly rose by an unknown amount during the 1990s, creating some new opportunities for some Irish businesses, it is important not to overestimate the extent to which this happened.

Ó Riain's second globalisation – indigenous spin-offs that were not directly linked to the foreign sector – appears to be significant only in software. The thousands of engineers and technicians who qualified in Ireland but emigrated, and others who stayed in Ireland but left their TNC employers, were a pool of potential entrepreneurs with knowledge of the software industry and who were eager to set up as small employers. They did so in record numbers during the 1990s. By the year 2000, the media reported that Ireland was the second largest exporter of software, behind the United States, having surpassed Israel and India. They stressed the importance of the indigenous sector in this result. Half of the employment in software was in indigenous Irish firms. Nearly eighty per cent of Irish software companies exported some of their product and nearly half exported most of their product.[16] Yet eighty-two per cent of these firms had no alliances of any kind with TNCs.[17]

In reality, however, the indigenous software sector is very weak. The industry is dominated by TNCs in every respect except employment. With only half of software employees, TNCs account for eighty-seven per cent of Irish software sales, ninety-two per cent of software exports and eighty-nine per cent of software revenues. Microsoft alone accounted for forty per cent of exports in 1995.[18] Indigenous software firms are mostly very small, with average employment less than fifteen. According to Ó Riain, their low levels of investment in research and development are 'worrying' and expenditure on training actually fell during the 1990s. This indicates that Irish software, like the rest of the economy, is essentially dualistic – with highly developed TNC giants alongside a scattering of very small and vulnerable domestic firms. The Irish software sector 'cannot bear the burden of the huge expectations which have been placed on [it]'.[19]

Overall, the sustainability of Irish indigenous industry had become very questionable by the end of the 1990s. Indigenous exports and profit performance remained weak. While the rise of TNC profits was spectacular between 1990 and 1999, rising more than sixfold, indigenous profits remained stable, even dipping at the end of the decade. Thus, the indigenous share of profits fell from over fifty per cent in 1990 to less than ten per cent in 1999.[20] While foreign profits are undoubtedly inflated by TNC profit-shifting behaviour, this does not detract from the fact that indigenous profits were not rising substantially during Ireland's most significant phase of rapid economic growth. This weakness was also reflected in a sharp rise in the numbers of indigenous company failures at the end of the decade.[21]

This duality between a rapidly growing foreign sector and a relatively stagnant indigenous one is shown most clearly in productivity figures for the 1990s. Output in the three US-dominated sectors of computers, electrical engineering and chemicals grew by 375 per cent during 1990–99, while employment grew by only seventy-three per cent. Thus, output per employee grew by 215 per cent, nearly nine per cent annually. Elsewhere in the economy – mainly Irish-owned services, construction and basic manufactures – output rose by just fifty-five per cent, while employment grew by forty per cent. Output per employee grew by about one per cent annually, which is quite a low figure by international standards. By 1999, the average worker in the foreign sector produced nearly eight times more output by value than did the average worker in the rest of the economy.[22] Again, productivity figures in the TNC-dominated sectors are so unreal that comparison with them cannot be taken to imply anything about the productivity growth of indigenous sectors. On the other hand, productivity growth of the indigenous sectors is low by any international standard and challenges the dominant assumption in Ireland that the indigenous sector was a dynamic partner in the Celtic Tiger growth experience of the 1990s.

Macroeconomic change: components of GDP

How have the dramatic changes of the 1990s affected the overall shape of the southern Irish economy? One of the most dramatic changes during the Celtic Tiger period was a change in the components of GDP/GNP. Indeed, when conservative economists proclaim the success of Irish macroeconomic stability, they are essentially praising a model that has effected a change in the composition of GDP that has entailed a declining proportion going to forms of income and expenditure that benefit the wider population, and a rising proportion being devoted to those that favour private corporations and the rich.

In all the excitement about rapid economic growth, which was certainly spectacular in the latter half of the 1990s, commentators often missed more fundamental changes that were taking place in the distribution of the national product. GDP was growing rapidly, but certain components of GDP were growing especially rapidly while other components changed much more slowly. Moreover, the distinction between what was growing very rapidly and what was growing much less rapidly had a class character and a global character. That is, the components that rose most rapidly favoured the richer segments of Irish and global society alike, while the other components disproportionately affected the wellbeing of the general Irish public.

The changing components of GDP (measured on an expenditure basis) are given in Table 2.4. The most profound increase was in the export surplus, which tripled its share of GDP over the course of the 1990s, from less than five per cent to over fourteen per cent. The export surplus is practically equivalent to repatriated profits of the TNCs,[23] so it is clear that *transnational capital* was the primary recipient of the benefits of Irish growth. The TNCs' share of GDP rose dramatically, from less than five per cent in 1990 to nearly fifteen per cent in 2000. In other words, their share tripled, while in absolute terms TNC incomes grew many times over.[24] This should be hardly surprising if, as I have argued, the overwhelming *raison d'être* of the Celtic Tiger from the global perspective was the creation of a regime that was amenable to the accumulation of profits by US transnational capital.

In return for creating this amenable environment, there were distinct advantages for the Irish state and for *sections* of the Irish public (to which I will return shortly). But, leaving distributional income aspects aside for the moment, what of the general Irish public?

The most striking thing about the changing distribution of southern Irish GDP during the 1990s is the move *away from* consumption, both private and public. Private consumption, which made up nearly two-thirds of GDP in 1990, fell to less than half in 2000. Irish public consumption, which, at sixteen per cent of GDP, was already at one of the lowest levels in Europe in the early 1990s, fell even further, to twelve per cent in 2000. As a whole, the share of GDP represented by public and private consumption fell dramatically, from seventy-seven per cent in 1990 to sixty-two per cent in 2000.[25] I will consider the negative consequences of these trends on social welfare below.

Table 2.4 Changing composition of GDP during the Celtic Tiger period (%)

Year	Private consumption	Public consumption	Investment	Export surplus
1990	61.3	15.3	18.7	4.7
1991	61.6	16.1	17.3	5.0
1992	60.0	16.1	16.3	7.5
1993	58.4	15.9	15.2	10.5
1994	58.2	15.7	16.3	9.8
1995	56.3	15.0	17.2	11.5
1996	55.4	14.3	18.6	11.6
1997	53.1	13.9	20.3	12.7
1998	52.6	13.4	22.4	11.6
1999	50.2	12.7	23.4	13.7
2000	49.4	12.2	23.8	14.3

Source: *National Income and Expenditure* (Cork: Central Statistics Office, various years).

Finally, it is worth noting that there was a distinct and rapid recovery of investment, the stagnation of which had exercised many experts during the early part of the 1990s.

The TNC profits explosion, fiscal policy and inequality

These broad changes in the Irish economy during the 1990s are crucial, because there is strong evidence that growth has been associated with inequality under the Celtic Tiger. On the one hand, economic growth encouraged a large rise in profits and unearned incomes, without a corresponding rise in wage levels, so that the class distribution of income moved rapidly away from the working classes and the poor and towards capital and high-income professionals. Rapidly rising outflows of profits to TNCs, combined with inflows of profits and fees to the upper strata of the Irish population, created a level of class inequality that was previously unknown in modern Ireland. Where factor shares of non-agricultural income were relatively stable before 1987, with wages accounting for seventy per cent and profits thirty per cent, they shifted drastically thereafter, until the profits share from non-agricultural activities was virtually equal to the wage share in the year 2000.[26]

On the other hand, factor income inequality was accompanied by increased disparities in incomes, including wages. The Irish labour market became more segmented during the growth phase of the 1990s, with a clear distinction between high-waged core jobs and low-waged peripheral jobs. As labour market segmentation became more pronounced, income distributions became more unequal. The available data show that both wages and disposable incomes became more unequal after 1987. The disposable incomes of the top forty per cent of households grew *twice as quickly* as those of the bottom forty per cent between 1987 and 1994. They continued to diverge thereafter. The share of the nation's disposable income of the bottom forty per cent of households fell from 16.2 per cent in 1994 to 15.2 per cent in 1998, while the share of the bottom ten per cent fell from 2.3 to 1.8 per cent.[27]

In terms of the ratio of the income share of the richest ten per cent to the poorest ten per cent, Ireland was, in the mid-1990s, the most unequal country in Europe and second only to the United States in the OECD.[28] Barrett *et al.*[29] show that the increase in earnings dispersion (ratio of the top to the bottom decile) was greater in Ireland than anywhere else in the OECD in 1994. Nolan and Hughes found that the proportion of Irish workers on low pay in that same year was twice the EU average and five times the Scandinavian average.[30] The income data quoted above indicate that this probably got worse rather than better in the last half of the 1990s. Moreover, by some absolute as well as relative measures, poverty increased along with inequality. By the end of the century, according to the United Nations' *Human Development Report*, the Irish poverty rate, as measured by its Human Poverty Index, was the highest in the EU.[31]

This rising level of inequality and relative poverty during a period of rapid growth was *not* effectively countered by state policies, as one can clearly see in macroeconomic terms by the shares of GDP shifting towards capital and away from public welfare. To what extent was this failure due to policy? On the surface, the changing components of GDP were a combination of two processes: a rapid increase of profit incomes that accompanied the inflow of TNC activities in the 1990s, and a rapid reduction in the share of public consumption/expenditure due to liberalised fiscal policy (i.e., stable macroeconomic policies). The first process is part and parcel of the Celtic Tiger, which is based on foreign activities and foreign profits. It is therefore a *systemic* outcome of the kind of development model that was chosen by Irish governments as far back as the 1950s and which has been adhered to since.

The second process, however, may be thought of as a policy variable *within* that developmental system. In other words, the government *could have* held onto its public functions and even increased them as fiscal revenues increased. Alternatively, fiscal liberalisation could be considered to be part and parcel of the neo-liberal model that attracted the TNCs in the first place. In reality, government fiscal liberalisation was probably a combination of the two, that is, both a policy variable and a systemic one. There were strong international pressures on the Irish government to liberalise during the 1990s – a process that was mirrored throughout the EU and, indeed, the rest of the world. But liberalisation was promoted within the twenty-six counties with a relish that was unnecessary, either for Ireland playing its 'proper role' in Europe *or* for maintaining the expansionary phase of the Celtic Tiger. Successive administrations in Dublin drew away from providing public services and public welfare in the 1990s in favour of providing tax breaks that favoured the richer segments of Irish society.

Indeed, the overriding ideological position of the 1990s in the Republic of Ireland was that growth was the result of neo-liberal policies, including privatisation and 'responsible' fiscal policies. Successive state budgets after 1987 favoured tax cuts for the rich and failed to provide the necessary spending to correct Ireland's severe social problems.

According to Eurostat, Ireland in 1997 had the lowest levels in the EU of both government revenues and government expenditures as a proportion of GDP. Sweden raised the most revenues, at more than 60 per cent of GDP, while the Irish state received revenues worth a mere 36 per cent of GDP. Irish spending was even more conservative. It was the only state in the EU whose public expenditures were less than forty per cent of GDP, at 35 per cent (compared with Sweden at 63 per cent and Denmark at 60 per cent). While these low figures partly result from the fact that Irish GDP was growing rapidly, they nonetheless represent an extraordinarily low level of state spending on basic social programmes. Despite its much vaunted emphasis on educating IT professionals, Ireland had the second lowest per capita expenditure in the EU on primary education, less than forty per cent of the Danish level. And it had the fourth lowest level of per capita spending on health, ahead of only Greece, Spain and Portugal, and only about half the German level.

Due to such government policies, many social services ran down. A populist social housing regime that had provided affordable and reasonable accommodation for successive generations of low-income households broke down. Irish citizens no longer have assured access to affordable housing.[32] In health, only three EU member states reduced spending as a proportion of GDP between 1980 and 1996. Ireland's reduction, twenty per cent, was easily the largest of the three. Irish public health spending per capita as a percentage of the EU average remained around seventy per cent, despite Ireland's rapid growth. During the 1990s, the number of hospital beds in southern Ireland fell, even as demand for them rose, leaving the country with the fewest hospital beds per capita in the EU. Even after an increase in health spending in 1998, Ireland still ranked twentieth in a survey of twenty-seven OECD countries, with much of what the government called new 'health' spending actually going on social services.[33] Between 1970–75 and 1995–2000, Ireland's global ranking with respect to life expectancy at birth fell by seven places.[34] In the field of education, Ireland has performed poorly, in spite of the public image that growth is due to a highly educated population. Almost twenty-three per cent of the population are functionally illiterate, easily the highest level in the EU. Yet, in the late 1990s, Ireland ranked last in the OECD in terms of investment per pupil as a proportion of per capita GNP.[35]

One of the most notable economic features of the 1990s was a sustained and rapid increase in fiscal revenues, despite the fact that Ireland was the lowest tax raiser in the EU and despite a falling tax take as a share of national income. This was primarily a result of the large numbers of new employees in the economy after 1995 and of taxes on their incomes and expenditures. Income taxes consistently made up about fifty-four per cent of state revenues from 1995 to 2000, while taxes on expenditures (which are notoriously regressive) rose from forty per cent of revenues in 1995 to forty-two per cent in 2000. It is significant that corporate taxes were not a major source of rising state revenues, despite the fact that trading profits of companies tripled between 1995 and 2000!

Rapidly rising revenues gave the Irish state a historical opportunity to begin making the transition from being one of the low-service economies of the EU to joining the continental social democratic countries

that provide high levels of services and social welfare for their populations. Instead, Irish governments tightened their conservative fiscal
policy of spending restraint and ran higher and higher budget surpluses.
Where the southern Irish state ran a budgetary deficit of IR£460 million
in 1995, rising revenues and spending restraint enabled it to turn this
around to a huge budget surplus of IR£5.1 *billion* in 2000. In the period
between 1996 and 2000, the government ran budget surpluses totalling
more than IR£12 billion. During this period, governments made big
announcements about grandiose public programmes to fight poverty and
to build infrastructure. Yet their unwillingness or inability to spend money
meant that these programmes were, in the end, more words than deeds.

Instead of applying its resources to improving infrastructures and
public services, the Irish state introduced a series of 'give-away budgets',
which offered tax breaks. These budgets became an annual event in the
second half of the 1990s, with the Irish Finance Minister initiating a
series of high-profile tax cuts. This publicity was generally geared to
give the impression that the reductions in tax were of benefit to most
people living in the Irish Republic. Closer inspection, however, consistently showed that the tax packages were heavily weighted towards high-
income earners and had marginal effects on the incomes of lower earners.
Over the four years from 1997 to 2000, low-income couples (those earning up to IR£12,500 a year) received tax breaks averaging about IR£250
a year, while high-income receivers (couples on IR£100,000 or more a
year) received income tax breaks of more than IR£1,600 per year.[36]

This crude measure of tax breaks, however, hides an even greater bias
towards inequality in the state's recent budgetary policies. The Economic
and Social Research Institute (ESRI) in Dublin has a tax-benefit model
that estimates the distributional impact of Irish budgets on families in
different income deciles. The model compares actual budget outcomes
against a benchmark, where the percentage change in disposable income
would be similar across all income groups. This model found that every
budget from 1987 to 1998 was regressive, that is, favoured high-income
more than middle- and low-income earners. The 1999 budget was more
neutral and perhaps even slightly progressive. And then the budget for
the year 2000 was again highly regressive. The 2000 budget gave the
lowest decile of income earners a less than one per cent change in their
disposable incomes, but gave the top two deciles more than a four per
cent increase in disposable incomes.[37]

The evidence of the 1990s shows a clear trend towards inequality.
This trend is a feature of Irish economic development at all levels. At the
macro level, the aggregates of national income have shifted dramatically
towards increasing shares for the private sector and capital, while both
private and public consumption have decreased their share of national
income. At the same time, within these aggregates, there has been widening

inequality among income earners, in terms of earnings dispersion and household incomes. And, far from countering these trends, the state has exacerbated them through its policies of encouraging wage restraint, through its highly regressive tax policies and by its constraints on public spending. As the state's revenues increased in the mid-1990s, it had a choice of continuing its fiscal conservatism or using the resources that it gained from the Celtic Tiger for the purpose of raising public consumption and, hopefully, general levels of wellbeing. It chose the former. And when the state reduced taxes, it had the choice of concentrating tax breaks at the lower end of the income spectrum, thus taking the side of equalisation of incomes, or of giving the largest tax breaks to the wealthiest, thus increasing inequality. It chose the latter.

Conclusions: *re*characterising the Irish state

The Celtic Tiger boom of the latter half of the 1990s appeared to be coming to an end as the present decade began. In 2001, recession in the United States caused cutbacks and closures of US-owned subsidiaries in the Republic of Ireland, which had been the backbone of the boom. The initial shock created moderate job losses and a strong contraction of growth. It then began to work its way through the rest of the southern Irish economy, particularly in the sectors of high job growth, such as services and construction. Many official economists were optimistic about the economy's future, and assumed that the downturn was short term and that the economy would return to a moderate equilibrium growth path within a year or two.[38]

Regardless of the sustainability of even moderate growth in Ireland's economic model, which is so dominated by and dependent on TNC activities, the experience of the Celtic Tiger presents us with an opportunity to assess whether such a neo-liberal economic model is desirable on social grounds.

Such an assessment comes in two parts. First, there is the question of whether such a foreign-dependent, and thus neo-liberal, model as Ireland's *can* provide the distribution of growth and the progressive social policies that will enable growth to be translated into general social wellbeing. Second, could the Irish state itself have exercised sufficient autonomy, had it wanted to, to use the resources generated by growth for a more equitable social outcome?

As the evidence of the 1990s shows, the Irish growth model is highly dependent on foreign activities. Rapid economic growth created a dualistic economy. Economic growth, investments, high profits, high-technology products and higher wages were heavily concentrated in the TNC sector. As a result, the continuation of growth required the maintenance and even the deepening of a regime that was attractive to US capital. The most important characteristics of such a regime are low corporate taxes, low restrictions on business, and especially on the flows of money and commodities, and maximum integration into the EU market, where most US exports were targeted. Such a liberalised regime by definition requires the Republic of Ireland to follow the prescriptions of radical globalisation, including privatisation, liberalisation, wage restraint, flexible labour and fiscal restraint. By adhering to such a regime, the south of Ireland was reckoned in 2001 to be the 'most globalised' country in the OECD.[39] Without doubt, fulfilling the conditions that enabled growth by attracting TNCs in the 1990s placed severe constraints on the state's ability to pursue policies that might reduce the negative impact of growth on inequality, combat poverty and allow for greater social provision.

Within these constraints, however, the Irish state had room to manoeuvre. The creation of conditions that favoured the continued entry of and expansion of activities by the TNCs did not require either the severe restrictions on public spending or the highly regressive tax reforms that the state adhered to throughout the 1990s. The windfall of revenues that came to the state in the second half of the 1990s represented a fund that would have enabled it to ease the inequalities that resulted from the Celtic Tiger, while beginning a transformation towards the high-service and higher-welfare models of continental Europe. Instead, Ireland remained, along with the United Kingdom and the United States, one of the most shabby, low-welfare states of the OECD. As a result, Ireland, despite, or perhaps because of, its economic growth, now finds itself at or near the bottom of the OECD on measures of human welfare, such as poverty rates, inequality, infrastructure and the provision of health and general education. It is a sad legacy of what was, after all, *meant* to be an economic miracle.

Notes

1 The actual rate of unemployment was certainly much higher than official statistics would suggest.
2 In the 1980s, the majority of engineering students emigrated within a year of receiving their primary degree; engineers had the highest rate of emigration of all kinds of students in Ireland. J. Wickham, 'Industrialisation, work and employment', in P. Clancy, S. Drudy, K. Lynch and L. O'Dowd (eds), *Ireland: A Sociological Profile* (Dublin: Institute of Public Administration, 1986), p. 92.
3 European Commission, 'The economic and financial situation in Ireland', special edition of *European Economy* (Brussels: European Commission, 1996); J. Bradley, J. Fitzgerald, P. Honohan and I. Kearney, 'Interpreting the recent Irish growth experience', in D. Duffy *et al.* (eds), *Medium-Term*

Review: 1997–2003 (Dublin: Economic and Social Research Institute, 1997); R. O'Donnell and D. Thomas, 'Social partnership in Ireland, 1987–1997', paper presented to a seminar on social partnership in western Europe, Cardiff, 11–13 September 1998; International Monetary Fund, 'IMF concludes Article IV consultation with Ireland', public information notice no. 00/61, 10 August 2000.

4 Other factors were also present but less critical, such as demographic change. For one of the most recent and comprehensive discussions of mainstream and critical explanations of Irish economic growth, see P. Kirby, *The Celtic Tiger in Distress: Growth with Inequality in Ireland* (Basingstoke: Palgrave, 2002).

5 Transfer prices are the accounting prices at which a corporation sells things from one of its subsidiaries to another. By selling inputs cheaply to subsidiaries that are located in countries where taxes are low, and selling on the products from those subsidiaries at an expensive price, corporations can shift their profits (the apparent amount of value that is added above the costs of production) from higher-tax countries to lower-tax countries.

6 Central Statistics Office, *National Income and Expenditure: First Results for 2000* (Cork: Central Statistics Office, 2001).

7 M. Caniffe, 'Company failures up 65% in second quarter 2000', *Irish Times*, 19 December 2000.

8 Put simply, GDP is a measure of all of the goods and services that are produced in a country. GNP, on the other hand, is the (earned and unearned) incomes received and retained by the residents of the country, regardless of where the activities occurred that produced the incomes. Thus, unlike GDP, GNP does not include profits, dividends and interest that are removed from a country, for example, by foreign subsidiaries that are located there. GNP is a better measure of the degree to which economic growth benefits a country as a whole, because it measures the resources that remain there as a result of its economic efforts.

9 See the discussion in D. O'Hearn, 'Global restructuring and the Irish political economy', in P. Clancy *et al.* (eds), *Irish Society: Sociological Perspectives* (Dublin: Institute of Public Administration, 1995).

10 Paul Tansey reaches the positive conclusion that part-time work is 'chosen' by most workers who take it because it meets their lifestyle needs, but this is questioned by Phil O'Connell and Peadar Kirby, among others. P. Tansey, *Ireland at Work: Economic Growth and the Labour Market, 1987–1997* (Dublin: Oak Tree Press, 1998); P. O'Connell, 'Sick man or tigress? The labour market in the Republic of Ireland', in A. Heath, R. Breen and C. Whelan (eds), *Ireland North and South: Perspectives from Social Science* (Oxford: Oxford University Press, 1999), p. 228; Kirby, *The Celtic Tiger in Distress*, p. 54.

11 E. O'Malley, 'The revival of Irish indigenous industry 1987–1997', in *Quarterly Economic Commentary* (Dublin: Economic and Social Research Institute, 1998).

12 F. Barry, J. Bradley and E. O'Malley, 'Indigenous and foreign industry: characteristics and performance', in F. Barry (ed.), *Understanding Ireland's Economic Growth* (London: Macmillan, 1999); F. Ruane, 'Whither Ireland's industrial policy?', paper delivered to the conference of the European Network on Industrial Policy, Dublin, 9–10 December 1999.

13 S. S. Ó Riain, 'Development and the global information society', unpublished PhD dissertation, University of California, Berkeley.

14 M. Breathnach and D. Kelly, 'Multinationals, subcontracting linkages and the innovative performance of indigenous firms: some Irish evidence', paper

delivered to the conference of the European Network on Industrial Policy, Dublin, 9–10 December 1999.

15 Forfás, 'Optimising purchasing linkages in the Irish economy', mimeo (Dublin: Forfás, 1997).

16 Forbairt, *National Software Directorate Irish Software Industry Survey 1995: Results* (Dublin: Forbairt, 1996).

17 Ó Riain, 'Development and the global information society'.

18 Forbairt, *National Software Directorate*.

19 S. Ó Riain, 'The birth of a Celtic Tiger', *Communications of the ACM*, 40:3 (1997), p. 24.

20 Author's calculations from *National Income and Expenditure* and *Balance of International Payments* (Cork: Central Statistics Office, various years).

21 Caniffe, 'Company failures up 65% in second quarter 2000'.

22 Central Statistics Office, *National Income and Expenditure*, various years; Central Statistics Office, *Labour Force Estimates*, various years.

23 D. O'Hearn, *Inside the Celtic Tiger: The Irish Economy and the Asian Model* (London: Pluto, 1998), p. 128.

24 Of course, one must qualify this statement by noting that *reported* TNC incomes are inflated by the profit-shifting mechanisms I have already discussed in this chapter.

25 Of course, both public and private consumption grew over this period in absolute terms. But the rapidly falling shares of consumption in national income indicate how unequally the fruits of growth have been shared. A very small proportion of growth went to goods and services that benefit the wider Irish population. Thus, 'trickle down' is precisely that: a *trickle*. Arguably, a much slower growth strategy could achieve much greater results for the Irish population as a whole.

26 D. O'Hearn, 'Economic growth and social cohesion in Ireland', in M. Dauderstadt and L. Witte (eds), *Cohesive Growth in the Enlarging Euroland* (Berlin: Friedrich Ebert Stiftung, 2001), p. 187.

27 B. Nolan, B. Maitre, D. O'Neill and O. Sweetman, *The Distribution of Income in Ireland* (Dublin: Oak Tree Press, 2000), p. 31.

28 United Nations Development Programme, *Human Development Report 2001* (Oxford: Oxford University Press, 2001), p. 182.

29 A. Barrett, T. Callan and B. Nolan, 'Rising wage inequality, returns to education and labour market institutions: evidence from Ireland', *British Journal of Industrial Relations*, 37:1 (1999), p. 84.

30 B. Nolan and G. Hughes, *Low Pay, the Earnings Distribution and Poverty in Ireland*, working paper no. 84 (Dublin: Economic and Social Research Institute, 1997).

31 United Nations, *Human Development Report 2001*, table 2.4. The Human Poverty Index is based on longevity, life expectancy, standard of living and social exclusion. The data used to construct the index are from various years, mostly in the latter half of the 1990s.

32 T. Fahey, *Social Housing in Ireland: A Study of Success, Failure and Lessons Learned* (Dublin: Oak Tree Press, 1999). The breakdown in social housing was not entirely a discretionary policy variable: increased population and employment led to rising demand. Nonetheless, the crucial point is that the state, having chosen a neo-liberal low-tax, low-spending regime, was unable to do anything effective about the housing problem, which was exacerbated by liberal zoning practices, favourable conditions for speculation and substantial corruption.

33 M. Wren, 'Health system needs urgent funding', *Irish Times*, 3 October 2000.

34 United Nations, *Human Development Report 2001*, p. 141.
35 OECD, *Education at a Glance: OECD Indicators, 1999* (Paris: OECD, 1999).
36 These figures are based upon a household that comprises a married couple, both of whom work.
37 T. Callan, 'Biased budget towards better-off marks return to earlier policy', *Irish Times*, 2 December 1999.
38 D. Duffy *et al.* (eds), *Medium Term Review 2001–2007* (Dublin: Economic and Social Research Institute, 2001).
39 A. T. Kearney, 'Measuring globalisation', *Foreign Policy*, 122 (2001), pp. 56–65.

3

Neither Boston nor Berlin: class polarisation and neo-liberalism in the Irish Republic

KIERAN ALLEN

The Celtic Tiger is dead. Between 1994 and 2000, real gross domestic product (GDP) in the Republic of Ireland grew at an annual average rate of nine per cent, taking per capita income from sixty-seven to eighty-six per cent of the European Union (EU) average by 1999.[1] In terms of conventional economics, this would seem to constitute a miracle. Growth rates for most industrial nations were sluggish in the 1990s and even the boom in the United States did not match this. The Celtic Tiger stood out as one of the fastest growing economies in the world. But the age of miracles appears to be coming to an end. 2001 started out with phenomenal rates of growth but, on 7 November, the Governor of the Central Bank of Ireland, Maurice O'Connell, proclaimed that 'the era of the Celtic Tiger is over'.[2] The pronouncement followed a spate of redundancies and factory closures. The government also warned that tax receipts were dropping and it might need to borrow to meet its spending targets. The housing market started to fall and even prestigious companies like Aer Lingus found themselves in extreme difficulty.

The signs of a comparatively sharp downturn are plainly visible. The dramatic announcement of the closure of the Gateway computer factory in north Dublin in 2001, with the loss of 900 jobs, was an important indicator of the turnaround. This was one of the flagship US companies in the computer industry, and the one whose factory was chosen as the location by President Clinton on his visit to Ireland in September 1998 to celebrate the commercial ties between Ireland and the United States. Yet, barely a year later, it had fallen to the growing recession affecting the information technology sector. Gateway was primarily of symbolic importance but behind the symbols there has been a major restructuring of the global high-tech sector.

Information and communications technologies account for 40 per cent of total exports from the Irish Republic, having grown at an annual average rate of twenty-three per cent between 1993 and 2000.[3] This sector is dominated by large US firms. There has been a strong pattern of agglomeration, whereby a cluster of rival US computer companies moved to Ireland to take advantage of its particular cost advantages of low tax rates, low wages and free access to EU markets.[4] The Industrial Development Authority (IDA) has claimed that twenty-six per cent of all greenfield projects established by US firms in Europe were located in Ireland.[5] These are mainly in computers and, to a lesser extent, in pharmaceuticals.

The Celtic Tiger differed from the Asian economies with which it has often been compared in at least one important respect. According to Bradley, the Irish state did not primarily select 'segments of indigenous industry with the objective of gaining in efficiency and capturing greater export market share' but rather it adopted 'policies designed mainly to encourage export-orientated foreign direct investment inflows'.[6] The consequence of this strategy was that the primary impetus for growth came from a number of highly specialised sectors in which US capital was dominant. By the turn of the century, Ireland had by far the highest level of direct US investment per manufacturing worker of any country in Europe, with the capital deployed per worker being a full seven times higher than the EU average.[7] The Celtic Tiger became an important bridgehead for US investment to capture growing segments of the European high-tech market. In the process, the Republic of Ireland became more dependent on US investment than many countries in Latin America, which has often been described as 'America's backyard'.

Yet, despite this growing dependence, there was little critical examination of the nature of the links with the United States. The dominance of neo-liberalism in Irish economics meant that the US boom of the 1990s was accepted simply as given – and as implicitly proving the benefits of deregulated markets. In reality, there were serious structural weaknesses.

The US boom

The US boom of the 1990s was much more one-sided than that of the 1960s, because it was not sustained by a pattern of rising living standards for the majority of the population. US corporations were more successful than their rivals in reducing the real wages paid to employees. The attack on living standards occurred in a variety of ways. One was through the increasing tendency to 'downsize' and replace permanent workers with 'contingent workers'. The latter are temporary employees, often hired on short-term contracts or through employment agencies. Between 1978 and 1995, the top 100 US companies laid off, on a net basis, no less than twenty-two per cent of their workforce.[8] Employment through temp agencies grew by 116 per cent between 1988 and 1996.[9] Another way in which living standards were attacked was through a series of 'give-backs' – a euphemistic term for wage cuts – followed by zero pay increases. Between 1985 and 1995, the average annual increase in hourly wages in US manufacturing was the lowest among the economies of the Group of Eight (G8), averaging 0.15 per cent, compared with 2.9 per cent in Japan and 2.85 per cent in Germany. By 1995, the average hourly wage for manufacturing production workers was $17.19 in the United States, $23.66 in Japan and $31.85 in Germany.[10] In brief, the US boom coincided with an increased rate of exploitation. This was well expressed by Stephen Roach, the chief economist at the Morgan Stanley investment bank:

> The American re-structuring model has three attributes: massive headcount reduction, real wage compression and outsized currency depreciation that took the value of the dollar down 50 percent from the early 1980s highs. And the US system of flexible labour is the glue that holds the whole thing together.[14]

Booms that depend upon an increased degree of exploitation face a major problem. Firms can raise their profits for a period, but they encounter more difficulties selling their goods, because wages have been depressed. This problem can be overcome as long as there are higher levels of investment in capital goods or if the wealthier sections of society engage in luxury spending. But if anything creates doubts about the prospects for these high profits, there can be a very sudden downturn. The result is often a pressure for ever increasing rates of return on investment to fuel the confidence of the wealthy. However, by creating near full employment, the boom itself placed limits on how far US industrialists could continue to restrain wages and by 1997 there were signs that the median wage had begun to recover. The expectation of ever higher profits eventually clashed with the demands of US workers to see some recompense for past losses.

Conventional economists easily ignored this contradiction because the US boom was also sustained by a tremendous infusion of foreign capital. The net inflow of foreign capital increased from $59 billion in 1990 to $264 billion in 1997, due to the stagnation of the European and Japanese economies.[12] This influx led to lower interest rates and, consequently, to a highly stimulated stock exchange. After 1991, the share of the US economy represented by FIRE – finance, insurance and real estate – overtook that of the whole of manufacturing industry.[13] The growth in the financial sector led to even greater pressure for higher dividend payments, which in turn were used to buy new shares and other financial derivatives. In the 1970s, dividend payments amounted to sixteen per cent of profits but by 1996 they had risen to thirty-six per cent.[14]

Companies also came to borrow more on the basis of their rising paper values and for a period this fuelled the boom. However, when the realisation eventually dawned that an escalation of share values did not represent real savings, there was a sharp decline in US consumer confidence. In brief, all the contradictions of the lop-sided boom came to the surface. The US economy is now suffering the hangover effects as the fraudulent culture of accounting which led to the Enron and WorldCom scandals has been revealed.

The Irish miracle

The growing dependence of the Irish economy on the United States and the underlying weakness of its boom were simply bracketed out of most commentaries on the Celtic Tiger. A myth emerged that the Irish boom would last well into the second decade of the twenty-first century. The normally cautious Economic and Social Research Institute (ESRI) set the standard for this consensus about growth. In its *Medium Term Review 1999–2005* it claimed that there would be 'an annual average growth rate of 5.1 per cent between 2000 and 2005, falling to 4.3 per cent per annum thereafter to 2010 and to something over 3 per cent in the period 2010–2015'.[15] A previous medium-term review had even claimed that 'over the next fifteen years Ireland may establish a standard of living among the highest in Europe'.[16] Paul Sweeney, the author of *The Celtic Tiger: Ireland's Economic Miracle Explained*, was even more confident and claimed that:

> The Irish miracle appears to have been built on a solid modern foundation on which a lasting edifice can be built. The foundation is good infrastructure, investment in the important capital – human beings – and a healthy demographic structure.[17]

This optimism about the prospects for the Irish economy was always highly ideological. In spite of their claim to be neutral and scientific, economists are usually deeply committed to the free market system. They dismiss any notion that capitalism may have inherent contradictions, which lead inevitably to business cycles. Instead, they often focus on extraneous or even psychological factors as the cause of recessions. Thus the 'oil crisis' is held up as the standard explanation of the global downturn which began in 1973, while the terrorist attacks on the United States on 11 September 2001 are supposedly the cause of a new downturn. (The notion that 11 September caused a global recession can be disproved by even the most cursory glance at the records. For example, on 25 August 2001, *The Economist* announced in its lead article, 'Welcome to the first global recession of the 21st century'.[18]) Concepts like 'consumer confidence' are also treated almost as psychological irreducibles that intrude on the otherwise smooth workings of a system that brings supply and demand into equilibrium. Of course, once you adopt this perspective there is often a danger of 'talking ourselves into a recession' – hence the pressure on conventional economists to see the brighter side of things.

The predictions of a long-term boom for the Irish economy have drawn heavily on an argument about demographic factors. In 1997, National City Brokers (NCB) published *Population and Prosperity*, which has since become a groundbreaking text among stockbroker economists, who have exuded extreme optimism about the future of the Celtic Tiger. The authors of the report pointed to a number of unique features of Ireland's demographic structure that could help to sustain a boom. These were a rising population, higher educational qualifications and, crucially, a falling age dependency ratio. Their argument is worth quoting at length, as it helped forge an important consensus in elite circles:

> Demographic change has played a crucial role in the strong economic performance of the past five years. The key features have been:
>
> • The capacity of the economy for non-inflationary growth has increased as the pace of labour supply accelerated to an annual two per cent on the back of a rising population in the economically active age groups.
> • The effectiveness of the workforce has been increased by higher educational attainment levels.
> • Falling dependency because of the lower numbers in the younger age groups has boosted wealth....
>
> The heightened rate of economic growth in recent years thus has a sound structural base and the demographic changes, which have their roots in the baby boom of the 1970s, will continue to have a strong influence on activity in the years ahead.[19]

On the basis of these demographic features, it was predicted that the Republic of Ireland would continue to grow at a rate of six per cent annually for the next five or ten years.[20]

This argument is extremely tenuous. The notion that labour supply was the decisive factor in 'non-inflationary growth' was soon disproved by the fact that the Celtic Tiger came to top the EU inflation league soon after the NCB made its pronouncements. The increase in higher educational qualifications has been a general feature in most industrialised countries. The link between age dependency rates and the state of the economy is crude in the extreme, or at the very least highly questionable. There are other countries which have experienced more dramatic falls in their age dependency ratios than Ireland but that have not been rewarded with a boom. Turkey and Thailand, for example, have seen their age dependency rate fall from 0.8 of the working population to 0.5 in the period 1980–99, whereas in Ireland it has fallen only from 0.7 to

0.5. Similarly, the United States maintained a relatively static age dependency ratio, of 0.5, in the same period but moved from recession to sluggish growth to boom at different stages.[21]

Conventional economists often have real difficulty in understanding the sheer chaos and disruption inherent in the free market system. Even where disruptions are recognised, they are seen as aberrant features that soon give way to equilibrium. The medium-term review of the ESRI published in September 2001 provides an extraordinarily candid acknowledgement of this. In their introduction, the authors note that the ESRI envisaged two scenarios for the future – their 'benchmark' estimate, which projected smooth growth, and their 'slowdown' forecast, which assumed a more malign scenario for the world economy. When writing the report they assumed that the 'benchmark' estimate was the more likely scenario but then, after 11 September, they switched to assuming that 'the slowdown scenario may be closer to reality'.[22] Yet, despite their sudden ad hoc adjustment, they still assumed that the overall growth of the Celtic Tiger would remain at 4.5 per cent per annum for 2000–05, 4.7 per cent for the next five years and 2.8 per cent for the following five. In other words, almost exactly the same figures for growth that were quoted in the previous medium-term review are used, even though cognisance was now apparently being taken of a global recession!

Less blinkered commentators on the Celtic Tiger make more realistic assumptions about the outcomes for Irish capitalism. The loosening of global controls on the movement of capital and the intense drive to increase both the relative and the absolute surplus value from workers make the system more chaotic and disruptive than ever. It is not necessary to invert the optimism of conventional economists and give an unremittingly pessimistic account of the prognosis of the Irish economy. It is simply important to discard ideological assurances about the benefits of deregulated markets or quasi-nationalist notions about the uniqueness of the Irish. The Irish economy may eventually benefit from a US recovery. Or the disruptions caused by changes in the global economy, and the US economy in particular, may bring a longer period of a downturn than many had expected. The point is to recognise that there are no automatic rewards given to those who follow the nostrums of neo-liberal economists and accept a 'downward flexibility on wages'.[23] The system is literally out of control and hence inherently more unpredictable than before.

Boston or Berlin?

The growing difficulties with the US model cast a new light on the 'Boston or Berlin?' debate which emerged in the last phase of the Celtic Tiger. The two cities have come to be employed as signifiers of a choice between two apparently different models of capitalism. On the one hand, there was the supposedly dynamic, tax-cutting form of neo-liberal capitalism of the United States, which had turned in a strong record of growth in the 1990s. On the other, there was the more regulated, social market in Europe, which allegedly sought to promote the values of social justice and solidarity. Advocates of a social partnership approach preferred the more regulated model which prevailed in Europe. This led the Irish Congress of Trade Unions, the Irish Labour Party and left intellectuals such as Fintan O'Toole to link up with the wider political establishment and advocate a vote for the EU's Nice Treaty. When the electorate rejected the Nice Treaty the first time around, in 2001, it was assumed that they were not fully informed about the workings of the EU and needed to vote on the issue for a second time. The fact that the Nice Treaty helped create the legal framework for a European Rapid Reaction Force or that a growing number of EU governments were also pushing for more 'flexible' labour markets barely took the gloss off the supposedly more progressive nature of Europe.

There is an important discourse prevalent in elite circles which links Irish 'social partnership' with the European social model and even suggests that the particular experience in Ireland may add to this model. The official documentation of the EU makes considerable play about concepts such as 'social solidarity' and removing forms of 'social exclusion'.[24] The various Irish social partnership agreements have taken up and amplified these themes. One writer has claimed that the Irish model of social partnership is an example of a 'competitive corporatist' strategy which has much to offer Europe as a whole:

> One of the futures that may prove appropriate for many European countries is that of 'competitive corporatist' social pacts which seek consensual and, in so far as is possible, an equitable adjustment of European welfare systems and labour markets. The EU is seeking to play a role in this process by encouraging a European employment pact and promoting further advances in the European social dialogue. Although such pacts may be criticised as 'national productivity coalitions' in which the power of capital is inevitably strengthened, they are certainly more desirable than unilateral neo-liberalism.[25]

Peter Cassells, the former General Secretary of the Irish Congress of Trade Unions, made a similar point when he claimed that 'from the way we have balanced the European approach with the culture of American inward European investment, it may be that Ireland could play a leading role in modernising the European Social Model'.[26] Europe, it appears, is identified with positively charged key words such as 'consensus', 'solidarity' and 'partnership'. Ireland has learnt the model well and is now in a position to instruct its old teacher on how to 'modernise'.

Table 3.1 Declining economic dynamism: average annual percentage change in gross domestic product

	1960–73	*1973–79*	*1979–90*	*1990–96*
United States	4.0	2.6	2.4	2.1
Japan	9.2	3.5	3.9	1.6
Germany	4.3	2.4	2.1	1.7
G7	4.8	2.8	2.5	1.6

Source: R. Brenner, 'The economics of global turbulence', special issue of *New Left Review*, May–June 1998, p. 235.

The problem with this whole approach is that it focuses on secondary features of regions of the global economy to claim the existence of radically different models of capitalism. It fails to look at the underlying dynamic of the wider system of late capitalism and, therefore, is unable to distinguish between different rhetorical forms used by political elites and the actual projects they seek to promote. When these projects are examined, it soon becomes clear that Boston and Berlin have far more in common than is supposed to divide them. In brief, the notion that there is a specifically 'European model' or 'social partnership model' which offers a real alterative to neo-liberalism needs to be critically questioned.

Since the end of the golden age of capitalism in the early 1970s, the economies of both the EU and the United States have faced declining growth rates, as Table 3.1 indicates. They have also experienced more frequent recessions, greater competition on a global arena and a decline in the rate of profit from manufacturing. These changes necessitated measures to raise the levels of profits through greater state support for capital. After all, it is an axiomatic law of our present society that capital, when faced with a decline in its rate of return, seeks to reduce unit costs and receive larger amounts of 'corporate welfare' from the state.

The nature of the EU, however, meant that the political elite went about achieving these objectives in a different way than their US counterparts. The strength of social democracy in Europe compared with that in the United States meant that far greater emphasis was placed on co-opting social partners and bringing them to see the necessity and 'inevitability' of new measures. This emphasis on social partnership is virtually institutionalised in the EU, in the Protocol on Social Policy, which has created the legal basis for the so-called 'Social Dialogue'. According to Keller and Storries:

> [the] new, more formalised dialogue guarantees representation of the interests of management and labour.... This means prioritising consultation, negotiations and agreements by social partners instead of legislative enactments

proposed by the Commission and adopted by the Council without the legal interference of private sector actors.[27]

The ethos of social partnership suggests that all sectors of society must pull together to face the challenges posed by 'globalisation'. To co-opt subordinate social groupings, a distinct type of technical language is often employed, which poses social change in terms of 'inevitable transitions' and as a process which does not involve unequal amounts of pain.

Another significant factor was that much of the strength of organised workers within the EU has been concentrated in public enterprises. Europe saw a major expansion in state ownership after 1945 and even by the mid-1980s the French state owned thirteen of the twenty largest French companies.[28] One of the key objectives of the EU bureaucracy has been to break up these concentrations of public ownership. Often this has been expressed in terms of responding to consumer demands for greater quality of service. But, as anyone who has had the misfortune to travel on the British railway network lately can testify, there is no necessary link between privatisation and consumer satisfaction. Rather, a considerable part of the political agenda has been to undermine traditional pockets of trade union strength and pave the way to a greater 'flexibility' of labour. Some of its commissioners have been quite open about the real objectives of EU policy. Leon Brittan, for example, has stated that the objective of EU competition policy has been 'to help European capitalism become more healthy, vibrant and competitive and prevent its decline into the cosy corporatism that so much of the European left used to espouse'.[29]

Key instruments for achieving this objective have been the transition to the single European market and the single currency. On one level, these were designed to stimulate the emergence of stronger EU companies that can compete more effectively on a global scale. But the moves to a single market and currency have also been accompanied by a shift to a greater adoption of neo-liberal economics. Far from the EU embodying the values of social solidarity, therefore, it seeks to provide a framework for national governments to carry through policies which transfer wealth back to the already privileged. This can be seen in three main areas.

First, there has been pressure to privatise, or 'liberalisation' as it is often called. Privatisation has become an openly stated objective of the EU Commission. It used a round of the General Agreement on Trade in Services (GATS) negotiations to promote a policy of privatisation around the world.[30] In slightly coy language, the EU Commission declared in 1995 that:

additional progress is necessary in reinforcing competition rules, reducing State aid and reducing the role of the public sector. Privatisation, to the extent that Member states judge it compatible with their objectives, could further the progress already made in this direction.[31]

Typically, the EU provides a framework behind which national governments can seek shelter from local public and trade union pressure when pushing privatisation. By presenting the matter as one that is out of their control and 'inevitable', the political elites within member states seek to disempower ordinary people. Specifically, the EU has been the main agent to have pressed for the deregulation of the airline industry, the removal of the postal monopoly for cross-border post and for items weighing over 350 g, the granting of third-party access to electricity markets and the full-scale privatisation of the telecommunications industry.

Second, spending cuts have helped to undermine the welfare state. The EU insisted that annual budget deficits be kept to within three per cent of GDP and accumulated national debts should be no more than sixty per cent of GDP. The effect of this measure has been to encourage national governments to cut back on public spending. Sweden offers a clear example of the effects of this approach. The welfare state in Sweden continued to expand through the 1980s but then faced sharp cuts after Sweden's accession to the EU in 1995. One commentator described the effects as follows:

> social and public expenditure in Sweden has been reduced in recent years. There have been cuts to benefits and eligibility rules have been tightened up. Hospitals have had to declare staff redundancies and some services for the elderly have been privatised. Charges for visits to the doctor and for prescriptions have risen enormously.[32]

Third, the EU has developed an institutional structure which increasingly removes decision making from democratic pressures. The large bureaucracy in Brussels produces highly complex directives, which are virtually closed to public scrutiny. Typically, new treaties contain huge amalgams of clauses, which make public intervention in decision making even more difficult. Thus, the Nice Treaty of 2001 includes a reference to a chapter of rights, provision for the framework for an EU Rapid Reaction Force and an objective in Article 133 which calls for 'uniformity in measures of liberalisation'. Even Jurgen Habermas, who is broadly sympathetic to the EU project, has noted that:

> the more policy matters are settled though intra-state negotiation, and the more important these matters are, the more political decisions are withdrawn from arenas of democratic opinion formation and will-formation.[33]

All of this means that the EU should not be seen as a bulwark against the jungle capitalism of the United States. It has, rather, evolved a method of presenting itself as 'more progressive' in order to co-opt significant sections of the leadership of labour organisations. However, despite indulging in rhetoric about the importance of combating 'social exclusion', the political project of the EU elite has been to strengthen the hand of capital against labour. Noble talk about the value of social partnership has coincided with the transfer of wealth to those who are already privileged. Indeed, social partnership has been praised as an example of the 'competitive corporatism' that Europe is assumed to need. The Celtic Tiger shows that one can use the rhetoric about 'social solidarity' while actually implementing policies which increase class polarisation.

The myth of social partnership

The phrase 'social partnership' has a distinctly pleasing ring to it. It implies cooperation and sharing. It suggests that all sections of society should pull together to look after the excluded. It promises a system whereby dynamic economic growth can be reconciled with a policy that advocates social justice and equity. These noble ideals are explicitly articulated in the texts of the various corporatist arrangements that have been devised in the Irish Republic over the last fifteen years. The first partnership agreement, the *Programme for National Recovery*, committed participants to 'seek to regenerate the economy and improve the social equity of our society through their combined efforts'.[34] A recent agreement, the *Programme for Prosperity and Fairness*, states that 'the core objective of the Programme is to build a fair, inclusive society in Ireland'.[35] So laudable are these objectives that even critics who acknowledge the growing inequality in the twenty-six counties still assert that social partnership has ensured 'that integration into the global economy has not decimated social rights'.[36]

However, the problem is that the rhetoric about social partnership coincides with growing social inequality. Indeed, it could be argued that it has been the very ideological success of the partnership model in co-opting potential opposition from the unions and community organisations which has facilitated the direct transfer of wealth from the majority of the population into the hands of a small elite.

Social partnership began in 1987 and since the early 1990s it coincided with the boom years of the Irish economy. Over that period living standards rose, but this is hardly remarkable. With near full employment and growing labour shortages, the bargaining position of workers had increased. This was supplemented by a huge increase in personal borrowing due to low interest rates during the boom years. In 1992, personal sector credit represented forty-two per cent of personal disposable income but by 2001 it had risen to seventy-one per cent.[37]

Table 3.2 Adjusted wage share of the total economy in Ireland and the EU (percentage of gross domestic product at factor cost)

	1987	*2000*
Ireland	71.2	58.0
EU total	72.0	68.3

Source: European Commission, *The European Economy*, no. 70 (Brussels: EU Commission, 2000).

The more interesting question concerns the role social partnership played in facilitating or hindering workers getting a bigger share of the growing economy. The clear evidence suggests that workers lost out relatively, with wages falling as a proportion of the various incomes generated within the southern Irish economy. Table 3.2 shows that there is a general tendency in the EU for workers' incomes to make up a decreasing share of the total economy. However, the decline in the share going to wages is much more dramatic in the country which claims to have the strongest institutions of social partnership.

The foundation for social partnership has been restraint on wages. Virtually every other area of the economy has been deregulated. There are no controls over rents, the price of building land, house prices or the level of profits. Only wages are controlled – apparently on a 'voluntary basis'. However, the dispute with the Association of Secondary Teachers Ireland (ASTI) in 2000 has shown that, even when a union leaves the partnership structures, the terms of these agreements are still enforced on it. If one major item of the economy is regulated in a boom while the other items are deregulated, it follows that there can only be a transfer of wealth upwards.

Irish workers have also lost out relatively because they have been poorly compensated for the increased productivity for which they have been responsible. 'Competitive corporatism' has meant that a premium has been placed on measures to encourage 'flexibility'. One study cf workplace innovations in Ireland found that ninety per cent of the surveyed establishments were using at least one high-performance work-organisation technique.[38] The Celtic Tiger has not witnessed a strong surge in investment in fixed capital and therefore labour has made an important contribution to rising productivity levels. In 1996, the EU average for wage-adjusted labour productivity was 139,000 ECUs per manufacturing worker. In the Republic of Ireland the figure was substantially higher, at 291,000 ECUs.[39]

Supporters of social partnership often concede that there has been a rise in inequality but argue that at least existing structures have taken care of the more 'marginalised'. The main basis for this claim is that social partnership agreements have led to the maintenance of the real value of unemployment benefits and assistance payments since 1997. However, this is, again, to view issues in isolation. The period of social partnership has, in fact, coincided with a wider change whereby the ratio of social security spending to GDP fell markedly in Ireland. By 1996, for example, the ratio of social security spending in Ireland converged with that of the United States, seven percentage points below the European average.[40] Moreover, the small increase in benefits to the unemployed stands in contrast to the tax benefits which higher earners have gained. The Justice Commission of the Conference of Religious in Ireland (CORI) has estimated that the government widened the gap between the incomes of couples who were long-term unemployed and those of higher earners by €159 a week between 1996 and 2000.[41] The irony is that, despite a period of unprecedented economic boom, the Irish Republic has slipped down the United Nations' Human Development Index, mainly because it has the second highest level of poverty in the developed world.[42]

One of the reasons why social security spending in the Republic of Ireland fell was because of the substantial decline in the number of people out of work. The boom itself was a major factor but the Irish state also spends more on active labour market programmes than many other countries. Unlike the British model, which has relied on measures such as the Job Seekers Allowance, it is sometimes assumed that the Irish schemes do not contain any element of compulsion. Yet the level of monitoring of the unemployed, the constant interviews and reviews that offer jobs or places on 'social inclusion' schemes mean that a large degree of compulsion is involved. The Celtic Tiger was often built on a regime of low pay and there has been a constant pressure on the unemployed to take up poorly rewarded employment. The Republic of Ireland comes second only to the United States in terms of the proportion of its workforce categorised as low paid, with twenty-three per cent of the workforce earning less than two-thirds of median earnings.[43] The numbers of workers on fixed-term contracts is below the EU average of thirteen per cent because of the boom conditions but, nevertheless, by 2000 it had risen to nine per cent.[44] Pension coverage is falling in the private sector and this has left many to rely on a very inadequate state pension. Far from social partnership protecting 'the weak', either inside or outside the labour force, it has ensured that they lost out significantly in the booming economy.

If one of the key foundations of social partnership has been wage restraint, its other main pillar has been a consensus on cutting taxes. Traditional forms of corporatism have often been linked to a Keynesian strategy of management of the free market, with a concomitant rise in state intervention and spending. The new 'competitive corporatism' which has been in operation in the Republic of Ireland has put this process into reverse by creating a culture whereby tax cuts are increasingly seen as the reward for participation in the partnership process. Thus, wage restraint is traded off against tax cuts and there are now even tax allowances for making union contributions! However, here again, the tax-cutting culture contains a powerful dynamic that exacerbates inequalities. This occurs for two main reasons.

First, the main beneficiaries of tax reductions are the wealthy. In 1987, the top rate of tax on companies that were not engaged in exporting manufactured goods stood at fifty per cent. By 2002, the rate had dropped to 12.5 per cent – the lowest in Europe. Capital gains tax was cut from forty per cent to twenty per cent. The social security contribution of employers at current prices had dropped from 3.2 per cent of GDP in 1988 to 2.7 per cent in 1996, the second lowest in the EU.[45] Those who have been asked to show the least restraint on their earnings have, quite simply, been awarded the greatest gains in terms of tax subsidies. This iniquitous process is illustrated most dramatically in the case of the banks. While the profits that the banks enjoy have grown astronomically, they now pay a lower proportion of tax on these than most workers.

Second, the overall effect of this cutting of taxes is that state spending is now the lowest by far in the EU. General government expenditure amounted to only 33.2 per cent of GDP, compared with an EU average of 46.2 per cent in 2000.[46] This creates severe disadvantages for poorer elements of southern Irish society, who are especially reliant upon public services. Widespread criticism has emerged, for example, over the state of the health service, which has produced growing pressure on people to take out private medical insurance. The average time spent on a waiting list is sixteen weeks for a medical cardholder but only eight weeks for someone on private insurance.[47] The main reason for this has been the systematic policy of under-funding the health service until very recently. Total health expenditure per head of population in the Irish Republic amounted to only sixty-two per cent of the EU average in 1996.[48]

Social partnership has also brought about an extraordinary co-option of oppositional elements within southern Irish society. Indeed, its very efficacy arises from this facility. The mid-1990s, for example, were characterised by mounting revelations about the intricate networks which linked a small elite of business people and top politicians. It emerged that the former Taoiseach, Charles Haughey, was paid IR£5,500 a week between 1988 and 1991 from a special fund, known as the Ansbacher accounts, which were opened by top business people.[49] A subsequent report on the affair revealed that this fund was administered from an office in the headquarters of Cement Roadstone Holdings company. Almost 200 leading business people were named as being involved in the account, which was established for the purpose of tax evasion. Two government ministers, Michael Lowry and Ray Burke, resigned after it emerged that they had close financial links with business people who had a vested interest in

their decisions. These revelations provoked considerable anger and dele-
gates at the conferences of two major unions, the Services, Industrial,
Professional and Technical Union (SIPTU) and the Irish Municipal Professional and Civil Service Union (IMPACT), called for national protest
demonstrations by the unions. Yet the close relationship that had
developed between the political elite and the union leaders meant that
these calls were simply discarded.

One of the key items of the neo-liberal agenda has been the privatisation of the state sector and the wider deregulation of the economy.
This is the agenda pushed by agencies such as the Organisation for
Economic Cooperation and Development (OECD), which has noted that
economic liberalisation began later in Ireland than elsewhere but
gathered pace in the 1980s and 1990s. It claimed that, 'by the end of
1997, Ireland was one of the less regulated OECD countries in terms of
barriers to entry and entrepeneurship, market openness and labour
markets'.[50] In other words, support for deregulation grew precisely as
the social partnership process deepened. The OECD also noted that 'policies
on privatisation have been developed in close consultation with trade
unions'.[51] The acceptance of privatisation is often driven by a notion
that it will not follow the British example but rather there will be a
distinct Irish model of privatisation, based, of course, on social solidarity. Union leaders joined the National Competitiveness Council, which,
as the OECD points out, 'has promoted increased competition in energy,
telecommunications, transport and many other areas of the economy'.[52]
While many British unions have expressed vigorous opposition to the
Private Finance Initiatives, the union leaders in the Republic of Ireland
have explicitly committed themselves to support for such schemes in the
social partnership agreements. Under a framework for public–private
partnership, the unions even agreed that some state employees would
transfer to private companies.[53]

Conclusions

The Celtic Tiger has been hailed as a model for developing countries
because of its success in attracting multinational corporations that have
engaged in an export programme. Social partnership was held to be an
essential accessory to this strategy. As long as Irish society was willing
to bow to the interests of capital, it was assumed that economic prosperity would continue for decades to come. The reality was that the
Celtic Tiger grew in the tailspin of the US boom. It functioned as the
bridgehead for US investment, which sought to capture a larger share of
the markets of its European rivals. Few conventional economists examined the contradiction of the US boom because of their own ideological

support for neo-liberalism. Yet those contradictions are now emerging with a vengeance – and were clearly in evidence even before the events of 11 September 2001.

Social partnership was highly successful in co-opting potential sources of opposition to the growing inequality in the Celtic Tiger. It was linked with the wider European social model, which stresses social solidarity and presents itself as an alternative to the jungle capitalism of the United States. Yet the irony was that discourse about 'social solidarity' and 'opposition to social exclusion' was a more appropriate way of carrying through a neo-liberal project in a country with strong unions.

That neo-liberal project is best exemplified in the saga of taxes on wealth. For more than two decades, the top business people in Ireland used reserves such as the Ansbacher accounts to send their money off-shore in order to evade tax. It would appear that this scheme, which was used by nearly 200 business people, was only one of about twenty or thirty. A key section of the Irish elite engaged in a criminal conspiracy to deprive the public sector of valuable resources that could have been used to alleviate the suffering of the sick or to provide better education. But, at some point, all criminals attempt to legitimise their activities and recycle their money. The Mafia do it through laundering money into respectable businesses. It appears, however, that the wealthy in the Irish Republic have simply decided to buy the loyalties of the state's political elite, for they now legally enjoy some of the lowest rates of tax on profit and wealth in the industrialised world. Instead of shifting their money offshore, they have turned the whole island into an Atlantic tax haven. And all of this occurred while Ireland was supposed to exemplify a form of 'social partnership'.

It seems reasonable to conclude that, far from offering a real alternative to neo-liberalism, social partnership and the wider European social model represent, in fact, political methods intended to advance the project of privatisation, deregulation and redistribution in favour of the wealthy.

Notes

1 OECD, *Economic Survey of Ireland 2001* (Paris: OECD, 2001), p. 23.
2 'O'Connell says era of Celtic Tiger over', *Irish Times*, 8 November 2001.
3 OECD, *Ireland: Survey, June 2001* (Paris: OECD, 2001), p. 47.
4 P. Krugman, 'Good news from Ireland: a geographical perspective', in A. Gray (ed.), *International Perspectives on the Irish Economy* (Dublin: Indecon Economic Consultants, 1997).
5 Industrial Development Authority, *Annual Report 1998* (Dublin: IDA, 1998), p. 12.
6 J. Bradley, 'The Irish economy in comparative perspective', in B. Nolan, P. O'Connell and C. Whelan (eds), *Bust to Boom?* (Dublin: Institute of Public Administration, 2000).

7 F. Barry, J. Bradley and E. O'Malley, 'Indigenous and foreign industry: characteristics and performance', in F. Barry (ed.), *Understanding Ireland's Economic Growth* (London: Macmillan, 1999), p. 46.

8 R. Brenner, 'The economics of global turbulence', special issue of *New Left Review* (May–June 1998), p. 200.

9 N. Klein, *No Logo* (London: Flamingo, 2001), p. 265.

10 Brenner, 'The economics of global turbulence', p. 20.

11 'Lessons in re-structuring', *Financial Times*, 22 October 1996.

12 F. Moseley, 'The United States economy at the turn of the century: entering a new era of prosperity', *Capital and Class*, no. 67 (1999), p. 34.

13 D. Henwood, *Wall Street* (London: Verso, 1997), p. 76.

14 Brenner, 'The economics of global turbulence', p. 209.

15 D. Duffy, J. Fitzgerald, I. Kearney and D. Smyth, *Medium Term Review 1999–2005* (Dublin: ESRI, 1999), p. 64.

16 D. Duffy, J. FitzGerald, I. Kearney and F. Shorthall, *Medium Term Review 1997–2003* (Dublin: ESRI, 1997), p. 109.

17 P. Sweeney, *The Celtic Tiger: Ireland's Economic Miracle Explained* (Dublin: Oak Tree Press, 1998), p. 15.

18 'A global game of dominoes', *The Economist*, 25–31 August 2001.

19 National City Brokers, *Population and Prosperity* (Dublin: NCB, 1997), p. 4.

20 *Ibid.*, p. 12.

21 World Bank, *World Development Indicators* (Washington, DC: World Bank, 2001), table 2.1.

22 D. Duffy, J. FitzGerald, I. Kearney, J. Hore and C. MacCoille, *Medium Term Review 2001–2007* (Dublin: ESRI, 2001), p. vii.

23 *Ibid.*, p. 142.

24 See C. Cousins, 'Social exclusion in Europe', *Policy and Politics*, 26:2 (1997), pp. 127–45.

25 M. Rhodes, 'Defending the social contract', in D. Hine and H. Kassim (eds), *Beyond the Market* (London: Routledge, 1998), p. 52.

26 P. Cassells, 'Recasting the European social model', in R. O'Donnell (ed.), *Europe: The Irish Experience* (Dublin: Institute of European Affairs, 2000), p. 74.

27 B. Keller and B. Storries, 'The new European social dialogue: old wine in new bottles?', *Journal of European Social Policy*, 9:2 (1999), pp. 111–25.

28 D. Parker, *Privatisation in the European Union: Theory and Policy Perspectives* (London: Routledge, 1998), p. 10.

29 L. Brittan, *A Diet of Brussels* (London: Little, Brown, 2000), pp. 44–5.

30 'Secret documents reveal EU tough stance on global trade', *Guardian*, 17 April 2002.

31 European Commission, 'Broad economic guidelines', in *European Social Policy*, no. 60 (Brussels: European Commission, 1995), p. 15.

32 A. Gould, 'The welfare state in Sweden', *Journal of European Social Policy*, 9:2 (1999), p. 166.

33 J. Habermas, 'The European state and the pressures of globalisation', *New Left Review*, no. 235 (May–June 1999), p. 49.

34 *Programme for National Recovery* (Dublin: Government Publications, 1987), p. 5.

35 *Programme for Prosperity and Fairness* (Dublin: Government Publications, 2000), p. 3.

36 S. Ó Riain and P. O' Connell, 'The role of state in growth and welfare', in B. Nolan, P. O'Connell and C. Whelan (eds), *Bust to Boom? The Irish*

   Experience of Growth and Inequality (Dublin: Institute of Public Administration, 2000), p. 338.
37 Central Bank, *Annual Report 2001* (Dublin: Central Bank, 2002), pp. 131–2.
38 J. McCartney and P. Teague, 'Workplace innovations in the Republic of
   Ireland', *Economic and Social Review*, 28:4 (1997), pp. 381–99.
39 Eurostat, *Eurostat Yearbook 2000* (Brussels: European Commission, 2000),
   pp. 370–1.
40 Ó Riain and O'Connell, 'The role of the state in growth and welfare',
   p. 331.
41 CORI Justice Commission, *Poverty Low Pay and Social Welfare* (Dublin:
   CORI, October 2001), p. 10.
42 United Nations Development Programme, *Human Development Report
   2001* (Oxford: Oxford University Press, 2001), p. 153.
43 A. Barrett, T. Callan and B. Nolan, *The Earnings Distribution and the Return
   to Education in Ireland*, working paper no. 85 (Dublin: ESRI, June 1997),
   p. 8.
44 European Foundation, European Industrial Relations Observatory, *Annual
   Review 2000* (Dublin: European Foundation, 2000), p. 34.
45 European Commission, *Eurostat Yearbook 2000: A Statistical Eye on Europe*
   (Brussels: European Commission, 2000), p. 243.
46 European Commission, *EU Economic Data Pocket Book*, no. 9 (Brussels:
   European Commission, 2001), p. 35.
47 'GMS patients wait twice as long on hospital lists', *Irish Times*, 24 August
   2001.
48 European Commission, *Eurostat Yearbook 2000*, p. 81.
49 *Report of the Tribunal of Inquiry (Dunnes Payments)* (McCracken tribunal)
   (Dublin: Stationery Office, 1997), p. 48.
50 OECD, *Regulatory Reform in Ireland* (Paris: OECD, 2001), p. 27.
51 *Ibid.*, p. 26.
52 *Ibid.*, p. 28.
53 'Government expects building costs to be static', *Irish Times*, 2 November
   2001.

4

Welcome to the Celtic Tiger:
racism, immigration and the state

STEVE LOYAL

The 'Celtic Tiger' has come to provide a convenient shorthand for Ireland's prosperous and rapidly growing economy. Like all metaphors, it occludes as much as it includes; as a way of representing, it is just as much a way of misrepresenting. The implication of a prosperity in which 'a rising tide lifts all boats' masks the growth of poverty and inequality and generalises what is, in fact, only a restricted experience of newly found wealth, within a broader context of class and gender stratification and regional underdevelopment. It also masks growing racism within Irish society.

The central aim of this chapter is to examine the current hegemonic construction of Ireland as an open, cosmopolitan, multicultural, tourist-friendly society. It will argue that underlying the celebrated liberal values of freedom, choice and opportunity, which are supposedly intrinsic to the cultural renewal ushered in by the 'new Ireland', is the harsh reality of capitalist production, exclusionary nationalism and growing xenophobia, in relation to both the state and the general populace. Far from conforming to the Irish Tourist Board ideal of *céad míle fáilte* – one hundred thousand welcomes – the Irish state, both before and, more specifically, since the emergence of the boom economy, has consistently treated non-national immigration as a political problem. This chapter will map the 'dark side' of contemporary Irish society by examining briefly the experiences of racism of two groups within the field of migration, namely asylum seekers and non-nationals with work permits.[1]

The implementation of stricter border controls and the current rise of racism are not, however, unique to Irish society but mirror – albeit within a different time scale – the earlier development of exclusionary policies and racism in other parts of Europe during and after the mid-1970s. Yet the exclusionary and racist processes within Irish society have assumed a specific configuration unlike that in most other developed nation states. The development of anti-immigrant policies and the increase in racism have challenged the belief that the colonialism and persistent emigration experienced by the Irish population will automatically engender in them sympathy towards others who are in poverty and are forced to emigrate. Instead, a paranoid belief that Ireland is being overrun by immigrants has become common currency.

The exclusionary processes characterising Irish society, I will argue, may usefully be understood in terms of a tension between three discursive poles:

1   a logic of capital accumulation which points towards open borders
     and the free flow of capital – this imperative has come to the foreground as a consequence of the labour market dynamism of the Celtic Tiger;
2   a narrative of ethnic and national identity inherited from the process of state formation before and after independence;
3   within the field of international relations, a commitment to constitutional liberalism and the rule of law – this expresses itself in support for the United Nations and the 1951 Convention Relating to the Status of Refugees.

Migration in Ireland

The two central pieces of legislation which currently shape Irish immigration policy are the 1996 Refugee Act (which was not fully passed until November 2000) and the Immigration Bill of 1999. These pieces of legislation, however, have only a restricted application, since they cover specific aspects of Irish immigration policy. In fact, the Irish state still lacks an official overarching or coherent immigration policy comparable to that of other European countries. The two principal mechanisms through which 'third area nationals'[2] can enter into Ireland are the asylum system and the work permit system.[3]

Despite a history of restriction on immigration and the predominance of outward migration, it would be mistaken to believe that contemporary asylum seekers and economic migrants are disrupting the contours of an otherwise unitary and homogeneous Irish society. Such notions of homogeneity invariably form a central part of nationalistic state discourses.[4] The presence of Travellers and Protestants and Black-Irish people bears witness to the fact that Irish society, although relatively homogeneous in terms of whiteness and Christianity, was always more diverse than it claimed to be.[5] Moreover, a limited, but culturally significant, degree of Jewish immigration at the turn of the century, in addition to the arrival after the 1950s of a number of 'programme refugees', including Hungarians, Chileans, Vietnamese and Bosnians, means that the experience and impact

on society of asylum seekers and work permit holders was not unprecedented.[6] Although there was and there still is no systematic method of
recording racism, many of these groups experienced racism, particularly
the Travellers and Jews.[7]

Asylum seekers in Ireland

Immigration into Ireland refers to the arrival not only of people from
Africa and Asia, who are predominantly 'people of colour', but also of
people from Romania and Poland, as well as from Australia, Canada
and the United States. The semantic correlation of non-Irish immigrants
with black asylum seekers or refugees is an ideological effect of social
relations of domination, specifically those of state and media discourses.
Between 1995 and 2000, asylum seekers constituted less than ten per
cent of all immigrants who entered Ireland.[8] Asylum seekers, in addition
to being classified according to country of origin or nationality, can be
subdivided further in terms of ethnicity, tribal group, caste, gender, age
and social class, such that they are far from constituting a homogeneous
group. Although exact figures are difficult to calculate, the main countries
of origin of asylum seekers seem to be Nigeria, Romania, Moldova and
the Democratic Republic of Congo. In 1992, Ireland received only thirty-
nine applications for asylum. By 1996, this figure had risen to 1,179; it
had risen to 7,724 in 1999 and to 10,325 in 2001 (Figure 4.1). In total,
there were approximately 40,000 applications for asylum in Ireland
between 1992 and 2001.

As we noted above, such a rise in the number of asylum applications
was not peculiar to Ireland but reflected wider trends throughout western
Europe, although a significant time lag must be taken into consideration.
In absolute terms, Ireland in 2000 received the lowest number of asylum
seekers within the European Union (EU), with only 2.4 per cent of the
total number of applications. However, while the absolute figures may
be low, Ireland does have the fifth highest number of asylum seekers per
capita.[9] Inevitably, the emergence of the Celtic Tiger partly explains the
increase in the number of asylum applications in Ireland but other factors
are also relevant.[10]

In Ireland, there is a dual-track system for determining refugee status:
the normal determination procedure, which is based on the 1951 Convention Relating to the Status of Refugees, and what is known as the
'manifestly unfounded' procedure. Both procedures embody aspects of
institutional racism, that is, patterns of social exclusion persist in the
assumptions and principles of the organisations and institutions and
how they operate. Since the dominant ethnic group has all the institutions of the state in its control – from the education system to the

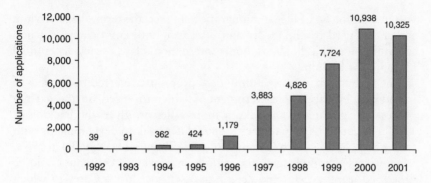

Figure 4.1 Annual numbers of asylum applications in Ireland, 1992–2001. (Source: Department of Justice, Equality and Law Reform.)

media and the legal system – and decides how and to whom these resources will be allocated, it also controls issues tied to ethnicity and power.

Such institutional racism is clearly evident in the asylum interview. As a result of institutional bias, not all asylum applications receive a fair and complete hearing. The aim of the interview is to establish the veracity and feasibility of the applicant's claim. In an interview, it is the investigator, as Bourdieu argues, who starts the 'game' and sets up its rules by assigning to 'the interview its objective and use'. This 'asymmetry is reinforced by a social asymmetry since the investigator occupies a higher place in the social hierarchy of different types of capital', including, in this case, cultural and linguistic capital.[11] The asylum interview not only entails a large power difference between the interviewer and interviewee, in both social and linguistic terms, but also is driven by the principle of establishing contradictions and minor inconsistencies in the asylum seeker's account, rather than the principle of the 'benefit of the doubt'. The investigator, through the exercise of symbolic violence, therefore wields considerable power in deciding whether the asylum seeker's account 'counts'. Moreover, in contrast to most other EU states, where officers examining asylum seekers have a legal background or university degree, there is no statutory provision relating to the training and skills of these officers. In Ireland, many immigration officers are retired gardaí or former civil servants. In the absence of full training, many of the assessors involved in the determination of asylum claims have little knowledge, understanding or experience in either the field of asylum claims generally or matters pertaining to refugee status, including the human rights situation in the applicant's country of origin.[12] Instead of considering each application for asylum individually and in depth, asylum seekers are collectively framed by both state institutions and the media as a threat, within a discourse of illegal immigration. In fact, the term 'illegal asylum seeker', as used by the media and increasingly by politicians, is a non sequitur, since all individuals, under international law, are legally entitled to apply for asylum.

The second, 'manifestly unfounded' procedure referred to above was introduced by the Irish government in order to speed up the asylum processing system and to make it more efficient, given the backlog of 12,600 of cases. This dual-track system dates back to developments with the United Nations High Commissioner for Refugees (UNHCR) in 1983, when it was acknowledged that certain categories of claimant could be processed using accelerated determination procedures. Cases to which such provisions could apply were those 'that were so obviously without foundation as not to merit full examination at every level of the procedure'. A 'manifestly unfounded' claim was one that was 'clearly fraudulent', that is, it was a claim which did not warrant being put through accepted United Nations Convention procedures. Since 1999, this procedure has been increasingly used to deal with asylum claims. In 1999, 133 claims out of a total of 7,724 claims were perceived to be manifestly unfounded (1.7 per cent); by 2000, this had increased to 2,263 out of a total of 10,938 claims (18.8 per cent). According to a report by the Irish Refugee Council, such procedures are being used on exceptionally broad grounds, with little basis in natural or constitutional justice or international human rights law.[13] Asylum applications are unfairly processed both through the normal procedure and, increasingly, through 'manifestly unfounded' procedures. Both procedures reproduce forms of institutional racism in their dealings with asylum applications.

Moreover, mirroring the restrictive practices which developed in Europe in the mid-1990s, the number of asylum seekers granted refugee status relative to the number of applications in Ireland has remained consistently low, as the government's interpretations of what constitutes asylum continually narrows.[14] In 1999, 166 asylum seekers out of 7,724 applicants were granted refugee status at first instance; by the end of 2001, 456 applicants out of 10,325 were granted refugee status. In both absolute and comparative terms, such a recognition rate remains very low, even though this number increased after the appeals stage.[15]

In Ireland, asylum seekers are not permitted, before the final determination of their case, to leave the state or to seek or enter into employment nor to carry on any business or to trade.[16] Those asylum seekers who entered Ireland before April 2000 are usually in receipt of full Supplementary Welfare Assistance payments and rent supplementation if they secure private rented accommodation. However, by contrast, asylum seekers who arrived after April 2000 are provided for through a system of dispersal and direct provision. Under this system, asylum seekers are involuntarily housed around the country in hostels, prefabricated buildings and mobile homes. In contrast to earlier asylum seekers, they receive only €19 per week per adult and €9.50 per week per child, in addition to the provision of fixed meals and basic accommodation.

At the beginning of 2002, there were approximately 5,000 asylum seekers dispersed in eighty-one centres in twenty-four counties.[17] Asylum seekers on direct provision represent the poorest of the poor. With an income which is below twenty per cent of the national household average income, they live in cramped conditions, sometimes with three or four individuals or a family sharing one room, and those living in remote areas in Ireland often have little social and cultural support.[18] However, a large number of dispersed asylum seekers have disappeared from the asylum system. Many are believed to have returned to Dublin and many to be working in the black economy. Overall, notwithstanding the social and juridical division between those arriving before and after the introduction of dispersal and direct provision, asylum seekers have the least entitlement and access to social and material resources of all the groups who live in Irish society. They are the most disempowered group, since they lack the right to work and their access to education and training is severely limited. Their presence marks the nadir of the putative values of the Celtic Tiger: they are marginalised, excluded, poor and, in many respects, they lack freedom.

Economic migration

The second major institutional mechanism for immigration is the work permit/work visa route. As a result of acute labour shortages in the Celtic Tiger economy, work permits and visas began to be issued increasingly often to non-EU migrants.[19] Given the rate of labour market expansion, the government estimated that some 200,000 new workers would be needed by 2006 as part of its National Development Plan. It was envisaged that about half these workers would be returning Irish migrants, one-quarter would be from the European Economic Area (EEA)[20] and the remainder would be non-EU workers.[21]

Evidence of such labour shortages was underlined in the Small Firms Association employment survey of 2000. This stated that, of the sixty-nine per cent of companies which had vacancies, ninety-one per cent were unable to fill them. A large source of demand came from unskilled sectors, such as hotels and catering, and other low-grade services, with forty-four per cent of employers in these areas claiming that they could not recruit, primarily as a result of the low rate of pay.[22] As the Tánaiste (deputy prime minister), Mary Harney, warned, a failure to address the labour shortage could undermine the Irish Republic's economic growth, since wage rates and the availability of skilled workers remain central concerns for multinational companies in relation to investment decisions.[23] As a result, work permits, renewable on a yearly basis, were issued to meet labour demands. However, such permits were tied to specific jobs and employers had to demonstrate that it had not been possible to fill the vacancy with indigenous labour or with EEA workers. The holders of work permits were allowed to be joined by family members after one year. In 1993, 1,103 work permits were issued. By the end of the year 2000, this figure had risen to 18,017, and by the end of 2001 it stood at 36,431. Significantly, there were three times as many applications for work permits by non-EU nationals as there were claims for asylum.

In 2001, the majority of the 36,431 permits issued were given to individuals from Latvia, Lithuania, Poland, the Philippines, South Africa and Romania.[24] Most of the countries of origin of the holders of work permits contained white populations, in contrast to the countries of origin of asylum seekers. The Department of Employment and Industry seems implicitly to have targeted specific countries for the recruitment of employees, through work fairs, advertising and so on. Thus, the first international jobs fair conducted by Foras Áiseanna Saothair (FÁS), in April 2000, was held in Newfoundland and was swiftly followed by others in London, Berlin, Cologne, Hanover, Manchester, Prague, Birmingham, Cape Town and Johannesburg.[25] In 2001, there were also visits to Poland, France, Croatia, Estonia, Australia, New Zealand, Russia, India and, again, Canada and South Africa.[26] As a result of this recruitment drive, the majority of permits went to non-African, non-Asian countries (with the exceptions of South Africa and India). These nation states are generally populated by white Christians, who are, from the state's point of view, more easily 'assimilatable' into Irish society.[27] This systematic racialisation of work permits by the state can be seen in terms of a straightforward attempt to regulate internal ethnic and religious diversity.[28]

As a result of continuing labour shortages, business organisations and government bodies such as the National Competitiveness Council and FÁS called for the creation of a fast-track work authorisation visa system. These fast-track visas were introduced specifically to facilitate the recruitment of workers in specialist categories: professionals in information technology and construction, as well as nurses. Work visas are more flexible than work permits in that they allow the recipient to move jobs within a specified sector. Moreover, visas are easier to obtain, since the employer does not have to petition the bureaucratic Department of Enterprise, Trade and Employment for a work permit.[29] Under the proposal, immigrants could get a work visa from an Irish embassy or consulate abroad, simply by producing a valid job offer from an Irish employer. Unlike work permits, visas are renewable on a two-year basis and allow family reunion in Ireland after three months, depending on the migrant's financial assets. The result is a two-tiered work regime with different rights for highly skilled visa immigrants, on the one hand, and lower-skilled work permit immigrants, on the other. The top five countries in receipt of the 3,870 work permits issued in the eight months up to the end of August 2001 were the Philippines, India, Russia, Slovakia and Yugoslavia. In contrast, the top five countries for work visas, of which 396 were issued, were South Africa, Australia, the United States, Canada and New Zealand. Significantly, no North African nations appeared in these figures.

Capitalist economic expansion has led to the formation of a dual labour market structure in Ireland's Celtic Tiger, which juxtaposes secure, permanent, highly skilled and well paid jobs, on the one hand, with unskilled, low-paid, insecure jobs, on the other. Specifically, the expansion of highly skilled, well paid computer and information technology work can be contrasted with the expansion in the unskilled services sector. The latter has generally been characterised by difficult, unpleasant and low-paid work. The marked increase in need for office cleaners, dishwashers and fast-food operatives, agricultural workers, factory workers, nurses, builders and waiters and waitresses has meant an increase in vacancies in these areas. Seventy-five per cent of all applicants for work permits in 2000 were for unskilled work,[30] with over one-fifth of these permits being for catering jobs.[31] Such unskilled positions lack a career path and are characterised by wages that fall well below the national average. Whereas, in the past, women and young people had filled these positions, migrant workers, some working in the black economy or illegally, were increasingly taking their places. The economic boom not only led to more women entering employment and thereby creating work for foreign childminders but, in addition, saw the aspirations of indigenous workers rise, so that it became increasingly difficult to fill '3-D' jobs (jobs that are dirty, difficult and dangerous).[32]

Another area in the skilled sector in which demand for workers has remained high, especially given its unsuitability for mechanisation, is the health service. The health sector has been estimated to be short of over 1,800 nurses.[33] As a result, a conscious attempt was made by the government to recruit nurses from the Philippines and it was this which partly prompted the introduction of the visa system. The Philippines has been exporting over 3,000 nurses a year.[34] In 2000, a staff nurse in Manila could earn approximately $200 per month, compared with approximately €2,000 a month in Ireland.[35]

Given the precarious, non-unionised and often illegal status of those employed in the unskilled sector, again reflecting a wider European pattern, exploitation in these areas has been rife.[36] Immigrant workers constitute cheap, flexible labour and, because they lack some important social and political rights, also in many cases lack certain economic rights. In 2001, for example, the Labour Inspectorate in the Department of Enterprise, Trade and Employment examined 108 cases of possible breaches of employment law involving foreign workers.[37] These investigations into employment violations included a variety of offences: the employment of migrant workers with unequal pay and conditions in comparison with Irish or EEA staff; failure by employers to pay workers prearranged wage rates; workers being paid below the minimum wage and being subject to excessive working hours; illegal pay deductions, with recruitment costs to be borne by the prospective employee; and the non-payment of overtime or holiday pay.[38]

The increase in the number of work permits being granted also saw the growth of racism in the workplace.[39] However, since many foreign workers were not aware of their legal rights or were afraid that they would be deported or that their work permits would not be renewed, few spoke out against abuse and exploitation – a problem that was often exacerbated by linguistic barriers. Such pervasive exploitation is a consequence of Irish government policy, which has focused on migrant workers largely in terms of economic criteria. Thus, rather than examining the consequences of increased immigration in terms of access to housing, education, health services, transport, social welfare, and civil and political rights, government policy focuses exclusively on the numbers of workers needed to meet the demands of the economy. The increase in work permits has been one method for reducing wage pressure and so clearly benefits business. However, this narrow economic concern has always been mediated by a restricted notion of Irish nationhood, in which the Irish government expects non-EEA workers to return (voluntarily or otherwise) to their country of origin once their labour is no longer needed. Such a standpoint echoes the restrictive policy of other European nation states and effectively denies the reality of long-term trends in immigration.

Despite the differences between those given work permits – described as 'bonded labour' – and those holding visas, both lack social and political rights, including access to free education, medical care and social welfare entitlements. Neither group benefits from any holistic integration strategy or even from access to language classes. As a result, asylum seekers and some economic migrants have a great deal in common. They are generally at the bottom end of the socio-economic ladder, share similar racialised disadvantages in terms of housing and educational opportunities, experience low standards of living, poverty and social exclusion, and are equally targets of informal and institutional racism, discrimination and hostility.

Classification and the state

Through legislation and social policy, most European states attempt to define and sanction acceptable types of social behaviour and activity. As the dominant force in the field of power, which controls the nation and citizenship through legislation, the state actively encourages some forms of social life while downplaying and repressing others. This ability to regulate social life depends in part upon the capacity to sustain and impose categories of thought through which institutions and individuals make sense of the world. This potential to impose what Bourdieu calls a 'vision of divisions' is the 'power of making social divisions and hence the political power *par excellence*'.[40]

An important aspect of this vision of divisions is the way in which individuals are encouraged to identify themselves predominantly in narrow national terms. Processes of nation state formation invariably invoke homogeneous narratives of ethnicity and national identity.[41] In Ireland, this narrative was originally predicated upon the idea of a white Celtic people, defined in opposition to British colonisers. Irishness in this sense leaves no room for non-white, non-Celtic people or for those who cannot participate in its collective historical experience.[42] National identity is defined by exclusions, which mark its limit. This ideal and undifferentiated 'imagined community', which has been reconfigured in the Celtic Tiger, elides difference and often draws attention away from the material experiences of domination and subordination which are intrinsic to bourgeois society.

The administrative categories and classifications used by the state play an important role in defining broader discourses of identification and exclusion. Both dominant and marginalised groups come to define themselves and each other through such categorisations. In 'imagining' a national community in terms of such categories, the state orchestrates a wider *conscience collective*, which is both descriptive and normative while reflecting and prioritising the values of the dominant class and ethnicity. This conscience collective is a continual object of struggle, since real-life experiences contradict, on a daily basis, the imaginary of national myth.[43]

The hegemonic sense of Irish identity established during the 1920s and 1930s has been severely challenged by the rise of the Celtic Tiger. The two main pillars and regulators of Irish identity and conservatism since the foundation of the state – the Catholic Church and Fianna Fáil[44] – have both been partly undermined by economic growth and various media discourses referring to clerical and political scandal.[45] In addition, the assumption of shared values and experience so central to the Celtic imaginary has been challenged by the recent increase in foreign immigration. Migrants often expose the social and political fault lines of religion, ethnicity, class, gender and culture, which lie beneath the veneer of any 'imagined community', and Ireland is no exception.

The new articulation of nationalism with racism can be understood in terms of this new tension between the re-imagined Irish community of the 1990s, to which corresponds a narrowly conceived sense of ethnic citizenship, on the one hand, and the reality of increasing social diversity characterising the Ireland of the Celtic Tiger, on the other. It is in this context that we can read the subtext of government policy, both in the ongoing maintenance of a restrictive and exclusionary definition of Irishness as white and Catholic, and also in the overt immigration policies, which are straightforwardly aimed at deterring the entry of non-nationals. The articulation of nationalism with racism also explains the reluctance to advance the structural integration of immigrants in social, political, cultural and economic terms. Here, the process of state categorisation is also important. Through administrative categorisation as 'significant others', those with power and authority (in this case the state) are in a position to impose their definition of an individual and situation, and thus to mould those people's subsequent careers in terms of their identity. As a result, individuals may adjust their identity correspondingly over time. The disempowered often come to see themselves through the eyes of the dominant, as self-images merge with public images:

> Dominated agents, who assess the value of their position and their charac-
> teristics by applying a system of schemes of perception and appreciation
> ... tend to attribute to themselves what the distribution attributes to them ...
> adjusting their expectations to their chances, defining themselves as the
> established order defines them.[46]

Rather than providing all residents with the same civil and political rights, bureaucratic classification schemes engender systematic patterns of discrimination. The legal and administrative categories of 'asylum seeker', 'refugee' and 'economic migrant' are important in that they confer different rights and entitlements. These categorisations have been used by state service providers during the period of the Celtic Tiger as a basis for judgements about individual entitlements to social, political and economic support. In many respects, this discourse of entitlement echoes older distinctions between the 'deserving' and 'undeserving' poor. Thus, both government and media make much of the putative difference between 'genuine' refugees (deserving), of whom there are few, and 'bogus' refugees (undeserving), of whom there are too many. Government statements frequently refer to the way that 'our' welfare regime is attracting 'economic migrants'. For instance, in 1999, John O'Donohue, the Minister for Justice, Equality and Law Reform, in a speech to the Irish Business and Employers Confederation, argued:

> In the early years of this decade and prior to that, our relatively high
> unemployment rates and low social welfare payments ensured that illegal
> immigrants invoking the asylum convention targeted the more prosperous
> countries – even small ones like Denmark and Finland. Let us be clear
> about it. Our current economic boom is making us a target.[47]

Such speeches often tell us more about the categorisers and how they perceive themselves than they do about the classified. The implication here is that an overly generous and prosperous Ireland, the land of a hundred thousand welcomes, is being systematically abused by unscrupulous asylum seekers. Similarly, a recent statement by a Fianna Fáil TD, Noel O'Flynn, reinforced such a negative view of asylum seekers:

> We're against the spongers, the freeloaders, the people screwing the system. Too many are coming to Ireland and too many to Cork in my view ... I'm saying we will have to close the doors. The majority of them are here for economic reasons and they are thumbing their noses up at Irish hospitality and demanding everything under the guise of the Geneva Convention while the taxpayer is paying for it all.[48]

Instead of provoking outrage, such populist rhetoric – which speaks directly to the collective unconscious – earned O'Flynn increased popularity in his Cork North Central constituency, where he topped the pole in the recent general election. Further, this statement was never retracted by O'Flynn, nor were formal sanctions brought against him by the Taoiseach. Such indifference to racist political narrative is part of a broader picture of government inaction. Despite the newly accumulated wealth and the move towards cultural renewal which have come to symbolise contemporary Ireland, the government has failed to take any systematic stance against racism. A failed awareness campaign has been matched by the failure to establish an independent body to monitor racism, or to introduce legislation to protect individuals from racist crimes, or to introduce comprehensive anti-racism instruction as part of education and public service training.

Historically, Ireland has experienced both colonialism and economic hardship. Many Irish citizens travelled to the United States and worked illegally while their regularisation was formally sought.[49] Given the significance of these events, it may have been expected that the Irish government would show sympathy to others who have suffered hardship. However, instead of treating immigrants, including asylum seekers and economic migrants, within a generous humanitarian framework which recognises the global nature of both political persecution and poverty, foreign immigrants coming to Ireland have been judged solely according to an economic cost–benefit criterion. As Sayad notes, from the point of view of the state and the economy, immigration and the immigrant have no meaning and *raison d'être* unless they 'bring in' more than they 'cost'.[50] The question facing policy makers is how to maximise the 'profits' (primarily economic) while minimising the 'costs' (economic, but also social, cultural and national). However, as Sayad rightly points out, the very accounting conventions which determine what is 'cost' and what is 'benefit' are loaded and systematically underplay the positive gains associated with immigration. For instance, these conventions emphasise the monetary transfers associated with welfare payments but rarely quantify the impact of savings transfers into the economy from abroad. More generally, they obscure the point that immigrants actually create more jobs than they take and are likely to pay more in taxes than they receive in welfare.[51]

Racism in Ireland

It is in relation to these state practices that we need to understand racism. Racism can be broadly defined as any belief or practice which attributes negative characteristics to any group or persons either intentionally or unintentionally, on the basis of their supposed 'race' or ethnicity, within the context of differential relations of power.[52] Despite Ireland's image as a welcoming, hospitable nation and its unparalleled economic boom, many members of black and ethnic minority groups have experienced racism since arriving in Ireland. In a recent Amnesty International survey, seventy-nine per cent of individuals from black or ethnic minority groups living in Ireland claimed they had experienced some form of racism or discrimination.[53] Moreover, many of these racist attacks were not one-off or incidental occurrences. When asked how often they had received insulting comments, 36.2 per cent of respondents stated that this had occurred 'frequently' and 32.3 per cent said that it had occurred 'occasionally'. The overwhelming majority of these racist incidents took place in public spaces. Over forty-four per cent of the experiences of racist abuse took place on the street, twenty-four per cent in shops and twenty-three per cent in pubs. For black and ethnic minorities, such abuse was a feature of everyday life and occurred in a multiplicity of social situations: in pubs, from neighbours, in banks, on buses and taxis, with regard to housing, at school and even at the cinema. Notwithstanding the fact that these statistics are geographically and contextually dependent, the high proportion of racist incidents experienced at the hands of the gardaí (twenty-five per cent) and employers (twenty per cent) is a particular cause for concern, since both groups hold a significant degree of power within Irish society. Such statistics underline the fact that, despite economic growth and cultural and political liberalisation, racism is steadily becoming an endemic feature of Irish society.

The economic boom has had massive social, political and cultural repercussions for Irish society, including the realignment of notions of ethnicity and class. With the creation of almost half a million new jobs since 1990, and the reversal of historical patterns of emigration, the Celtic Tiger signifies an emphatic shift in the context for the reception and integration of would-be immigrants. At the same time, however, there has been a dramatic increase in wealth inequality and a similar expansion at the lower end of the labour market in low-paid, insecure and part-time service jobs, often in the informal economy. As a result, poverty levels have increased dramatically. The growing gap between rich and poor has also been reflected in other social processes, for instance the emergence of a two-tier health system and growing numbers of homeless people. Government policy with respect to taxation and the wage restraint agreements negotiated under the rubric of 'Partnership 2000' have seen corporate profits rise while the poorest have slipped further behind.[54] It is important, therefore, to acknowledge, in opposition to the liberal view of a society composed of sovereign individuals, a more radical view which emphasises the importance of racialisation within a context of broader cultural and economic differences in power and social domination.[55]

The recent development of contemporary Irish society is inherently paradoxical. At the same time as producing unprecedented wealth, it has created poverty and social exclusion. It is largely, although not exclusively, by reference to this paradox that we can attempt to understand the growth of racism in Ireland. Although racism may take the form of a relatively coherent theory, it can also appear in the form of a less coherent assembly of stereotypes, images and attributions, and as an explanation that is constructed and employed by individuals to negotiate their everyday lives. As Miles notes, racism can be characterised as practically adequate, in the sense that it refracts, in thought, certain observed regularities in the social world and constructs a causal interpretation which is presented as consistent with those regularities.[56] Such images and stereotypes rarely emerge spontaneously and often arise from state and media discourses, given their monopoly over the powers of governance, diffusion and representation. Thus, refugees in Ireland, and Europe generally, are often represented as being responsible for a number of social and economic problems (which usually existed well before their arrival), such as housing shortages, unemployment and the general lack of adequate statutory provisions. For many disempowered sections of the population, racist discourses often constitute a description of, and explanation for, the world they experience on a day-to-day basis. Racist discourse is an ideological account of the social world which recognises and offers an explanation for the housing crisis, for the lack of jobs, for the continuance of poverty – experiences which many marginalised groups face. As a correlate of racialisation, racism therefore serves to make a causal link between observed, material differences in Irish society and signified phenotypical and cultural differences of black and ethnic minorities. It helps to make sense of the economic and social changes accompanying poverty, urban decline and social exclusion, as they are experienced by sections of the working class within the context of a booming Celtic Tiger economy.

In a study carried out by Amnesty International in 2002, forty-four per cent of respondents believed that asylum seekers were depriving indigenous Irish people of local authority housing, ninety-five per cent believed that some asylum seekers were in Ireland illegally and fifteen per cent believed that asylum seekers could obtain grants to buy cars, while ten per cent believed that they were given free mobile phones.[57]

In research carried out by the Irish Refugee Council, many asylum seekers referred to the hostility they encountered from other excluded and marginalised groups.[58] It was felt that such indigenous excluded groups often perceived asylum seekers and refugees as welfare scroungers, or as preventing them from receiving certain scarce social resources:

> I think Irish people ... are racist people but I think the racist people are from Ireland's cities, the people who are getting Social Welfare. I really think that educated people are not racist ... even if in their roots they have some racism they learn to control it or they learn what it is to be racist.[59]

> In inner city areas these people are thinking that refugees and asylum seekers are their competitors, or in competition with them.[60]

Such explicit, potentially violent hostility concurs with 'popular' definitions of racism as well as those definitions used by the media and government. However, such a view occludes the more silent but equally pernicious forms of institutional racism which also operate through state organisations. And, of course, asylum seekers are more likely to encounter such overt racial hostility from inner-city working-class communities because of their similar social and geographical position.

Yet, it is important not to oversimplify or homogenise the causes of racism in Irish society. Processes of racialisation and racism are heterogeneous, contradictory and uneven, and cannot simply be reduced to a consequence of the practices of state, media and capital. The argument that is proposed here is merely that these practices have been particularly important in understanding *some* forms of racism which have emerged in modern Irish society. Other sites where racism operates and is reproduced also need to be acknowledged. These include playgrounds, streets, classrooms, hospitals and the workplace. As Rattansi argues, such sites often embody racialised power relations which are tied to various power/ knowledge configurations.[61] However, in contrast to many postmodern approaches – which, often reflecting the position of their advocates in social space, tend to concentrate on the concepts of difference and 'other' to explain nationalism and racism – the importance of the state and the economy should not be downplayed.[62] Such postmodern standpoints often disarticulate the social and economic conditions of the emergence of forms of signification and racialisation. As Hall notes, however:

the question is not whether men-in-general make perceptual distinctions between groups with different racial or ethnic characteristics, but rather, what are the specific conditions which make this form of distinction socially pertinent, historically active.[63]

Signification of 'otherness', as a basis for racialisation and racism, can have effect and meaning only within determinate economic and political relations of social domination. Language as a practice, as Wittgenstein rightly notes, is always embedded in other, broader practices or forms of life.[64]

Conclusions

It was argued earlier that it is impossible to understand racism in contemporary Ireland without making some reference to the Celtic Tiger. On an ideological level, the Celtic Tiger has come not only to characterise Ireland's unprecedented economic boom and a new-found confidence in the arts but also to represent an endorsement of liberal values, including cosmopolitanism and multiculturalism, as well as a commodified international image of tourist friendliness, hospitality and openness. The underlying reality, however, remains starkly different. Rapid economic growth has created a structural tension between the logic of capital accumulation and that of political nationalism. The 'imagined community' which emerged during the early years of the Republic embodied a highly restricted notion of citizenship and ethnicity which, despite undergoing significant modification during the economic boom, have remained essentially exclusionary. Since the foundation of the state, Irishness and citizenship have been correlated with whiteness and Catholicism, both of which implicitly acted as the measure against which difference was constructed.[65] However, this restricted, hegemonic view of 'Irishness' is now coming into conflict with the labour market imperatives of the increasingly globalised Tiger economy. Hence, there is a need for immigrant labour, yet at the same time a racialisation of that labour. The free movement of people has not matched the free and accelerating movement of goods and capital across national borders. Despite the acute labour needs of the Irish economy, the Irish government has remained stringent with regard to the entry of non-nationals, as is witnessed by the low number of asylum seekers who have actually been granted refugee status and the racialisation of those given work permits. To this tension between historic nationalism and the contemporary economic revival can be added the issue of Irish constitutional liberalism. As a small state with a history of neutrality and a commitment to democracy and to the international rule of law, and coloured by its own experience of colonial oppression, Ireland has always voiced strong support for the

United Nations, and, specifically, the 1951 Convention Relating to the Status of Refugees, although this support was often more in terms of image than substance. Since the emergence of the Celtic Tiger, the Irish state has increasingly interpreted international protocols and legislation relating to migration in an illiberal spirit. In addition, it has failed to adopt a number of international laws relating to human rights and racism. This liberal internationalism further complicates the political response to what is, for Ireland, the new problem of immigration.[66] Here we see the overdetermination[67] of a structural contradiction between, on the one hand, nationalism – closed, Janus-faced, insular, selective, discriminating and particular – and, on the other, capitalism – open, expansionary, indiscriminate, global and universal.

In order to have any purchase in this context, antiracist struggles will have to be carried out at a number of different levels. Exclusionary forms of nationalism cannot be simply replaced by anodyne notions of multi-culturalism or by calls for more inclusive forms of national identity, which leave unequal forms of power in place. Nor can material shifts towards economic equality through the challenging of private property be secured without major ideological shifts which relate to classification, social recognition and the valorisation of difference. These remain the fundamental challenges for Irish society as the Celtic Tiger, coming under increasing pressure, continues to throw up new social and economic problems.

I would like to thank Alice Feldman, Stephen Quilley, Louise Campbell and Colin Coulter for their very helpful comments on this chapter.

Notes

1 As a result of the limited focus of this chapter, it needs to be constantly borne in mind that the word 'immigrant', which has come to stand for black and minority groups, is a much broader concept and its conflation with blacks, and more recently with refugees, is the effect of ideological and political processes instituted by political and media discourses. To that extent, this chapter, by concentrating largely on black and ethnic groups, reproduces this ideological correlation.
2 That is, nationals not born in Ireland or a member state of the European Economic Area.
3 Other methods of entry include student visas and tourist visas.
4 C. Calhoun, *Nationalism* (Basingstoke: Open University Press, 1997).
5 B. Rolston and M. Shannon, *Encounters: How Racism Came to Ireland* (Belfast: Beyond the Pale, 2002).
6 'Programme refugees' differ from 'Convention refugees' in that they are invited by the government in groups.
7 E. Ward, '"A big show-off to show what we could do" – Ireland and the Hungarian refugee crisis of 1956', *Irish Studies in International Affairs*, 7

(1996), pp. 131–41; D. Keogh, *The Jews in Ireland* (Cork: Cork University Press, 1998); K. Goldstone, '"Benevolent helpfulness?" – Ireland and the international reaction to Jewish refugees 1933–9', in M. Kennedy and J. M. Skelly (eds), *Irish Foreign Policy 1919–1966* (Dublin: Four Courts Press, 2000).

8 P. MacÉinrí, 'Immigration policy in Ireland', in F. Farrell and P. Watt (eds), *Responding to Racism* (Dublin: Veritas, 2001), p. 56.

9 P. Faugnan and M. Woods, *Lives on Hold: Seeking Asylum in Ireland* (Dublin: Social Science Research Council, 2000); Comhlámh Refugee Solidarity Group, *Refugee Lives* (Dublin: Comhlámh, 2001). In contrast, the United Kingdom received 21.6 per cent of all European applications and Germany 17.4 per cent.

10 These include the role of traffickers and European refugee policies generally, especially those in the United Kingdom, which have had repercussions on the situation in Ireland.

11 P. Bourdieu (ed.), *The Weight of the World* (Cambridge: Polity, 1999), p. 609.

12 L. Almirall and N. Lawton, *Asylum in Ireland: A Report on the Fairness and Sustainability of Asylum Determinations at First Instance* (Dublin: Irish Refugee Council, 2000), p. 24.

13 S. Mullally, *Manifestly Unjust: A Report on the Fairness and Sustainability of Accelerated Procedures for Asylum Determinations* (Dublin: Irish Refugee Council, 2001).

14 The usual distinction between asylum seekers and refugees will be used throughout this chapter. According to the 1996 Refugee Act, an asylum seeker is a 'person who, owing to a well founded fear of being persecuted for reasons of race, religion, nationality, membership of a particular social group or political opinion, is outside the country of his or her nationality or, owing to such a fear, is unwilling to avail himself or herself of the protection of that country'. By contrast, refugees are asylum seekers who have successfully fulfilled these requirements as stipulated in the 1951 United Nations Convention and are thereby (usually) entitled to full citizenship rights.

15 Moreover, many asylum seekers were also given humanitarian leave to remain. In 2000, this figure stood at 2,473.

16 The exception here is a select number of asylum seekers who were given the right to work. Asylum seekers who had made their applications in Ireland at least twelve months before 27 July 1999, as well as those who had applied for asylum in Ireland on or before 27 July 1999 and had been in the state for twelve months, were all given the right to work. As a result, an estimated 3,500 asylum seekers were permitted to work.

17 Department of Justice, 24 March 2002; B. Fanning, S. Loyal and C. Staunton, *Asylum Seekers and the Right to Work in Ireland* (Dublin: Irish Refugee Council, 2000).

18 B. Fanning, A. Veale and D. O'Connor, *Beyond the Pale: Asylum Seeking Children and Social Exclusion in Ireland* (Dublin: Irish Refugee Council, 2001).

19 Employers who apply for work permits are generally required to establish that it has not been possible, in spite of reasonable efforts being made, to fill the vacancy with an Irish or other person for whom a work permit is not required. A permit is granted when the employer has no alternative but to employ a non-EEA national. For more detailed information, see *Changes to Work Permit Requirements in Ireland: Information Note*, available from the Department of Enterprise, Trade and Employment.

20 The EEA includes the fifteen states in the EU, plus the members of the European Free Trade Association, Norway, Iceland and Liechtenstein.

21 *Irish Times*, 22 January 2001.

22 *Ibid.*

23 *Irish Times*, 22 December 2000.

24 The top countries granted work permits were as follows: Latvia, 4,355; Lithuania, 2,907; Poland, 2,490; Philippines, 2,471; South Africa, 2,031; Romania, 1,572; Czech Republic, 1,454; Russian Federation, 1,440; Ukraine, 1,331.

25 FÁS (Foras Áiseanna Saothair) is the labour development authority in Ireland and provides job placements for workers.

26 *Irish Times*, 22 December 2000.

27 The one exception to this was the Philippines, although it should be noted that between eighty and ninety per cent of Philippinos are Catholic.

28 Thanks to T. Ward for this information.

29 However, following signs of an economic downturn, the Taoiseach has re-emphasised the need for Irish industry to employ Irish workers before seeking to recruit non-EU workers (see *Irish Times*, 23 November 2001). In addition, the policy requiring employers to prove that an Irish person (or other EEA national) was not available for a job instead of a non-EEA migrant has been strengthened. Annual work permit fees, as a disincentive, have also been increased, from €159 to €400.

30 *Irish Times*, 5 July 2001.

31 *Irish Times*, 23 December 2000.

32 In the skilled employment sector, the effect of skilled migrants leaving the country of origin to seek work abroad has thrown up issues relating to 'brain drain' and the continued economic exploitation of developing societies by more economically developed ones.

33 *Irish Times*, 3 March 2000.

34 P. Stalker, *No-Nonsense Guide to Immigration* (London: Verso, 2001), p. 26.

35 *Irish Times*, 17 April 2000.

36 *Irish Times*, 7 July 2001.

37 *Irish Times*, 8 June 2001. Of 108, thirty-three involved foreign workers in the hotel and catering sector, twenty-four in agriculture sector, sixteen in nursing and nine in the retail sector.

38 The extensive exploitation of migrant workers is not a phenomenon peculiar to Ireland but increasingly reflects global practices. Hence, in South Korea in 1999, workers from China, Thailand and Pakistan employed officially on public work programmes were paid only forty-five to seventy-six per cent of what Korean workers were paid. In Hong Kong in 2000, Chinese workers from the mainland were paid $8 a day for unloading vegetables when the average daily pay for Hong Kong residents was $28 for day labour. Stalker, *No-Nonsense Guide to Immigration*, pp. 26–7.

39 *Report of the Equality Authority* (Dublin: Government Publications, 2001).

40 P. Bourdieu, *Distinction: A Social Critique of the Judgement of Taste* (London: Routledge, 1984), p. 468.

41 A. Smith, *National Identity* (Harmondsworth: Penguin, 1991); E. Hobsbawn and T. Ranger (eds), *The Invention of Tradition* (Cambridge: Cambridge University Press, 1983).

42 This is not to say that Irish nationalism has not changed. Nationalism is ever in the process of being reproduced and, as such, must inflect broader social and political transformations. For this reason, one should be wary of

equating the peculiar exclusionary doctrines of the newly born Irish state of the 1930s with contemporary discourses of nationalist governance and moral regulation, which have emerged in relation to very different economic and social problems.

43 P. Corrigan and D. Sayer, *The Great Arch: State Formation as Cultural Revolution* (Oxford: Blackwell, 1985).

44 K. Allen, *The Celtic Tiger: The Myth of Social Partnership in Ireland* (Manchester: Manchester University Press, 2000).

45 T. Inglis, *Moral Monopoly: The Rise and Fall of the Catholic Church in Modern Ireland* (Dublin: University College Dublin Press, 1998).

46 Bourdieu, *Distinction*, p. 471.

47 John O'Donohue, speech to the Irish Business and Employers Confederation, Dublin, September 1999.

48 *Irish Times*, 29 January 2002.

49 M. Corcoran, 'Clandestine destinies: the informal economic sector and Irish immigrant incorporation', in J. MacLaughlin (ed.), *Location and Dislocation in Contemporary Irish Society* (Cork: Cork University Press, 1997), pp. 236–52.

50 A. Sayad, '"Costs" and "benefits" of immigration', in P. Bourdieu *et al.* (eds), *The Weight of the World* (Cambridge: Polity, 1999).

51 Stalker, *No-Nonsense Guide to Immigration*.

52 Under this broad definition, racism is being used here only as a generic or class concept. That is, it signifies what particular social actions and practices may, loosely, have in common. Racism, as such, does not exist *per se* but exists only in its empirical instantiations, which we must identify on a shifting social and historical basis. Racism can also be broadly seen as a form of 'exclusionary practice', which occurs when a specified group is shown to be in unequal receipt of resources and services. However, in order to avoid the interrelated dangers of supposing that the explanation for disadvantage is mono-causal and that the disadvantaged position of 'refugees' is necessarily consequent upon racialisation, it should be assumed that exclusionary practices have a number of determinants, which refract and reinforce one another.

53 E. O'Mahony, S. Loyal and A. Mulcahy, *Racism in Ireland: The Views of Black and Ethnic Minorities* (Dublin: Amnesty International, 2001).

54 Allen, *The Celtic Tiger*.

55 As Marx states in the *Grundrisse*: 'This so called consideration from the point of view of society means nothing more than to overlook precisely the differences which express the social relation (relation to civil society). Society does not consist of individuals, but expresses the sum of the relationships and conditions in which these individuals stand to one another. As if someone were to say: for society slaves and citizens do not exist: both are men. They are both men, if we consider them outside society. To be a slave and to be a citizen are social determinations, relations between human beings A and B. Human being A as such is not a slave: he is a slave in and through society'. K. Marx, *Grundrisse: Foundations of the Critique of Political Economy* (M. Nicolaus, trans.) (Harmondsworth: Penguin, 1993).

56 R. Miles, *Racism* (London: Routledge, 1989).

57 Opinion poll for Amnesty International (Dublin: Lansdowne Marketing Research, April 2002).

58 Fanning *et al.*, *Asylum Seekers and the Right to Work in Ireland*.

59 *Ibid.*, p. 20.

60 *Ibid.*, p. 21.

61 A. Rattansi, 'Just framing: ethnicities and racisms in a "postmodern" frame-work', in L. Nicholson (ed.), *Social Postmodernism* (Cambridge: Cambridge University Press, 1995), p. 262.
62 See P. Bourdieu, *The Logic of Practice* (Cambridge: Polity, 1990) for a dis-cussion of the academic tendency to privilege the symbolic.
63 S. Hall, 'Race, articulation and societies structured in dominance', in *Socio-logical Theories: Race and Colonialism* (Paris: UNESCO, 1980), p. 338.
64 L. Wittgenstein, *Philosophical Investigations* (Oxford: Blackwell, 1957).
65 D. Haraway, *Primate Visions* (London: Verso, 1992).
66 However, the gap between the appearance of international constitutional acceptance and the reality of policy is also evident. See the treatment of the Hungarian programme refugees in Ward, '"A big show-off to show what we could do"'.
67 L. Althusser, *Reading Capital* (London: Verso, 1974).

5

Irish women and the Celtic Tiger economy

SINÉAD KENNEDY

The term 'Celtic Tiger' has connotations that extend well beyond the realm of the purely economic. It has, for instance, become a metaphor for a new national consensus that constantly reminds us how 'we have never had it so good'. This chapter takes issue with this consensus and argues instead that, while the recent boom in the Irish Republic has produced enormous wealth for a small minority, the majority of Irish people have benefited little from this apparent economic miracle. In fact, there has been a direct transfer in wealth from the poorest sections in society to the richest. The chapter will offer a critical examination of the realities of the Celtic Tiger for Irish women.

The changing position of women in Irish society is one of the most overlooked aspects of Ireland's recent economic prosperity. In this context, there is a consensus among political commentators and academics that the shift towards a more liberal and secular Ireland is the inevitable result of the process of modernisation or a result of the liberalisation inspired by the European Union (EU). The premise of this chapter is that the changes that have occurred in Irish society over the past ten years can be better understood if they are viewed in terms of the shifts in patterns of economic production. Changes in capitalism have resulted in a transformation of family structure, sex and sexuality and, ultimately, the lives of Irish women. One of the defining features of the Celtic Tiger era has been the sheer number of women with children who are returning to the workforce. Since the early 1990s, women have been entering the workforce in large numbers but this radical shift in labour market dynamics has received little more than a passing comment in the growing literature on Ireland's recent apparent economic success.[1] Furthermore, feminist analysis frequently attempts to create a seamless connection between women regardless of their class position. All too often there is an assumption, albeit frequently an unconscious one, that 'we are all in this together'. This perspective ignores, of course, the fact that class position mediates one's experience of oppression.

The feminisation of the workforce

Ireland's membership of the EU, infrastructural development and a decreased economic dependence on the United Kingdom had transformed the Irish economy by the late 1970s. Irish women grew up expecting and demanding a life outside the home, wanting to be more than wives and mothers. Between 1971 and 1983, the number of women in the workforce grew by thirty-four per cent. The number of married women in the workforce increased by 425 per cent over the same period. More remarkable are the changes that we have seen over the past decade, in the era of the Celtic Tiger. The majority of new female employment is in the service sector, many in jobs that used to be relatively well paid, high-status male jobs, such as in computers and banking, but which have been deskilled and demoted in the job hierarchy. By 1996, there were 488,000 women working in Ireland, an increase of 212,000 since 1971, compared with an increase in male employment of just 23,000 for the same period.[2] Between 1991 and 1996, female employment grew by 102,000, equalling the growth of the previous twenty years. A further 128,000 women entered the workforce between 1996 and 2000.[3] One of the principal reasons for this shift was that women no longer saw marriage or having children as a reason to leave the workforce. Participation in the labour force is highest among women aged between twenty-five and forty-four, running at around ninety per cent and equalling the EU average.[4] The overall level of female participation in the workforce had risen from thirty-nine per cent in 1994 to over fifty per cent in 2002, equalling the EU average.[5]

This feminisation of the formal workforce has been a contradictory experience for the majority of women. While women have entered employment in growing numbers, they continue to earn less than men, and sometimes less than men who are doing the same job. Women's low pay is related to their concentration in occupational groups which are predominantly female, understood as low skilled and poorly paid.[6] The differential is even greater among the lowest-paid women. Research conducted by the Irish Congress of Trade Unions (ICTU) in 1993 found that low pay in Ireland was most common in areas of traditional female employment, such as textiles, clothing and cleaning and at the lower grades of the civil service.[7] Four years later, in 1997, despite an unprecedented economic boom and successive national wage agreements, the average weekly earnings of women employed in the industrial sector, while increasing, were still just sixty-five per cent of men's. For women who were employed in white-collar employment and senior management, it rose to eighty-three per cent.[8]

This clear wage differential between men and women can, in part, be explained by the number of hours worked. There is an increasing trend among women to work part-time and part-time employment in Ireland is a primarily female activity. In 1994, eighteen per cent of women worked part-time; by 2000, that figure had increased to twenty-nine per cent.[9] This increase in part-time employment has been one of the ways that women have attempted to get around the inadequate provision of child-care. The 1996 *Living in Ireland Survey* showed that seventy-three per cent of those who were in part-time employment were women and that women with children under ten years of age made up forty-one per cent of part-time female workers.[10] The majority of these part-time jobs are regular rather than occasional and can, thus, arguably be seen as part of the restructuring of the labour force and capitalism's increasing need for a flexible and cheap workforce.

Irish women's participation in the labour force is still below the EU average, especially if we consider parental rather than marital status.[11] Ireland has the lowest level of labour market participation in Europe among women with children under five years of age. In the Irish Republic, as well as in Italy and Greece, less than fifty per cent of women with young children work outside the home. Yet, in Denmark, for example, eighty per cent of women with children of preschool age work.[12] Provisions for early childhood education and publicly funded childcare services are lower in Ireland than the rest of Europe. Just one per cent of three-year-olds in Ireland have access to preschool education, compared with forty-five per cent in the United Kingdom, sixty per cent in Germany and ninety-eight per cent in Denmark.[13] Irish parents spend a higher proportion of their earnings on childcare than their European counter-parts, with at least twenty per cent of maternal earnings going towards paying for it. The lack of state-sponsored childcare and its privatised provision discriminate against working-class mothers and force them out of the workforce.[14]

Unsurprisingly, childcare has become an important issue among women in Ireland, yet successive governments have failed to create an adequate solution or even to address the question. The average cost of a Dublin full-time crèche place in December 2000 was €500 per month. This had risen to €1,200 per month by June 2002. Over thirty per cent of nurseries operate from converted houses and only thirteen per cent use purpose-built facilities.[15] The Expert Working Group on Childcare, which commissioned the *National Childcare Strategy* report, argued the case for tax relief for childcare providers who upgrade their facilities and personal tax relief for parents. The issue has created a dilemma for policy makers trying to juggle a desire for more women to enter the labour force, in order to redress labour shortages, and a desire to reduce public spending and maintain a low-tax regime for the wealthy.[16] Unfortu-nately, the trade union movement, while continuing to lobby for better childcare facilities, has capitulated to this tax credit solution. Needless to say, this is not an adequate resolution. The care of children should not be subject to the demands of the marketplace. Furthermore, tax relief is a solution that benefits the rich. Two high earners will get more tax relief, especially if they are in higher tax bracket, than a low-paid single parent.

The principal effect of the feminisation of the workforce has been to increase the already stark class divisions among women. Between 1997 and 1998, over fifty per cent of all workers (fifty-six per cent of women and fifty-one per cent of men) earned less than IR£13,500, or two-thirds of the average wage. At the other end of the spectrum, fifteen per cent earned in excess of IR£40,000, or more than twice the average wage. While two-thirds of the latter were men, it is clear that there is a layer of women who are doing considerably better than the average man or woman.[17] According to the 1996 *Labour Force Survey*, fifty-three per cent of those in professional or technical occupations are women. In the survey's sectional categories, sixty-five per cent of those in the professional services sector and sixty-two per cent of those in the personal services sector are women.[18] Women at the higher end of the scale do suffer from discrimination but not all women's work is low paid.[19] However, the point that is often missed is that these figures highlight a sharp class divide. While all women suffer serious difficulties fulfilling childcare and work commitments, not all women experience these difficulties equally. A checkout operator in Dunnes Stores cannot afford to pay for domestic backup, whereas a well paid professional woman can afford a full-time nanny or au pair.

The gap between rich and poor continued to increase during the years of the economic boom and, despite government protestations to the contrary, there has been little attempt to distribute the benefits of the Celtic Tiger equally. The Justice Commission of the Conference of Religious in Ireland (CORI) estimates that the average income gap between rich and poor in Ireland for 2001 was a staggering £IR191 per week, the largest difference in the entire EU. This disparity is particularly evident when one examines the situation of women and children during the Celtic Tiger years. A study by Nolan and Watson found that the risk of poverty for women living alone was twenty-four per cent.[20] The risk of women being low paid, while being equal to that of men when below the age of twenty-five, becomes much greater between the ages of thirty-five and forty-four.[21] Even more worrying is the fact that for female lone parents, who are heads of households, the risk increases to 31.7 per cent.[22] The single-parent organisation Cherish, in its 2002 pre-budget submission, recommended a weekly payment of €253.96 for single parents with one or two children in order for them to avoid serious and persistent poverty.[23] Child Benefit, which is paid to all parents with children, regardless of financial position, increased to €117.60 in 2002 for each of a family's first two children. Child Dependant Allowance, which is targeted at children in poor households, had not increased since 1996 and remained in 2002 a paltry €16.76 per week and will make no significant difference for families living in poverty according to the Irish National Organis-ation of the Unemployed.[24] Therefore, a class analysis concerning the position of women in society cannot just be about creating a league table of poverty: it must involve a strategy to end class society and the in-equalities – not least those of gender and sexuality – which it produces.

An Irish solution to an Irish problem

An examination of abortion law in Ireland illustrates the difficulties facing many women today and the class forces that operate in Irish society. Abortion is illegal in almost all circumstances in Ireland, but it is very much a reality for Irish women.[25] Between 1967 and 1998, almost 95,000 women who had abortions in Britain gave Irish addresses.[26] In their comprehensive study of Irish abortion, Mahon, Conlon and Dillon, on the basis of available statistics,[27] estimated that the Irish abortion rate was 5.6 abortions per year per 1,000 women of childbearing age (fifteen to forty-four years) (this figure had risen to 7.2 in 1999).[28] British statistics show that the numbers of Irish women having abortions has steadily increased and that, in 2000, 6,381 women who had abortions in Britain indicated that they were resident in the Irish Republic; this is approximately eighteen women every day.

It is widely accepted that many women resident in the Irish Republic who travel to Britain to have an abortion do not give their real address. It is impossible, therefore, to be precise about the number of Irish women who have terminations every year, except to say that the figure is far higher than official data would indicate. British statistics also indicate that eighty per cent of Irish women have their pregnancies terminated in the first twelve weeks, although the percentage of Irish-resident women having later abortions is higher than that of British-resident women.[29] The fact that Irish women have later abortions than their British counter-parts may indicate that many women encounter difficulties in accessing information. Furthermore, the need to raise funds necessary to pay the cost of travelling to Britain and obtaining accommodation there, as well as paying for the abortion itself, is likely to cause significant difficulties for less well-off women.

The Mahon report is the best available qualitative study of the reasons why Irish women decide to terminate their pregnancies, comprising as it does data collated from interviews with eighty-eight Irish-resident women availing themselves of abortion services in British clinics.[30] The reasons given by the women for choosing a termination were varied and included job- and education-related concerns, fear of the effects of the stigma of lone parenthood, financial difficulties, concern for existing children and the desire to exercise their right to control their fertility. There is no evidence that the lack of legal abortion in Ireland has had any effect on the Irish abortion rate, although the expense entailed in travelling to Britain and the cost of paying for the abortion itself may cause difficulties, particularly for less well-off women and other vulnerable groups. In some instances, this may mean that Irish women cannot travel to Britain, but more often this means that they have abortions later than they would wish. The Women on Waves Project and the visit of the Dutch ship *Aurora* to Dublin in June 2001 saw over 200 women seeking abortion services. Clearly, requiring women to travel abroad to obtain abortions has resulted in extreme hardships for a significant number of Irish women.[31]

In November 1992, the Irish electorate voted in favour of proposals to liberalise the law relating to abortion information and the freedom to travel abroad to obtain an abortion, and voted to reject a proposal that would have restricted the constitutional right to life of pregnant women identified by the Supreme Court in the X case, the details of which will be outlined later in this chapter. More recently, in March 2002, a government led by Fianna Fáil once again attempted to restrict risk of suicide as grounds for obtaining a termination in Ireland.[32]

It is difficult to establish the views of Irish people on abortion, as, for example, in both 1992 and 2002, some of the electorate who voted against the government's proposal to exclude suicidal risk as a ground for the termination of pregnancy did so because they thought the proposal would undermine women's right to life, whereas others did so because they felt it did not give sufficient protection to the foetus. Furthermore, some people may have voted in favour of the proposals because they (mistakenly) assumed it would provide increased protection for Irish women. However, the net effect of the vote in 1992 was to support proposals to liberalise the law relating to abortion information and travel and, in both 1992 and 2002, the electorate rejected proposals that would have restricted the constitutional right to life of a pregnant woman identified by the Supreme Court in the X case. It is worth remembering that, despite protestations from anti-abortion campaigners about the democratic right of the people to vote to outlaw abortion, Irish people have never been give the right to vote for the liberalisation of abortion law. Yet when, in 1992 and 2002, they have been given the opportunity to vote on the issue at all, they have refused to restrict abortion rights.

Surveys asking people whether they support the holding of a referendum on abortion are meaningless unless it is indicated what the motivation is for the referendum. Surveys consisting of questions as to whether or not they favour a particular legislative or constitutional proposal are of limited value unless respondents understand the proposal. For example, just after the announcement, in October 2001, of the 2002 referendum on further restrictions to access to abortion, *Ireland on Sunday* carried out a survey. It showed that fifty-three per cent of people supported the referendum proposal, thirty-five per cent opposed it and twelve per cent did not have an opinion. Conversely, forty-nine per cent of people favoured liberalising Irish abortion law, with only thirty-one per cent wishing to make abortion legally more difficult to obtain. This evidently reflected a lack of understanding of the nature of the government's proposals. In-depth surveys may provide a more definitive illustration of public opinion. A survey carried out by Landsdowne Market Research Limited for Abortion Reform in March 2001 is a good example.[33] In that survey, 1,200 persons over the age of fifteen were asked to give their opinions on three options (which were fully explained) put forward by the All-Party Oireachtas Committee. The survey found that only sixteen per cent of respondents thought that abortion should be illegal in all instances. Fifty-two per cent indicated that abortion should be permitted where a woman's life is physically at risk; forty-seven per cent thought that abortion should be available in cases of rape or incest; forty-one per cent thought that abortion should be permissible when continuation of pregnancy would cause irreparable damage to the woman's health; thirty-seven per cent thought that a woman at risk of suicide should be permitted to terminate her pregnancy; twenty-three per cent thought that it should be permissible in cases of foetal abnormality incompatible with life; nineteen per cent thought that abortion should be available on request. What the Abortion Reform poll illustrated is that people have a wide variety of opinions on abortion and that a significant percentage of the public favours greater rather than less access to abortion in Ireland.

No political party, including the Irish Labour Party, has been willing to introduce the legislation that would implement the judgement in the X case and allow suicidal risk as grounds for abortion. The only political consensus that exists on the issue is to do nothing and, meanwhile, eighteen women on average are forced every day to travel to Britain to have abortions. The cowardice of traditional left parties, which are unwilling to stand up to the dictates of the Catholic Church, goes back to the 1940s and 1950s. Many Labour TDs were more worried about what the Church would say than about their female voters. Furthermore, there has always been a reticence, even within the pro-choice movement in Ireland, about openly arguing the position of a woman's right to choose, primarily out of a fear that it will alienate the middle ground, but also from an approach that sees change as a gradual process of persuasion and mitigation.

The X case

On 6 February 1992, the then Attorney General, Harry Whelehan, obtained an interim injunction restraining a fourteen-year-old girl, pregnant as a result of rape and reportedly suicidal, from obtaining an abortion in Britain. The injunction was confirmed by the High Court eleven days later, when Justice Declan Costello ruled that the girl and her parents were prohibited from leaving Ireland 'for a period of nine months from the date thereof'.[34] The story of the 'internment' of a fourteen-year-old rape victim was leaked to the media and across the country there was an explosion of anger.

> Dublin's traffic police had to escort march after march down O'Connell St. Thousands took part in a silent, candlelit march to Leinster House, the parliament buildings, and festooned the railings with white ribbons on behalf of the girl and her family. A group of several hundred stood outside the gates of the parliamentary debating chamber, chanting the telephone number of an abortion information line in between cries of 'Not the Church, Not the State. Women must decide their fate'.... In Waterford in the south, thirty-seven girls at the Sacred Heart of Mary's Convent walked out of class to join fellow students from the city's Mercy Convent in a demonstration. They said they had 'made their stance for freedom of choice' because of their profound sympathy for the girl. Their disobedience led to mass suspension.[35]

The case became known as the X case and would prove to be a turning point in Irish society.[36] The protests shook the political establishment to its core and forced a dramatic U-turn by the judiciary. The case was appealed to the Supreme Court and the injunction was overturned. The court stated that, because Ms X was suicidal, not only did she have the right to travel to Britain for an abortion but she also had the right to an abortion in Ireland, an unusual interpretation, by any standards, of the 'pro-life' clause inserted into the Irish Constitution in 1983. An examination of the events of February/March 1992 show that the judgement had at least as much to do with the fear of further mass mobilisations on the streets as it had with abstract legal logic.

Political commentators usually underestimate the significance of mass mobilisations such as those provoked by the X case. This is mostly because there tends to be a general reluctance to believe that change can come from below, when ordinary people storm onto the stage of history. Commentators tend to be more comfortable with the notion that changes come slowly from on high, from the actions of enlightened men. Yet, as Kieran Allen argues:

> slow molecular changes in quantitative relations can at some point transform into decisive qualitative changes.... These struggles sometimes stop

short and often simply force our rulers to reorder the manner of their rule, but they are nonetheless the decisive conjunctures on which historical changes pivot.[37]

The years following the X case prove this point to be true. In 1993, the sale of condoms in vending machines was legalised and homosexuality decriminalised. In 1995, Irish people voted to legalise divorce and the changed atmosphere in Ireland following the X case gave people who had been victims of clerical sexual abuse the confidence to speak out.

However, one should also be careful of overestimating the changes that have occurred in Ireland in the past decade or so. It became popular in the late 1990s, particularly in the pages of the *Irish Times*, to speak of the completion of the liberal agenda. Nonetheless, a broader ideological offensive against the power and influence of the Catholic Church has not emerged – schools and hospitals, for example, remain under the control of the Church. Middle-class women can afford to travel to Britain for abortions but their working-class counterparts, at best, struggle to get the money together or, at worse, are forced to continue with pregnancies against their will. The struggle that emerged in the context of the X case was sudden and dramatic but it was not sustained because those catapulted into power after it failed to push through reforms. The X case allowed people to see abortion not as an abstract moral issue but rather as a real concern, with serious implications for the type of society people want to live in. What is clear is that rights have to be fought for and won and a liberal abortion regime will emerge in Ireland only when a mass movement emerges that is willing to fight for and defend those rights.

Backlash

The changes in the lives of Irish women during the era of the Celtic Tiger have been varied and profound, as we have seen, and the myth of equality – that women have achieved it all – dominates Irish society. We are constantly told in the pages of newspapers and glossy magazines that women everywhere are enjoying the fruits of liberation. Women outperform men in school and university, dominate the business world, feel good about sex and refuse to accept discrimination or abuse. Women have excelled to such extents that it is now men, we are told, who are discriminated against in society. A variant of this argument can be found in the writings of John Waters, who regularly devotes his *Irish Times* column to polemics against the horrors of what he calls a 'feminazi' conspiracy that pervades all aspects of Irish society. Waters, who is also the consultant editor of the political magazine *Magill*, uses his influential position in the media simultaneously to bemoan his status as a male in feminist-dominated Ireland and to exalt his heroic status as the one lone voice daring to speak out.

Few people in Irish society have the access to the media, to promote their views, which Waters enjoys; he seems to participate in most major political media programmes in Ireland.[38] He is particularly passionate about the mainstream media's unjust representation of the issue of domestic violence:

> The domestic violence issue is one of the key areas of propaganda-creation in the now relentless attack on the character of men and fathers.... I would hope that men would begin to take a look at the society they are alleged to dominate, and ask themselves: where is the evidence of such domination in a society which demonises and denigrates them at every turn, which conspires to steal their children at the whim of mothers and institutions.[39]

He chides the Irish government for having succumbed to 'nearly thirty years of relentless campaigning by misandrist forces ... having developed a multimillion pound industry out of the demonisation of the adult male'.[40]

Waters returns to this theme again and again, usually quoting the *British Home Office Survey*. Waters claims that the core finding was that an identical proportion (4.2 per cent) of women and men had been assaulted by a current or former partner in the previous year and argues that this shows that domestic violence is roughly a similar phenomenon among men and women. The study he refers to did find that the same proportion of women and men reported a physical assault by a current or former partner in the previous year (1998). However, the study also found that women were twice as likely as men to have been injured by a partner in the last year and three times as likely to have suffered frightening threats. They were also more likely to have been assaulted three or more times. Not only are women more likely to have been injured in assaults but also they are far more likely to be 'living in fear of their partners'. These findings Waters has conveniently ignored. Men who suffered from domestic violence were typically working part-time or suffering from a long-term illness or disability. Regardless of sex or age, men and women living in poverty were most likely to suffer violence.

Moreover, it is essential that, when statistics on domestic violence are quoted, the nature of the research and in particular the methods used are closely scrutinised. To argue from the results of a particular survey that women and men are equal perpetrators of violence is to ignore the fact that all the other evidence indicates that men are overwhelmingly the instigators of violence in intimate relationships.

Domestic violence has only recently even been defined as a crime in the Republic of Ireland. Marital rape, for example, has been directly covered by sexual assault legislation in Ireland only since the 1990 Criminal

Law (Rape) Amendment Act. At the time of writing, only three cases of marital rape had come before an Irish court, and only one conviction had been secured. Research has shown that rape, sexual assault and sexual coercion are often used by abusive men as part of a pattern of violent and coercive behaviour intended to control their partners. Almost one in five Irish women have experienced some form of violence in their relationships with men. Of these, just over twenty per cent experienced sexual assault.[41] For women in violent relationships, forced pregnancy, pregnancy as a result of rape and actual or threatened use of violence during pregnancy are common strategies employed by abusers.[42] In a major literature review on the subject of violence against women and reproductive health, Lori Heise *et al.* cite several studies (from 1994 to 1998), spanning more than fifteen countries, which clearly document sexual coercion as a major component of domestic violence. In the studies cited, women frequently reported being 'physically forced to have sex and/or engage in sex they found degrading or humiliating'. Large numbers of women also reported 'defensive acquiescence', whereby they agreed to sex with a violent partner 'out of fear of the consequences of refusal, such as physical abuse, loss of economic support or accusations of infidelity'.[43]

Waters' other target is the judicial system, which, he argues, is prejudiced against men in child custody cases. He argues that when custody is contested, judges are more likely to rule in favour of the mother than the father, because of the feminist agenda that dominates the Irish law courts. Due to the nature of the family court, statistical data are difficult to acquire. Waters may well be right but his conclusions are wrong. The fact that members of the judiciary are more likely to grant custody to the mother has more to do with the conception of women and the family in Irish society than it has to do with a feminist conspiracy. Instead of attacking an archaic system that sees women as the primary source of childcare, a system that benefits neither men nor women, Waters blames women, who, he argues, deliberately prevent men from having access to their children. His argument stems from a failure to understand the function of the family in society and the essential role it plays within capitalism in the creation of a future source of labour and a unit of consumption.

Waters' argument has found an echo among men, especially working-class men, who experience injustice at the hands of family courts. On the surface, the family does not have an obvious economic role. While the conventional couple is usually presented in terms of individual romantic love, this should not obscure the family's economic function as a source of care and education for a future workforce in a crisis-ridden, profit-oriented system. Historically, it was women who were associated both with childcare and domestic labour and, while changes in capitalism have seen women enter the labour force, they still bear the primary responsibility for housework and childcare. The judiciary is notorious for being out of touch with how people live their lives and is dominated by middle-class men, the majority of whom have nannies or partners who bear the primary responsibility for childcare. It is hardly surprising, then, that judges tend to assume that childcare is a predominantly female responsibility.

The family can operate a contradictory role: as well as being a place of comfort, it can also be the source of horrendous violence, and so it is inevitable that men also suffer. If one considers the central role that the family has played in Irish society, it is no surprise that Ireland has one of the highest rates of child sexual abuse, higher than in either Europe as a whole or North America. *The Sexual Abuse and Violence in Ireland Report*, commissioned by the Dublin Rape Crisis Centre, showed that forty-two per cent of women and twenty-eight per cent of men in Ireland had been subjected to sexual abuse in their lifetime.[44] These figures are unusually high. Similar studies in Europe show that seventeen per cent of European women have experienced sexual abuse as children. In Ireland, that figure is thirty per cent.[45] Among men, five per cent in Europe and seven per cent in North America have experienced abuse as children. In Ireland, however, twenty-four per cent of men were sexually abused as children. The majority of abuse occurs within the family or by an individual close to the family unit, such as a teacher or a priest.

The report also found that forty-seven per cent of those interviewed said that they had never told anyone about the abuse. Just one per cent of men and eight per cent of women had disclosed the abuse to the gardaí. This is not surprising if one considers the finding by Sue Lees, reported in her book *Carnal Knowledge*, that, increasingly, rapists are known to their victims and are former boyfriends and husbands. During a trial, sexual history is frequently called into account and raped women are often not believed in court. Lees monitored a series of rape trials in Britain over a two-week period and found that grounds for disbelieving a woman included: 'Whether she had suffered from depression, taken Prozac, been in care, been abused, had an abortion, allegedly had more than one relationship or invited home someone she had just met'.[46] More disturbing is the recent trend towards the commodification of sexual violence, particularly towards women. Sexual violence is becoming something that is no longer deplored by society but something that can be commodified to sell everything, from sports bras to popular music.[47]

Conclusions

Irish women have seen their lives transformed in recent years. This transformation has been a result of the interaction of changes in women's relationship to production. Women workers, such as nurses and teachers, have been among the first to demand their share of the Celtic Tiger. However, the feminisation of the workforce has also been a contradictory experience for most women. On the one hand, becoming economically independent has led to women having more choices about what they do with their lives. On the other hand, the 'double burden' faced by women because of their role in the family means that the lives of women workers are incredibly difficult, as they try to reconcile work and family life. Attitudes to female sexuality, in particular, have changed but not always favourably. Ireland now has a burgeoning sex industry. The country that banned *Ulysses* as a pornographic text for much of the twentieth century now has shelves full of pornography,[48] Irish versions of 'New Lad' magazines, a growing prostitution industry and a selection of lap-dancing clubs.

However, as we live in an increasingly globalised world, it is important to situate the experiences of Irish women in an international context. The changes and challenges faced by Irish women workers are similar to those being experienced by women across the world. The global development of capitalism over the past twenty years has depended almost everywhere on large numbers of women entering the formal workforce. Women's oppression has its roots in the contradiction between social production and privatised reproduction. Childcare remains the responsibility of the individual family and, overwhelmingly, of the female parent. Even most non-parental carers are women. While there are many alternatives to this in an advanced capitalist society, the logic of economics raises its head and the privatised family, with the woman at the centre, continues to provide the majority of care-giving under capitalism. The family reproduces the next generation of workers, ensures that there is a constant replenishment of labour power, which is cared for, educated and socialised to enter the marketplace.

A small number of women across the world have been able to sidestep the worst oppression and have made it into the parliaments and the boardrooms. Yet the exploitation and oppression of the majority of women and men is necessary for the survival of global capitalism. If the Celtic Tiger cannot deliver the needs of the majority of women – and men – it is clear that capitalism never will. Perhaps, therefore, the only real alternative for women across the world is the emerging anti-capitalist movement, which challenges the fundamental inequalities in society and champions a world that is about people, not profit.

Notes

1 For example, D. O'Hearn, *Inside the Celtic Tiger: The Irish Economy and the Asian Model* (London: Pluto, 1998), P. Sweeney, *The Celtic Tiger:*

Ireland's Economic Miracle Explained (Dublin: Oak Tree Press, 1998) or
R. MacSharry and P. White, *The Making of the Celtic Tiger: The Inside
Story of Ireland's Boom Economy* (Cork: Mercier Press, 2000).

2 Central Statistics Office, *Women in the Workforce* (Dublin: CSO, 1997).
3 Central Statistics Office, *Quarterly National Household Survey* (Dublin:
CSO, December 2000).
4 Central Statistics Office, *Labour Force Survey 1987* (Dublin: CSO, 1987);
Central Statistics Office, *Quarterly National Household Survey First
Quarter 2001* (Dublin: CSO, 2001).
5 Central Statistics Office, *Labour Force Survey 1996* (Dublin: CSO, 1997);
Central Statistics Office, *Quarterly National Household Survey Third
Quarter 2002* (Dublin: CSO, 2002).
6 P. O'Connor, *Emerging Voices: Women in Contemporary Society* (Dublin:
Institute of Public Administration, 1999), p. 197.
7 Irish Congress of Trade Unions, *ICTU: Mainstreaming Equality* (Dublin:
ICTU, 1993).
8 Irish Congress of Trade Unions, *Delivering Gender Equality 1999–2004.
Fourth Equality Programme* (Dublin: ICTU, 1999), p. 11.
9 T. Fahey, H. Russell and E. Smyth, 'Gender equality, fertility decline and
labour market patterns among women in Ireland', in B. Nolan, P. O'Connell
and C. Whelan (eds), *Bust to Boom? The Irish Experience of Growth and
Inequality* (Dublin: Institute of Public Administration, 2000), p. 263.
10 *Living in Ireland Survey* (1996), cited by Fahey *et al.*, 'Gender equality',
p. 264.
11 A. Barrett and T. Callen (eds), with A. Doris, D. O'Neill, H. Russell,
O. Sweetman and J. McBride, *How Unequal? Men and Women in the Irish
Market* (Dublin: Oak Tree Press, 2000), pp. 18–21.
12 European Commission, *Key Data on Education in the European Union*
(Luxembourg: European Commission, 1997), p. 144.
13 *Ibid.*, pp. 144–4.
14 Partnership 2000 Expert Working Group on Childcare, *National Childcare
Strategy* (Dublin: Stationery Office 1999), p. 12.
15 *Ibid.*, pp. 12–13.
16 K. Allen, *The Celtic Tiger: The Myth of Social Partnership in Ireland*
(Manchester: Manchester University Press, 2000), pp. 91–2.
17 Revenue Commissioners, *Statistical Report* (Dublin: Stationery Office, 1999).
18 *Labour Force Survey 1996*, cited in O'Connor, *Emerging Voices*, p. 199.
19 See O'Connor, *Emerging Voices*, p. 199 and chapter 8 for fuller discussion.
20 Nolan and Watson (1999) cited in P. Kirby, *The Celtic Tiger in Distress:
Growth with Inequality in Ireland* (Baskingstoke: Palgrave, 2002), p. 65.
21 O'Connor, *Emerging Voices*, p. 61.
22 Nolan and Watson (1999) cited in Kirby, *The Celtic Tiger in Distress*,
p. 65.
23 Cherish, pre-budget submission 2002, available at www.cherish.ie (accessed
February 2002).
24 Department of Social Welfare, www.welfare.ie (accessed December 2001).
25 Abortion is also illegal in most circumstances in Northern Ireland. Therefore women from both Northern Ireland and the Republic of Ireland must
travel to Britain to obtain an abortion. All figures relate to women from the
Irish Republic unless otherwise stated.
26 *Green Paper on Abortion* (Dublin: Stationery Office, 1999), p. 5.
27 Figures calculated on the basis of the number of women giving Irish
addresses to British clinics between 1967 and 1998.

28 All-Party Oireachtas Committee, *Fifth Progress Report: Abortion* (Dublin: Stationery Office, 2000), p. 86.

29 *Ibid.*, p. 86.

30 E. Mahon, C. Conlon and L. Dillon, *Women and Crisis Pregnancy* (Dublin: Stationery Office, 1998).

31 See R. Gromperts, *Women on Waves* (Amsterdam: Women on Waves, 2002) and www.womenonwaves.org.

32 The 2002 Protection of Human Life in Pregnancy Act, which Irish voters voted on in the referendum, also attempted to extend the scope of the criminal law and enshrine the criminality of abortion in the constitution, in that, if the Act was passed, it would have had constitutional status.

33 Details of the poll are available at www.abortionreform.ie.

34 See A. Smyth, 'A sadistic force: women and abortion in the Republic of Ireland 1992', in A. Smyth (ed.), *The Abortion Papers, Ireland* (Dublin: Attic Press, 1992).

35 W. Holden, *Unlawful Carnal Knowledge: The True Story of the Irish X Case* (London: Harper Collins, 1994), p. 80.

36 C. Hug, *The Politics of Sexual Morality in Ireland* (London: Macmillan Press, 1999), pp. 6 and 199f.

37 Allen, *The Celtic Tiger*, p. 166.

38 The list includes mainstream radio and television programmes such as *Five-Seven Live*, *The Last Word*, *Agenda* and *Prime Time*.

39 J. Waters, *Irish Times*, 12 January 1999.

40 J. Waters, *Irish Times*, 8 June 1999.

41 P. Kelleher and M. O'Connor, *Making the Links: Towards an Integrated Strategy Towards the Elimination of Violence Against Women in Intimate Relationships with Men* (Dublin: Women's Aid, 1995).

42 H. Amaro, L. E. Fried, H. Cabral and B. Zuckerman, 'Violence during pregnancy and substance use', *American Journal of Public Health*, 80:5 (1990), p. 575.

43 L. Heise, M. Ellsberg and M. Gottemoeller, *Ending Violence Against Women*, Population Reports, series L, no. 11 (Baltimore: Population Information Program, Johns Hopkins University School of Public Health, December 1999).

44 See H. McGee, R. Garavan, M. de Barra, J. Byrne and R. Conroy, *The SAVI Report: Sexual Abuse and Violence in Ireland* (Dublin: Liffey Press, 2002).

45 K. Holland, *Irish Times*, 20 April 2002.

46 S. Lees, *Carnal Knowledge: Rape on Trial* (London: Penguin, 1997), p. 13.

47 J. Freedland, *Guardian*, 17 July 2002.

48 *Playboy* sells more issues per capita in the Irish Republic than in any other European state.

6

Globalised Ireland, or, contemporary transformations of national identity?

G. HONOR FAGAN

The influential US magazine *Foreign Policy* issued a 'Globalization Index' in 2001, which, to the surprise of many, found the Republic of Ireland to be at the top of the list.[1] The indicators used to construct the index included information technology, finance, trade, travel, 'politics' and personal communications, all designed to evaluate the degree of global integration. We learn that 'Ireland's strong pro-business policies' have made the country (or more precisely the Irish market) 'a hugely attractive location for foreign investors'.[2] To make itself even more attractive, 'the country has cut corporate tax rates (already among Europe's lowest)'.[3] There is even better news on the financial front: while in 1996 financial inflows and outflows totalled a meagre 1.6 per cent of the national economy, by 2000 portfolio flows in Ireland were the largest in the world, in terms of gross domestic product (GDP). Those running investment funds, corporate finance, international banking and insurance companies could, with *Foreign Policy*, say to themselves, 'Don't Worry, Be Happy'.[4] That Ireland (or at least the twenty-six counties) is doing well in terms of the index constructed by the global managers of economic internationalisation seems beyond doubt.

What is perhaps more interesting from our point of view, and leads nicely into the arguments of this chapter, is the way the globalisation index deals with (or rather does not deal with) culture. In an obscure appendix on how the index is calculated, we are told that the various indicators referred to above 'only scratch the surface of globalisation's complexity. Many other aspects of global integration – including culture – defy measurement'.[5] Perhaps culture cannot be measured in the same way as GDP but it is arguably a central element in the globalisation process and thus a vital element in any critical analysis of its impact. In future, it will not be good enough simply to leave out culture when dealing with globalisation or constructing indices. From an Irish 'grass roots' perspective, globalisation may not look as rosy as it does to the international financial sectors and their political supporters in Ireland.

The global

Studies originally heralded the globalisation of communications, capital and culture, more or less in that order, and the argument was made that these forces were, in effect, decomposing the nation state and the distinctiveness of individual societies.[6] This argument was followed immediately by critiques of the notion of an all-encompassing globalisation process, and the work in this mode emphasised uneven, complex and contingent aspects of globalisation.[7] This chapter seeks to position itself outside either of these established approaches to the study of globalisation. Whereas, in general, the trend has been to show how global processes affect the production of single events or social change at the local or national level, I propose to reverse the trend by approaching an explanation of the global with specific reference to the national or local. Basically, I wish to ask the question 'What can a study of Ireland do for our understanding of the phenomenon called globalisation?' rather than 'How can globalisation theory explain contemporary Ireland?' In examining the specificity of Irish international and national dynamics, and the linkages between cultural and economic processes at play in 'developing' or 'imagining' Ireland, we can see tendencies and counter-tendencies towards a globalising dynamic.

This chapter addresses the complex articulation between the cultural and the economic in the discursive construction of Ireland in the era of globalisation. The basic argument is that, if we are to understand how Ireland has 'produced' itself in its current form, within and around the dynamics of the global forces of capitalism, then we need to examine the phenomenon of 'Ireland' through the analytical framework of cultural political economy. This should throw light on globalisation tendencies and counter-tendencies from a specific location and, likewise, show how culture implicates itself daily in the cultural political processes that have produced 'Ireland'.

The most common reading of Ireland and its current state of development is as a country that has done well in the era of globalisation, much as it had earlier done very badly in the era of imperialism. Has there really been such a turnaround? What dynamics does this debate uncover that the emerging 'global studies' approach might need to take on board? This chapter moves towards an answer in three parts: first, it examines the problematic 'placing' of Ireland in the world; second, it traces its constant (re)invention from a cultural political economy approach; and, finally, it turns to its moving parts on the global scene – its exiles and diasporas. I hope to contribute to an 'Irish' perspective on globalisation, but one that avoids the difficulties associated with taking a banal either nationalist or post-nationalist approach.

Placing

We can usually, fairly unproblematically, 'place' a given country in the global order in terms of its economic, political or strategic importance. Yet, with Ireland, there is little agreement on 'placing'. Recently, a historian of the Americas, James Dunkerely,[8] sought to place Ireland 'across the Atlantic', as it were. Dunkerely follows the tradition of 'Atlanticism'[9] but is more sceptical of 'globalism'. However, he argues for 'the idea that Ireland is really an American country located in the wrong continent'.[10] It was the Great Famine of the mid-nineteenth century and subsequent mass migrations which, supposedly, converted Ireland from an Atlantic country to an American one. This shift in cultural geography was sustained, according to Dunkerely, by a 'superabundance of myth'[11] but was also validated by the one million Irish people who became US citizens in the second half of the nineteenth century. From this perspective, it is easy to leap to another end of century and an economistic reading which would 'place' Ireland as an 'outpost' of Silicon Valley. O'Hearn argues, for example, that US computer and pharmaceutical companies have set the tone for the 'Celtic Tiger', which has transformed the economic, social and cultural make-up of the country.[12] Whether the economic growth of the 'Celtic Tiger' is perceived to have set the scene for the cultural trans-formation of Ireland, or conversely whether cultural development is thought to have set the scene for economic growth, we have here an argument that Ireland can be historically and economically placed as 'American'. Recent Irish political and social reaction to the 'terrorist' threat to the United States, on the part of conservative and radical politicians alike, seems to confirm the view of many in Ireland who see themselves as an extension, or even a part, of 'America'.

However, the 'American' perspective seems to ignore the facts of British colonial rule in Ireland and what many authors argue is a neo-colonial pattern of development in the years since independence, itself, of course, geographically incomplete. Not so long ago the question 'Is Ireland a third world country?'[13] did elicit a mainly affirmative, albeit qualified, response. The colonial legacy is seen as enduring and all attempts to 'revise' Irish history beyond the nationalist myths are rejected out of hand. Thus, for example, Robbie McVeigh argues that this move to 'decolonise' (or 'postcolonise') Irish history is 'factually incorrect and intellectually dishonest' and we are enjoined 'to address the colonial legacy directly in order to transcend its negative and corrupting conse-quences'.[14] This point may be taken simply as a truism but it does point to an apparent blind spot of the new 'postcolonial' pro-globalisation perspectives. Ireland's colonial legacy is also taken up in the literary post-colonial studies, in a more subtle way.[15] The point is that the colonial legacy is inescapable in any long view of Irish history and it has had a range of complex effects on politics, on society and, of course, on the cultural make-up of Ireland as we know it.

Returning to the question of placing Ireland, at the economic level the Republic is certainly not simply a 'third world' (itself an anachronistic term) country. The Republic of Ireland is today one of the top performers in the European Union – the once poor and 'underdeveloped' western periphery has given way to the thriving economy and cultural revival of the 1990s, albeit with all the inequalities and problematic long-term prospects all apparently thriving economies have. In terms of the debate over whether Ireland is a 'first world' country of a US variety or a 'third world' country, I do not think we need to adjudicate between these admittedly rather starkly painted alternatives. However, I do wish to use this debate as a marker for the analysis that follows.

First, though, I wish to argue for a slightly different approach to 'global studies' than the one that dominates in the literature. It would seem that, from Malcolm Waters[16] onwards, global studies, as a subject, have become parcelled out into discrete economic, political, social and cultural domains, or levels. While mindful that this may simply be a research or presentation strategy, I would be wary of going back to the old Marxist topographical analogy of 'levels'. Society is simply not a building with a structure and a 'superstructure', or roof. This type of structural determinism has long since received a decent burial and we would not really benefit from its resurrection within the new global studies. This approach is at its best when it analyses processes and flows, not bound by any determinisms and also self-consciously eschewing disciplinary boundaries. If the 'global studies' approach is to become a new paradigm in the fullest sense of the word, it will need to shake off the last vestiges of disciplinary 'ownership'. In terms of economics, there are indeed signs that Ireland is a 'satellite' of the United States, given its dependency on US companies. In terms of politics, there are indications of the same, as Irish leaders rush to support the United States in its campaign for world domination. Likewise, cultural considerations feed into both economics and politics and have to be taken into account in 'placing' Ireland. Hence my suggestion is to merge the political economy and cultural studies approaches into a new cultural political economy paradigm.

We can take up the recent call by Ngai-Ling Sum[17] to create a 'cultural political economy', which is at once sensitive to cultural or discursive dynamics and the role of economic and political factors. Nigel Thrift has also referred suggestively to the 'cultural circuits of capital'.[18] Thinking about 'culture' in Ireland (the 'Irish pub', Irish films, U2, *Riverdance*, etc.) and the new capitalism (software companies, the e-economy) has made me even more conscious of the need to build an integrated cultural political economy approach. A 'cultural' element is clearly an integral part of the Celtic Tiger and the 'political economy' element certainly has a strong 'cultural' component. From the critique of political economy (not its existing disciplinary forms) and from reflexive cultural studies (not an unthinking application) we may derive a critical optic which is adequate for the study of the complex reality we call 'Ireland' today. All I would add would be the need for a strongly historical approach, only sketched in here, given constraints of length, which would be necessary to make any sense of the current situation. This is, of course, a highly contested historical terrain and my rendering is not the only possible one.

Inventing

The cultural critic Declan Kiberd once wrote that 'If Ireland had never existed, the English would have invented it…'.[19] One could add, conversely, that because England existed, Ireland was forced to 'reinvent' itself, much as what the west knows as the 'Orient' and 'Islam' is inseparable from western discourses. It is common now to understand that nationalism is, indeed, an 'invented tradition'[20] or an 'imagined community'.[21] However, it would seem that in the 'era of globalisation', this approach has even greater validity for Ireland in particular. What passes for Irish 'culture' today – the musical dance show *Riverdance*, the 'supergroup' U2 or the ubiquitous global 'Irish pub' – does not spring from the eternal wells of the Irish soul. Rather, these phenomena are, to a large extent, manufactured by the global cultural industry. They reflect fully all of the hybridity, syncretism and even, arguably, the 'postmodernism' typical of the cultural political economy of globalisation. If globalisation can be said to have produced a 'world showcase of cultures',[22] then on this stage Ireland has achieved a paradigmatic position. Ireland today, or at least Dublin, is witnessing a culture-led process of regeneration and insertion into globalisation in terms more favourable than could be expected from its economic weight.

Historically, Ireland gained its partial independence from Britain in 1921 but it was not until the Wall Street Crash of 1929 and the Great Depression of the 1930s that a consistent path of inward-oriented growth began. While De Valera's notions might today smack of right-wing romantic isolationism, his industrialisation policies did lay the basis for a more independent development strategy in Ireland. This process of conservative modernisation can be compared to the 'passive revolution' Antonio Gramsci analysed in Italy: a case of 'molecular changes which in fact progressively modify the pre-existing composition of forces and hence become the matrix of new change'.[23] That new process of change occurred in the late 1950s, as protectionism gave way to free trade and inward-oriented growth turned into outward-oriented growth. As T. K. Whitaker, the architect of the post-1958 turn towards foreign loans and investments, put it at the time, 'there is really no choice for a country wishing to keep pace materially with the rest of Europe'.[24] So, Ireland joined the European Economic Community in 1973 and the removal of protectionism proceeded at full pace.

When Ireland 'joined' Europe in 1973, it was very much as a poor relation and major beneficiary of all the 'structural funds' made available for 'less developed' regions. It seemed that Ireland was exchanging self-reliance for dependency in a wilful shift away from the independence movement ethos. As Denis O'Hearn put it, a 'country which had virtu-ally clothed and shod itself in 1960 imported more than seventy-one per cent of its clothing in 1980'.[25] This shift away from indigenous industry towards transnational investment operated across the board. It coincided with a period in which US transnational corporations (TNCs) were seek-ing profitable, high-tech locations, particularly ones that would offer them access to the lucrative European market. The outward-oriented growth strategy led to mass unemployment as national industries collapsed, but by the 1990s a new era of prosperity seemed to begin. Officially, the boom began in 1994, when, in an obscure European investment assess-ment bulletin, the US investment bank Morgan Stanley asked, perhaps tongue in cheek, whether there was a new Celtic Tiger about to join the family of East Asian tiger economies.

So, the Celtic Tiger emerged just when 'globalisation' was beginning to make itself felt in earnest. This does not mean that globalisation pro-duced the Celtic Tiger, whose origins lay, as we saw in the bare outline above, in a series of economic transformations going back to the 1920s. And while the Irish boom may be real enough, it has its limits: growth rates are half those experienced in East Asia during the growth phase, and its sustainability is seriously in question, given the limited base of the growth sector. Dependency on the whims and market susceptibility of the transnational sector (essentially the computing and pharmaceutical sectors) is even greater than in the 1970s, insofar as in the mid-1990s this sector accounted for three-quarters of value added in manufacturing. A handful of computer companies, such as the giant processor manu-facturer Intel, literally hold the key to sustained growth rates in Ireland. As the United States began to move into a slowdown by the end of 2001, if not a full-blown recession, the Celtic Tiger was beginning to look distinctly more fragile than it did a couple of years previously. Indeed, by late 2001 the Irish growth rate was officially described as 'flat'.

Going back to Ireland as a 'US' country versus Ireland as a 'third world' country, what can we now say? Ireland does seem to be very much a 'US' country, given its reliance on American investment and its often unthinking support for the United States in all matters. Yet, Ireland

can still arguably be seen as a 'third world' country in terms of its conditions of structural dependency on the central locus of power in the era
of globalisation. In the world of globalisation, there are 'globalisers' and
'globalised', and Ireland fits the latter category in political economy
terms. However, Ireland is perhaps more accurately described in terms
of hybridity, meaning a condition of mixed temporalities within a process
of uneven development. Thus, to a large extent, cutting-edge technology
coexists with traditional social relations. Luke Gibbons wrote a while
back that: 'The IDA [Irish Development Authority, which helped bring
in foreign investment] image of Ireland as the silicon valley of Europe
may not be so far removed after all from the valley of the squinting
windows',[26] the latter being an image of traditional rural Ireland. This
image of uneven but combined development may serve as a useful and
evocative backdrop for our analysis of the cultural political economy of
contemporary Ireland.

Observers of the contemporary cultural scene in Ireland are impressed
by its dynamism. Conservative politician Gemma Hussey, in her book
Ireland Today, refers to a 'new exuberance of self-expression which the
country has never seen before' and notes the 'new Irish appetite for expression of its own identity'.[27] We get a picture of a pristine and whole
national identity proudly reasserting itself. Insularity is left behind as
Ireland enters the world scene but remains 'in touch' with its traditions.
Hussey remarks how 'Traditional music has been revived in its many
forms, and enthrals tourists as much as Irish people, who are themselves,
amazed by its richness'.[28] From the touching tones of the travelogue, we
receive an image of 'tradition' largely uncontaminated by unpleasant associations with a colonial past or a fierce anti-imperialist struggle. Faced with
the 'inexorable weakening of the Irish language', which Hussey seems
to see as the main repository of 'tradition', Ireland has been able to
avoid 'the pressure of Anglo-American media'[29] and construct for itself
the eminently valuable commodity known as contemporary Irish culture.

From the left of the political spectrum we get a not dissimilar reading
of Irish cultural political economy. Thus Denis O'Hearn, in his book
Inside the Celtic Tiger, refers to 'Ireland's cultural revival throughout
the Western world [which] was evidenced in the popularity of the musical
Riverdance'[30] and also makes an explicit link between 'an apparently
vibrant economy and a confident culture'.[31] As with Hussey, the parameters
of the nation state are taken for granted and one could be forgiven for
thinking that globalisation was not part of the picture at all. Where the
left analysis differs from the conservative one is only in its causation,
because its economism leads it more or less to 'read off' the cultural
transformations from the economic ones. Yet, ultimately, we get no explanation as to why Ireland has been part of 'a Pan-Celtic Revival in the
years leading up to the millennium' and living in 'what amounts to little

less than another Cultural Renaissance',[32] as one radical cultural critic put it. If we are not to fall back on mystical notions of 'national culture', we must begin with the cultural political economy of globalisation in seeking an explanation.

I find it helpful to start my alternative reading with a travel story of my own. If you were to visit Ireland you might wish to travel with 'Ireland's cheap fares airline', Ryanair. If you made a telephone booking you would be politely put on hold and left listening to the rousing theme music from *Riverdance*, as much flamenco and Broadway as 'traditional' Irish music. From this postmodern pastiche or melange your thoughts might turn to the company itself. Ryanair is typical of the new 'hollowed out' company, whose brash chief executive, Michael O'Leary, actually is the company, and epitomises the new confident Irish entrepreneurial classes. It contrasts with the bureaucratic, more formal national carrier Aer Lingus, which still lingers in the statist era and claims massive compensation for its alleged losses following the events of 11 September 2001. But you travel Ryanair and arrive in Dublin, along with thousands of European weekend tourists keen to sample the delights of the 'fashionable' Temple Bar area. As you get to passport control there is a billboard with a leprechaun (a traditional icon of Irish folklore) and a caption that reads 'If you think this is an icon of traditional Ireland you are away with the fairies'. A small symbol in the corner of the billboard indicates this is an advertisement for ICON, which is the marketing company for the 'traditional' global Irish cream liqueur Bailey's. Can we really talk about Irish traditions anymore?

It seems clear to me that globalisation has radically redefined what we know as 'tradition'. But then tradition was always invented. It was invented in the Ireland of the 1920s, the 1960s and the 1990s. In the 1920s, as Declan Kiberd puts it, the country engaged in 'the reconstruction of a national identity, beginning from the first principles all over again'.[33] De Valera and the founders of the Irish state were in the business of constructing a modernity based on 'tradition'. To refer to 'tradition' or cultural 'authenticity' today makes little sense when we realise how pragmatic an affair the construction of a national identity is. In the 1960s, there was a reconstruction based on transnational values, first 'American' and later 'European'. Then, in the 1990s, there was another reconstruction of Irish 'identity', within global parameters. The spectacle of *Riverdance*, the music of the Chieftains and the 'new' Irish films cannot be understood as national cultural forms. They may be partly constituted locally but it is with reference to a global cultural market: they are local cultural keys turning global locks.

I can only conclude by rejecting any essentialist notion of 'Irishness' that is fixed from time immemorial. Neither Irish culture nor identity can be seen as self-contained, immutable or closed. A new state of flux, typical of postcolonialism and globalisation, opens up a new era of more fluid and uncertain constructions of cultural identity. This is also manifest at the political level, where the future of the island is, as always, uncertain. There is hardly a comfortable situation of cultural diversity being constructed where gender, ethnicity and religious conflicts become safely defused. Ireland's culture is currently showing a more threatening side. Racism around the issue of immigration and refugees highlights some of the more worrying sides of the uncertainty we now face. This is hardly the positive scenario of Gemma Hussey, for whom insularity has been replaced by 'the confidence of an outward-looking young generation'.[34]

Moving

The cultural critic Terry Eagleton once wrote that while, on the one hand, Ireland signifies 'roots, belonging, tradition', it also spells at the same time 'exile, diffusion, globality, diaspora …'.[35] We could posit that Ireland was always, or at least already, part of the story of globalisation, which would mean pushing back its conventional temporal origins. Being 'Irish' was always associated with movement, even while being at 'home'. Irish migration and the substantial Irish diaspora across different parts of the globe meant that 'Irishness' was, in a very real sense, a globalised identity. That was the case at the last turn of century, but now, in the 'era of globalisation', migration is not so prevalent or economically necessary. It is perhaps ironic, then, that today 'Irishness' is finding confident home-grown roots and 'home' has a certain stability to it. Irish Presidents recently (Robinson and McAleese) have foregrounded the wish to bring the diaspora 'home', culturally and politically, if not physically. The confidence of 'Irishness' on the island of Ireland today has even led to intense hostility to today's migrants created by 'globalisation' – the asylum seekers and refugees.

Movement in the nineteenth century meant dislocation, rupture and trauma in Ireland. It was associated with the Famine, the British landlord and unemployment. Emigration was, indeed, the national trauma. Today, movement means travel or working abroad or 'coming home'. The Irish media portray Ireland's citizens as the 'young Europeans', computer literate, confident, citizens of the world. Migration, then, cannot have a simple meaning as a symptom of globalisation. It can signify expulsion or, as in Ireland today, success. The diaspora was once an integral element of Irish identity. Today, there is a move to 'bring it home' but home is not what it used to be. The Ireland of today has seen the full effect of the deterritorialisation of culture. Observer Fintan O'Toole notes that 'US culture is itself in part an Irish invention' and that 'Irish culture is inconceivable without America'.[36] Fluidity and hybridity have always been part of the Irish condition but today this occurs under the inescapable aegis of the United States, not some fuzzy, indistinct 'era of globalisation'.

Ireland was always part of broader flows of people and ideas, it was always 'globalised' and it was always a floating signifier. National 'tradition' was located as much in the diaspora as at 'home'. And 'home' today, as the accelerated movement of globalisation takes effect, is re-instated in the 'global Irish family' our politicians call the diaspora. National 'identity' is translated and appropriated by the new 'global culture'. When U2 refer to the Famine they do so in a way which makes it part of the new global history in the making. What might make an interesting analogy to extend this analysis would be John Urry's concept of sites of 'pure mobility'.[37] For Urry, society is today replaced by mobility, with such icons as the airport becoming truly 'non-places'. What if Ireland were to be conceived as a place of 'pure mobility', dominated by movement and fluidity? Although only an analogy, and one that cannot be stretched too far, it may help to understand why Ireland is significant for an understanding of globalisation, too often read from the perspective of stable, settled and dominant world powers.

Conclusions

It would seem that the cultural political economy of Ireland might take us beyond the stark 'American' and 'third world' options for placing Ireland. Nor can we retreat to an essentialist notion of 'Irishness' existing since time immemorial. The cultural political economy of Ireland has never been self-contained, immutable or closed. The era of globalisation, coinciding in Ireland with that of a postcolonialism, which put the British shadow firmly behind, has created the new context for Irish development. And yet Ireland was always part of a world of flows, never static, never fixed. The elements of uncertainty and undecidability, which many see as pertaining to globalisation and/or postmodernity, have always been Ireland's lot. We cannot, in Ireland, produce 'a finished image of finished reality'[38] because it has always been in flux. To engage with such a society, a writer such as Roddy Doyle is necessarily 'constrained to open meaning up rather than close it down',[39] as one cultural critic put it. The social and political scientist can hardly do otherwise.

At a recent International Studies Association conference, one contributor examined globalisation and the 'preservation of local identity' in Ireland.[40] Ireland was portrayed as one of those states that have 'taken advantage of the new opportunities afforded by contemporary globalisation'[41] and the conclusion was that 'The Irish have culturally escaped from a parochial sense of nationalism and become a proud member of

the international community'.[42] While certainly capturing something of
what is happening in Ireland today, I think it is clear, in the light of my
analysis above, why this approach is insufficient. It seems to 'buy in'
totally to the ideology of globalisation: if we 'take advantage' of it we
can escape 'parochial nationalism'. It was this patronising politics I
sought to contest in declaring at the start that this chapter was neither
nationalist nor postnationalist. Many social groups in Ireland, but many
women especially, have always contested the smug conservative self-
serving myths of Irish nationalism. Postnationalist accounts that imply
that we have moved into a sea of tranquillity, where all conflict will be
peacefully resolved in Brussels or Washington, are also problematic. The
world is more complex than the 'Jihad versus McWorld'[43] dichotomy, in
Ireland as elsewhere, as any critical and reflexive understanding of the
current world crisis would show.

An earlier version of this chapter appeared as 'Culture and globalization,
placing Ireland', *Annals*, no. 581 (May 2002), pp. 133–43.

Notes

1 'Globalisation Index 2001', *Foreign Policy* (with management consultants
   A. T. Kearney), no. 128 (January/February 2002).
2 'Globalisation's last hurrah?', *Foreign Policy*, no. 128 (January/February
   2002), pp. 38–51.
3 *Ibid.*, p. 4.
4 *Ibid.*, p. 5.
5 *Ibid.*, p. 2.
6 For example, see K. Ohmae, *The Borderless World: Power and Strategy in
   the Interlinked Economy* (London: Collins, 1990).
7 For example, see P. Hirst and G. Thompson, *Globalisation in Question*
   (Cambridge: Polity, 1996).
8 J. Dunkerely, *Americana* (London: Verso, 2000).
9 Compare this usage to that of P. Gilroy, *The Black Atlantic* (London: Verso,
   1993).
10 Dunkerely, *Americana*, p. xxii.
11 *Ibid.*, p. 37.
12 D. O'Hearn, *Inside the Celtic Tiger: The Irish Economy and the Asian
    Model* (London: Pluto, 1998).
13 T. Caherty, A. Storey, M. Gavin, M. Molloy and C. Ruane (eds), *Is Ireland
    a Third World Country?* (Belfast: Beyond the Pale, 1992).
14 R. McVeigh, 'The British/Irish "peace process" and the colonial legacy', in
    J. Anderson and J. Goodman (eds), *Dis/Agreeing Ireland* (London: Pluto,
    1998), p. 31.
15 For example, see P. Childs and P. Williams, *An Introduction to Post-colonial
    Theory* (London: Harverster, 1997).
16 M. Waters, *Globalisation* (London: Routledge, 1995).
17 N.-L. Sum, 'Globalisation and its other(s): three "new kinds of Orientalism"
    and political economy of trans-border identity', in C. Hay and D. Marsh

(eds), *Demystifying Globalisation* (New York: Palgrave, 2000), pp. 105–27.

18 N. Thrift, 'State sovereignty, globalisation and the rise of soft capitalism', in Hay and Marsh (eds), *Demystifying Globalisation*, pp. 71–105.

19 D. Kiberd, *Inventing Ireland: The Literature of the Modern Nation* (London: Jonathan Cape, 1995), p. 9.

20 E. Hobsbawn and T. Ranger (eds), *The Invention of Tradition* (Cambridge: Cambridge University Press, 1983).

21 B. Anderson, *Imagined Communities* (London: Verso, 1983).

22 M. Featherstone, *Undoing Culture: Globalisation, Postmodernism and Identity* (London: Sage, 1995), p. 13.

23 A. Gramsci, *Selections from the Prison Notebooks* (London: Lawrence and Wishart, 1971), p. 109.

24 T. K. Whitaker, 'From protection to free trade – the Irish case', *Administration*, 21:4 (winter 1973), p. 415.

25 O'Hearn, *Inside the Celtic Tiger*, pp. 41–2.

26 L. Gibbons, 'Coming out of hibernation? The myth of modernity in Irish culture', in R. Kearney (ed.), *Across the Frontiers: Ireland in the 1990s* (Dublin: Wolfhound Press, 1988), p. 218.

27 G. Hussey, *Ireland Today: An Anatomy of a Changing State* (London: Penguin, 1995), pp. 470–1.

28 *Ibid.*, p. 484.

29 *Ibid.*, p. 471.

30 O'Hearn, *Inside the Celtic Tiger*, p. 117.

31 *Ibid.*, p. 57.

32 G. Smyth, *The Novel and the Nation: Studies in the New Irish Fiction* (London: Pluto, 1997), p. 175.

33 Kiberd, *Inventing Ireland*, p. 286.

34 Hussey, *Ireland Today*, p. 484.

35 T. Eagleton, 'The ideology of Irish studies', *Bullan*, 1 (1987), pp. 5–14.

36 F. O'Toole, *The Ex-Isle of Erin: Images of a Global Ireland* (Dublin: New Island Books, 1997), p. 12.

37 J. Urry, *Sociology Without Society* (London: Sage, 2000), p. 63.

38 Smyth, *The Novel and the Nation*, p. 67.

39 *Ibid.*

40 T. White, 'Globalisation and the preservation of local identity: the case of Ireland', paper presented at the International Studies Association conference, Hong Kong, 2001.

41 *Ibid.*

42 *Ibid.*

43 B. Barber, 'Jihad against McWorld', *Atlantic Monthly*, no. 269 (March 1995), pp. 53–63.

7

Millenarianism and utopianism in the new Ireland: the tragedy (and comedy) of accelerated modernisation

KIERAN KEOHANE and CARMEN KUHLING

There is a mode of vital experience – experience of space and time, of the self and others, of life's possibilities and perils – that is shared by men and women all over the world today. I will call this body of experience 'modernity'. To be modern is to find ourselves in an environment that promises us adventure, power, joy, growth, transformation of ourselves and the world – and, at the same time, that threatens to destroy everything we have, everything we know, everything we are. Modern environments and experiences cut across all boundaries of geography and ethnicity, of class and nationality, of religion and ideology: in this sense modernity can be said to unite all mankind. But it is a paradoxical unity, a unity of disunity: it pours us all into a maelstrom of perpetual disintegration and renewal, of struggle and contradiction, of ambiguity and anguish. To be modern is to be part of a universe in which, as Marx said, 'all that is solid melts into air'.[1]

Thus begins one of the most influential books of the last quarter century, Marshall Berman's *All That is Solid Melts into Air: The Experience of Modernity*. Developing Berman's theme, other authors have described the contemporary zeitgeist as 'late-modern',[2] emphasising the intractability of modernity's ambivalence and paradox, or 'postmodern',[3] pointing to the intensification of the experiences of social fragmentation and individuation, the continuation of modernity, but without the utopian hopes and dreams that made the experience bearable. Beck, Giddens and Lash[4] use the concept of 'reflexive modernisation' to describe an acceleration of the processes of transformation in contemporary society, intensifying and accentuating the experiences Berman describes in a second wave of modernity, driven by the generation of risk and the unforeseeable consequences of technological development. In addition, all of these authors, as well as Bauman, Beck, Giddens and Jameson,[5] have used the term 'globalisation' to reiterate the transnational, world-scale nature of these collective social historical experiences, experiences that are 'shared by men and women all over the world today'.

We in Ireland are also caught up in these world historical processes of modernisation and experiences of modernity, all be it modulated and mediated by our own histories, our own insertion into the global political economy, and our own particular experiences as members of different socio-economic classes, religious and political persuasions, as men and women, as urban and rural dwellers, as native born and as newcomers, as Travellers and minorities. Furthermore, the unprecedented economic boom of the mid-1990s, the period of the so-called 'Celtic Tiger', short-lived, uneven in its effects, unstable and insecure, has amplified and exacerbated the experiences of accelerated modernisation. We are caught up in a world historical process. We are forced 'on pain of extinction' to adapt to the new mode of civilisation.[6] As Walter Benjamin puts it, the tragedy of development is that 'we are propelled along the road to catastrophe'. We cannot foresee this, Benjamin says – we can only see retrospectively the damage already done as we are thrown backwards into the future: 'The Angel of History stares in horror at a pile of debris heaping up before him as he is propelled backwards by a storm blowing out of heaven. This storm is what we call Progress.'[7]

The Faustian tragedy of development

One of the most perceptive accounts of the deep origins of the experience of modernity is the epic *Faust*, by the German poet/philosopher Goethe. Berman shows how Goethe's tragic story of Faust is the prototypical formulation of the paradoxes of modernity and modernisation, which, although written in the late eighteenth and early nineteenth century, is still pertinent to Irish experiences today. In Goethe's epic, when the Devil first tries to tempt Faust, he finds that Faust's wants are not the usual fare of money, power and sexual conquest that the Devil deals in. Sure, I would like these, Faust says, but these are merely means to greater ends, means to satiate desires that are higher, deeper and infinitely more expansive. What I want, Faust says, is to experience the outer limits of the realisation of human potential. He says to the Devil:

Do you not hear? I have no thought of joy!
The reeling whirl I seek, the most painful excess
Enamoured hate and quickening distress
     ... My mind
Shall not henceforth be closed to any pain, and what is portioned out to all mankind,
I shall enjoy deep within myself, contain within my spirit summit and abyss, pile on my breast their agony and bliss, and let my own self grow into theirs unfettered
'Til as they are, I too, at last, am shattered.

Like Goethe's Faust, many of the actors in the contemporary Irish tragedy of development are driven by noble aspirations and high ideals. Our Faustian desire for development is not just for wealth but for the freedom from want that wealth can bring about: freedom from ignorance and also from innocence; freedom of expression and riches of knowledge; cultural and emotional development; a quest for transformative experience, of ourselves, of others, of the world. This utopian dream is ambivalent and paradoxical: it is both emancipatory and megalomaniacal, for, as Marx says, we become like 'the sorcerer who is no longer able to control the powers of the netherworld whom he has called up by his spells'.[8] Although modernisation is foisted upon us from outside by the experience of imperialism and colonisation, and in a postcolonial era through exogenous forces of globalisation, we should not delude ourselves, as we so often do, that we are innocent victims of history. We are like Faust: the desire for development is our own desire, and that desire is for full and unlimited development, wherever it may lead us, even up to and including our self-destruction. Part of the tragedy of development in the magical/terrible Faustian world of contemporary Ireland is that the casualties of accelerated modernisation are swept away by a tide of events that they themselves have helped to set in motion. As Berman says, 'The deepest horrors of Faustian development spring from its most honourable aims and its most authentic achievements'.[9]

Goethe's Faust symbolises the aspirations of modern people for full and unlimited development and their often terrible and beautiful unforeseeable consequences. Homer Simpson sells his soul for a doughnut to the Devil in the form of Ned Flanders, and Irish people are at times happy to trade everything, if not for a doughnut then for designer clothes and a dormer bungalow with an unobstructed view. Our public representatives seem like so many cartoons: former Prime Minister Charlie Haughey, who liked to ape the lifestyle of a debauched minor aristocrat – a mansion, a yacht, horses, sex, drink and extravagant clothing; former government minister Michael Lowry, the price of whose corruption was no more than an extension to his house. But collectively, historically, modern people strike a better bargain with the Devil.

Faust sells his soul for knowledge and power, and this is what his Devil, Mephistopheles, grants him, but the catch is – the Devil, as always, is in the detail! – that he can never trade them back. Faust becomes damned to perpetual striving. He can never again say, 'Ah, linger still! Thou art so fair' or, as we might say in our own vernacular idiom, 'That's grand now. That'll do fine!' The desires of modern people are insatiable and, as Durkheim shows, 'insatiability is a sign of morbidity'.[10] Unlimited horizons and insatiable desires are the conditions of egoism, delusions of omnipotence, psychosis and anomie.[11] The ability to limit ourselves, to govern our individual and collective desires, collides with the Faustian spirit of the Celtic Tiger, whose appetites and desires can know no limit. As Berman so eloquently demonstrates through his interpretation of Goethe's Faust, modernisation comes at a price: the thorough penetration of the commodity form (Marx), the dominance of instrumental rationality (Weber), the ascendance of individualism and egoism (Durkheim). Ironically, the Faustian bargain that we made to extricate ourselves from the state of nature throws us back into that same state. The Devil wins; we end up in Hell. We are condemned to 'a perpetual and restless pursuit of power after power, ceasing only in death'.[12] Power, which began as a means to an end, is now an end in itself, the only end. Weber's critique of the irrationalism of rationalised acquisition,[13] and Marx's critique of capitalism's reduction of all value to a 'cash nexus', the 'bottom line',[14] is that these are forms of modern nihilism, the catastrophe at the end of the road to development.

In Berman's account, the paradox of modernity is represented as the ambiguous spirit of the Devil. On one hand, Mephistopheles is the personification of evil: his name spells corruption, destruction, death and decay – Lord of Flies, Prince of Darkness, Father of Lies, with associations of insatiability, lust, envy, pride, gluttony, sloth, avarice, wrath, the seven deadly sins of excess and boundlessness which the children of the Celtic Tiger commit freely and gladly. On the other hand, the Devil is the Fallen Angel, Lucifer, the Bearer of Light, the Morning Star, who does the work of God and has a positive role in creation by paving the way for more creation and redemption through his destruction and corruption. This ancient paradox that lies at the heart of Christian cosmology is fundamental to understanding the zeitgeist of contemporary Ireland.

Ireland's 'Great Hunger' for development

We can see this deep paradox of modern Irish life in Patrick Kavanagh's poem 'The Great Hunger'.[15] What is 'great' (positive) about the Great Hunger is that, in Lacanian terms, it is the original collective traumatic experience, the constitutive Lack that makes us what we are.[16] The Famine (in Irish *an Gorta*, meaning 'hurt', 'injury', 'wound') is the collective historical mortal wound that killed 'traditional Ireland', and at the same time *an Gorta Mór* – the great wound – is the primal scene of pain, horror and torment that gives birth to 'modern Ireland'. It is the constitutive moment, the point that collects us as a society: it is the death of the collective mythic father and mother, the ancestors from whom we are all descended. It creates and recalls generations of emigration; it collects the diaspora. It is the great agony that underpins modern Irish religiosity and legitimates the moral authority of the Catholic Church. It collects the various strands of national consciousness, from the lost motherland of romantic sentimentality, to the betrayal of reason that animates rational Home Rule,[17] to the murderous genocide that must be avenged that has inspired militant Republicanism. The Great Hunger lies at the heart of modern Ireland. The ambivalence which contemporary Irish people feel towards the Great Famine is apparent in President Mary Robinson's 150th anniversary Famine commemoration as *celebration*: the recollection of the Famine became the affirmative moment of historical continuity and the primal scene of the new birth, a second birth of modern Ireland, the birth of the Celtic Tiger.

Kavanagh's 'The Great Hunger', written one hundred years after the Famine and fifty years before the birth of the Celtic Tiger, pokes at and reopens this constitutive primal wound by showing how the 'Great Hunger' takes on different forms in changing historical contexts. The Great Hunger is usually taken to refer to the Famine of the 1840s, but for Kavanagh the famine is a scarcity of spirituality in the 'modern Ireland' of the 1940s. As Kavanagh sees it, the promise of modernity has been broken and instead of being a bright morning, modern Ireland is dark and dreary. He depicts the terrible world after independence but when the progress promised by independence had already become antiquated and ossified. Kavanagh depicts an Ireland that is spiritually stifling, intellectually dead and emotionally crippled; a world of hunger and scarcity – not just of material poverty in an underdeveloped political economy where people spent a lifetime not living but merely existing, scratching a living from peasant holdings – but of spiritual poverty in an underdeveloped libidinal economy, of emotional and sexual underdevelopment. 'Life dried in the veins of these women and men', Kavanagh says. 'There is no future but time stretched for the mowing of hay.' In this static world, a man's act means 'nothing, not a damn thing'. Ireland is a closed, narrow parochial world of ignorance and prejudice, where 'the chapel pressed its low ceiling' over the bent backs of a servile congregation.

For Kavanagh, the dreamer, the Great Hunger is the expression in his time and place of the modern Irish Faustian desire for change, progress and development. As soon as this process is set in motion and people begin to emerge from the shackles of a world that has become antiquated, the stage is set for an explosive confrontation between modern desires and sensibilities and the old, antiquated and outmoded world. Bearers of avant-garde cultures in backward societies, as Kavanagh was, experience the Faustian split with particular intensity. Their inner anguish has often inspired revolutionary visions, actions and creations, and no doubt this is the fissure that has produced talents ranging from Joyce to U2, from Flan O'Brien to Brian Friel. That Westlife or Meave Binchey should be seen to be the bearers of this torch should be a cause for concern, as it may herald that what was fraught, and fecund, in Irish culture is becoming scarred over, dead and insensitive.

But as people are torn and tear themselves free from traditional worlds, they are also free to fall in love with them again. The new virility, liveliness, awakening that accompanies the lifting of traditional morality, sexual freedom, hedonism rather than denial of the body and the mortification of the flesh, provoke ambivalence. We are thrilled by the new eroticism evident for the first time in the reawakened, reworked and reinvigorated traditional content of *Riverdance* but we are uneasy of Flatly's excess, and as it suits us we disavow him as an American. When freed from tradition we gain the ability to see good in it – integrity, solidity, stability, continuity, groundedness. This nostalgia for a lost world is very obviously the basis of the emigrants' desire and romantic yearning but it is also the basis of the modern continentals' interest in rural Ireland. The modern metropolitans would, as it were, trade in their cosmopolitan worldliness for a quiet retreat in the west of Ireland, where they fantasise that the authentic, the pure, somehow still resides: English New Age Travellers in West Cork and East Clare, spiritual refugees from post-industrial society; cynical, disillusioned Germans who come to Ireland in search of authenticity but who are let down by the modernity of the natives they hoped would be naive, and are now too long gone from German industry to get back into the business; Dubliners who become chronic 'weekenders', in Galway, Westport, Clifden, pushing westwards until they fall into the Atlantic or, exhausted from the eight-hour drive, collapse in the door of the suburban house in the private development of exclusive holiday homes that they have relocated from Dublin to Achill island. In this movement, Marx says, peasants are 'rescued from the idiocy of rural life' and metropolitans force villagers 'to adopt what it calls civilisation into their midst'.[18]

Asymmetrical love affairs between worldly metropolitans and innocent (or at least who are imagined to be innocent) country folk frequently end in disillusionment and tragedy. During the 1970s and 1980s, the tiny village of Doolin on the west coast of Clare became the object of desire for modern urban Irish people and continentals, who imagined that they saw in its pubs, its musicians and 'local characters' something essential, authentic that, if they could get close to it and possess it, might save them from transcendental homelessness, the spiritual vacuousness, cultural amnesia and loss of particularity characteristic of modern life. Within a short time, the car park at Gussie O'Connor's pub was crowded with Dublin- and European-registered cars, and fifteen- and twenty-roomed bed and breakfasts, Tourist Board approved, hot and cold TV en suite, all mod. cons., bourgeoned like mushrooms on horse manure as investors and locals cashed in on the interest. The biggest mod. con. turned out to be the complete destruction of the original cherished object. Doolin was emptied out of any particular local content, characters elevated to minor celebrities, only to be discarded as fashions changed and small farmers transformed themselves into petty-bourgeois hoteliers, speculators and property developers. After the brief but intense fling, Doolin is left today a tawdry, desolate, debauched cultural wasteland. 'The good is gone out of it', people say, a pithy figure of speech that applies to so much in Ireland today. The epitaph to life ruined by modern black magic is graffiti on the toilet door of a Doolin pub: 'Musicians turn publicans into millionaires, and publicans turn musicians into alcoholics.'

Goethe's Faust has three incarnations, the Dreamer, the Lover and the Developer. Kavanagh represents the Faustian incarnation of the Dreamer. He expresses the hunger and dreams for development, affluence, and the power and freedom that accompany them that lie in the hearts of modern Irish people, desires that are intolerable to repress, but when released are insatiable and impossible to fulfil and end in death and catastrophe. The nativists who search for the vestiges of traditional Ireland – the imaginary 'Real Ireland'[19] – represent Faust's incarnation as the Lover, who romanticises and yearns for a lost innocence. But the Real Ireland of the postcard is the Lacanian 'Real': the void in the symbolic order of modern Ireland, into which the lover projects his own romantic fantasy, and through pursuing the fantasy of the Real, succeeds only in destroying the imagined thing he thought he loved.

Irish incarnations of the Developer are similarly fraught with tragedy. Goethe's Faust becomes the Developer when he turns his attentions away from romance, the pursuit of pleasure and experience, to the transformation of the material world, and he systematically sets about building an enormous commercial enterprise. He pursues his own desires for wealth, power and fame, but this has the consequence of transforming – for better and for worse – the lives of others around him. Some are bulldozed out of the way but many others become employees and collaborators and find vitality and meaning through their activity. Idleness is transformed into thriving enterprise, waste ground bristles with new houses and communities, and bustles with business. Contemporary Ireland is swarming with Developers, and we celebrate and idealise dream development projects like Dublin's Temple Bar as material evidence of the Faustian self-transformation of our society and portents of what we may do in the future.

Such a Faustian Irish Developer is Brendan O'Regan. Beginning as a caterer to transatlantic flights refuelling at Foynes in the 1950s, O'Regan established the world's first duty-free airport shop. Later, at Shannon, he developed the world's first tax-free export processing zone, an initiative that has since become not only the cornerstone of Ireland's economic development strategy over the past fifty years but also a model for economic modernisation and development throughout the world. In addition, O'Regan initiated the restoration of Bunratty and other castles and national historical and heritage sites. A key adviser to Sean Lemass, the Prime Minister who oversaw the end of protectionism and the opening of the Irish economy in the 1960s, O'Regan has been a leader driving industrial and tourism development in Ireland for half a century. At least two generations and several hundreds of thousands of Irish people directly and indirectly owe their present affluence and prosperity to his vision and energy. In addition to his role in economic modernisation, in the 1980s, at the height of the conflict in Northern Ireland, O'Regan founded Co-operation North to foster cross-border community relations. O'Regan's life's work is that of a true Faustian Developer: his goal has been not simply profit as personal gain, but, in so doing, to transform and to improve the world for a broader public, to whom he remains largely unknown.

But Irish developers and their schemes are mostly pseudo-Faustian opportunists and speculators, exploiting the moment for a strictly personal profit, rather than, as Faust is, committed to a lifelong quest to transform the world and everyone in it and to build a future for all. Johnny Ronan, the brash young would-be Faust driving the Spencer Dock project in Dublin, is a typical Irish developer: the son of a farmer who moved to the city, whose vision of the city remains that of a farmer in its sense of space.[20] His Spencer Dock proposal is for a vast 'groundscraper', taken from a catalogue of global 'anywhere architecture', masked with the façade of a conference centre by a celebrity architect, concerned solely with exploiting to an absolute maximum the rentable square footage of office space: the same instrumental-rational calculus that a modern Irish pig-farmer would bring to the layout of farrowing pins for breeding sows. An older, mature Faust is represented by a builder whose construction company has become practically synonymous with suburban housing development in Ireland, a giant man, whose huge hands and lined face tell of a youth of physical labour as he built his empire up through lean years. This Colossus sat through a meeting of architects, planners and citizens convened by Cork City Hall to share views on the future development of their city. Dreams and schemes and talk of the future ground to a halt when the developer interjected, stating:

> Whatever about what the city needs, I'll tell you what people want. They want a three-bedroomed semi-detached house on a nice estate in the suburbs, with a patch of grass front and back. That's what they want, and that's what I'll give them.

Irish pseudo-Faustian Developers aspire to being high-flying global visionaries, but their visions are still bounded by the farmyard gate and the parish pump.

The globalisation of Irish culture by Irish cultural developers and entrepreneurs all too often produces cultural homogenisation that reduces Irish culture and identity to a repetitive, simplistic formula easily consumed on the global market. Oscar Wilde famously said, 'We are all in the gutter, but some of us are gazing at the stars', by which he means that what distinguishes visionary leaders from the ordinary masses is idealism. The Irish pseudo-Faustian Developer is the inverse of this and represents the disparagement of idealism and the cynical debasement of action to the lowest common denominator. A prominent Irish culture industry Developer, Louis Walsh, exemplifies the thorough penetration of the commodity form that globalisation entails, and the concurrent emptying out of any creative impulse from visionary ideals. Walsh, originally from rural Mayo, moved to Dublin, began his career as a booking agent for show-bands on the circuit of dancehalls in Irish provincial towns, and in the 1990s developed the boy-bands Boyzone and Westlife. Walsh's vision is unabashedly cynical: 'Catching sight of East 17 and Take That, he made the obvious observation, "They're getting away with it. Why can't we?" The next step was Boyzone'. His products are substitutes for the global culture industry, in the same way as Supermacs (founded by a schoolteacher from a small town in county Galway) copies the formula to substitute for McDonald's. Boyzone, Walsh says, 'are past their "sell-by" date', but 'Samantha Mumba could be the next Jennifer Lopez, Omera Mumba is the Irish Michael Jackson.' In the pipeline are two new tasteless and fattening fast-culture products: a new Irish 'rock band' 'in the style of Duran Duran and Spandau Ballet', and Bellefire, whom Walsh describes as 'Corrs lite'. Like Ronan, and a cohort of pseudo-Faustian business heroes of the Celtic Tiger, true to Wilde's definition of the cynic as 'one who knows the price of everything, but the value of nothing', Walsh says: 'I'm not interested in what people think. I just do what I do and it's very successful.'[21]

The Irish apocalypse and intimations of redemption

In the premodern cosmology of traditional Irish Catholicism, the interior that matters is the interior of the soul. In modern Irish consumerism, it is the interior of the house. Walter Benjamin says, 'The bourgeois interior is a dialectical image in which the reality of industrial capitalism is represented visibly.'[22] For Benjamin, the combination of clutter and fastidiousness characteristic of the turn-of-the-century living room was symptomatic of the crisis of overproduction at the heart of modern society, reproduced in the microcosm of the interior as a hysterical cycle of production and consumption. The bourgeois interior is 'apocalyptic', Benjamin says. The 'apocalypse' means to 'open the curtains', to 'reveal' the end of things, the final judgement.[23] Hence the Apocalypse is the Book of Revelation. By this analogy, Benjamin means that written in the interior of the modern home is a cryptic eschatology and teleology of modernity. By a cultural analysis that Benjamin likens to detective work, a 'hermeneutics of the profane' and 'a physiognomy of the interior', we can find 'traces', clues that foretell the end of modern forms of life. By the eschatological and teleological 'ends' of modern life, Benjamin means the goals it strives towards, which, when achieved or fully realised, mark the End: Hell and damnation, but also the possibility of salvation and rebirth. The damnation(s) foretold for modernity which Benjamin has in mind here are various forms of nihilism – the reduction of all value to cash (Marx), the iron cage of rationalised acquisitiveness, wherein the pursuit of wealth, stripped of higher religious goals and resting on mechanical foundations, becomes a form of mechanised petrification (Weber), the egotistic anti-social cult of the individual (Durkheim). If we take the Irish interior as such a microcosm of dialectical images that reveals the nihilistic pathologies of the broader social metempsychosis, what clues can we find that, in their ends (their goals), reveal the ends of contemporary forms of Irish life, and the end of Irish history?

James Joyce's interiors in *Dubliners*, especially and typically in the stories 'The Sisters', 'The Boarding House', 'Clay' and 'The Dead', are microcosmic representations of paralysis, darkness and death, the closed inner worlds characteristic of Dublin crushed and squeezed by the British Empire, the Holy Catholic Church, nationalism and commercialism.[24] More recently, the London-Irish playwright Martin McDonagh has provided a paradigmatic representation of the interior of the Irish house as a dialectical image indexing the pathologies of contemporary Ireland. *The Lonesome West*[25] is set in a contemporary kitchen in Connemara, the *locus classicus* of the Irish spirit in the symbolic order and imaginative structure of Irish culture and identity. Connemara is the heartland of traditional Ireland, as it is where the Irish survived, having been cleared and beaten westwards by successive colonial plantations – 'to Hell or to Connaught'; a heartland romantically imagined by Irish revivalists and global primitivists, but in reality a vast refugee settlement, filthy, hungry, teeming, demoralised, seething with resentment and violence. This is the kitchen of contemporary culture represented by McDonagh. The *mise-en-scène* consists of condensed hybrid fusions of forms of life from dialectically opposed worlds: traditional and modern, global and local. Two bachelor brothers, brutish Coleman, who has murdered his father, and avaricious Valeen, who blackmails Coleman to sign over his inheritance, occupy the house. The light is dim, although there is a profusion of electrical outlets and power-points, their orange 'live' lights glowing with potent malevolence.[26] Modernisation has been through here and has left its mark, but the old hobgoblins are still alive, too. Although meanly furnished, it is untidy; the most prominent objects amid the clutter are old religious icons juxtaposed uneasily with new and spotless appliances; these objects – religious and commodity fetishes – and the antithetical forms of life that they represent – traditional religious and secular modern – are locked in conflict in the Irish interior.

The material and libidinal economy of the household circulates between the claustrophobia of community, family, Catholic sexual morality and modern materialism, commodity fetishism – the brothers' neurotic fixations on a fashionable shirt and a hair-do, plastic holy statuettes, new kitchen appliances. The drama unfolds as an endless and pointless exchange: of insults between the two equally frustrated and impotent bachelor brothers, who homophobically call each other 'virgin gay-boys'; of vol-au-vents pilfered from wakes, weddings and local community functions, traded for potato crisps and *poitín*,[27] the commerce between the global and the local represented in their barest meanness and excess. The tragedy is that action is frozen; colliding forms of life are locked in static conflict, generating murder and suicide. There is no transcendence, no redemption, no third moment of dialectical reconciliation, no movement or progress in any direction except eternal recurrence, circularity, spiralling downwards into petty recrimination, pointless violence and meaningless catastrophe. This conflict/stasis of *The Lonesome West* is a metaphor for the interminable cycle of violence and recrimination in Irish history in general, and Northern Ireland in particular. Mirroring the Northern Irish Peace Process, in which politics is the continuation of war by other means,[28] at the end Coleman and Valeen go off to the pub for a drink together but, as they go, they are already gathering ammunition for the renewal of hostilities and the continuation of their conflict.

McDonagh's *The Beauty Queen of Leenane*[29] represents the same theme of dialectical conflict degenerated to static eternal recurrence in Irish culture and identity. Again the time/space of the play is an undefined 'contemporary' interior, but frozen in an ever present past. The old mother sits in a rocking chair, passively absorbing television. The rocking chair is emblematic of Ireland's paradoxical experience of accelerated modernisation and stasis – in motion, but going nowhere. The formulaic drama of soap opera flickers on the television, reminding us that the stasis of reflexive modernisation is a global problem, albeit accentuated in this local setting. She is just waiting for the news, she says, but it never comes. Time passes but there is nothing new in Leenane. The interior of the house in Leenane represents continuity despite apparent transformation. The walls are adorned with icons in niches, both sacred and profane. There are statuettes of the Virgin and a framed portrait of JFK and Bobby, the Irish American Holy Family. A flashy radio-tape deck plays a mix of schmaltzy modern Irish traditional muzak. The television soaps are Australian. The mother's daughter/carer/bonded labourer is depressive: on the threshold of old maidenhood, with frustrated dreams of marriage and escape. An electrical conduit runs around the walls, terminating in power-points with glowing 'live' lights. This is an old

Irish home, a traditional house rewired. But modernity is an overlay, tacked on, not fully integrated. A chip-pan stands on the electric cooker. Their diet is Irish fast food, a sickening mixture of fats and sugar – tea and fancy biscuits, chips, Complan, causing clogged arteries, obesity, sluggishness, deadening the life process. The house reeks of the mother's urine. She deliberately neglects her infection to annoy her daughter by reminding her of infirmity, decrepitude and death. Her cruelty is reciprocated: boiling fat from the chip-pan is used to torture and eventually murder the domineering mother. But even matricide is not enough to break the torturous stasis. Escape to Boston is the Beauty Queen of Leenane's psychotic delusion, and she eventually takes her mother's place rocking in the chair in front of the television.

That the 'D'unbeliveables' comedy duo of Pat Short and John Kenny[30] produced McDonagh's *The Lonesome West* is perfectly apt, as McDonagh's work is black tragicomedy, and their own comedy plays on the grotesque, tragic and darkly comic forms that are produced by cultural collisions: vanishing giants and trolls from our collective cultural childhood; the fanatically parochial GAA coach;[31] the sadistic and fatherly schoolmaster; the 'gombeen man'[32] – the megalomaniacal, obsequious 'cute hoor' local county councillor with his eye on the Dáil seat. But the utopian gesture of D'unbelievables is that these social types, who represent the shades of the past that still haunt contemporary Irish culture, are also hilarious caricatures, exaggerated to absurdity. The target of comedy, Samuel Johnson says, is 'the bad humour of the Father that keeps us in a state of bondage', that makes us slaves to the conventions of his house.[33] D'unbelievables target such 'Fathers' – priests, teachers, guards, councillors and minor 'offeecials' of all sorts, the 'little men' who constitute authoritarian and oppressive forms of Irish life. Freud says that comedy targets:

> people and objects that lay claim to authority and respect and are in some sense sublime. The degradation of the sublime allows one to have an idea of it as though it were something commonplace, in whose presence I need not pull myself together, but may, to use the military formula, 'stand easy'.[34]

The double action of comedy, according to Freud, is that it frees us from the tyranny of the Father, but without 'killing the Father'. Through comedy we renegotiate our relations with cultural authorities; we try to come to new terms with our inherited traditions. D'unbelievables' comedy enables us to free ourselves from the life worlds where priests, schoolmasters and minor 'offeecials' wield power and simultaneously allows us fondly to remember those worlds as real and meaningful. The interiors and dream sequences constructed by D'unbelievables – ideal homes and fantasy dream sequences used in television advertisements for the National Lottery;

satellite dishes made out of wheelbarrows propped outside red-brick, palisaded, galvanised-roofed monster houses; De Valera-esque comely maidens chasing through meadows with a hurley in a surreal fantasy of a feminised, eroticised GAA meets *Riverdance* scenario – comes very close to capturing the bizarre imaginative structure of the current Irish phantasmagoria: elements drawn incongruously from the symbolic registers of the traditional and the modern, the local and the global, dialectical images juxtaposed in an extravagant pastiche of hyper-real, postmodern contemporary Ireland.

Kenny and Short say that their comedy is inspired by the forms of life they are familiar with in Ireland's 'in-between' towns (Kenny and Short are from middling-sized towns in Limerick and Tipperary, between the city and the country, the global and the local), the places all over Ireland living through the experience of accelerated social change as well as the persistence of older forms of life; the same theatres of acceleration, stasis and cultural collisions where other young people, unable to laugh, or to laugh any longer, choose instead to cry and to die.[35] D'unbelievables test their new material in theatres in county towns, Tralee, Kilmallock, Tuam, before staging them in Dublin, saying that if they find resonance with audiences there, then they know it will work in Dublin. In other words, the secret of D'unbelieveables' comedy is not that a city audience laughs at a caricature of a rural 'other', as North American and continental comedy plays with the radical alterity of the bumpkin, the peasant or the hillbilly. In Irish comedy, the rural other is close to us and familiar: we are laughing at, and with, an aspect of ourselves. A large proportion of the population in Dublin is from the rural hinterland, and those who are not are intimately, nostalgically connected with it, as the symbolic order and imaginative structure of contemporary Ireland are still very much rural.

Comedy has two distinct moments: a critical disruptive moment that frees its audience from the tyranny of the dominant culture, lets us see the absurdity of the in-between culture that is our habitus; and it also has an affirmative moment that, as it estranges us from our habitus, simultaneously reconciles us with that world as familiar and continuous. In Ireland we need both, and the comedic art of Kenny and Short throws open the grotesque horrors of accelerated modernisation in contemporary Ireland, and simultaneously gives us the gift of laughter that shows colliding worlds – traditional and modern, global and local, past and future – in moments of fleeting reconciliation. Kenny and Short show us that what is unbelievable about contemporary Ireland is that people manage to live enjoyably in the liminal spaces typical of a strange and paradoxical world in which Irish people presently find themselves.

Conclusions

As we have shown above, the experience of modernity and modernisation in contemporary Ireland is illustrative of the end of history as interpreted by the Hegelian/Marxist dialectic, and its decomposition into eternal recurrence and stasis, a Nietzschean/Weberian end of Irish history. But, Beck asks, what of other possibilities? What has becomes of politics – 'the art of making oneself at home in the maelstrom, as Marshall Berman put it so nicely?'[36]

The development of contemporary Irish society is characterised by increasing fragmentation and individuation, but these processes themselves are historical and social (that is to say collective) experiences, experiences that cut across differences of class, gender, ideology, region and so on. Individuation and fragmentation of collective identities are perceived from within the interpretive horizons of particular life worlds to be unique and irreducible and entirely different from others' experiences. But that perception is itself a social phenomenon, and one with profoundly political implications to boot. It was Margaret Thatcher who said, 'There is no such thing as society. There are individual men and women, and there are families.' One of the great dangers facing those of us who are interested in a politics that would make us more at home in the maelstrom of accelerated modernisation, that would, as Marx says, help us to 'make our own history with will and consciousness' rather than simply have it happen upon us, is that the scepticism towards unifying projects and the emphasis on the particularity of identity eschew the notion of collective experiences, the interdependency of identities, the reciprocity of their material and symbolic exchanges, and even of society as such. Against this, we hold to the notion that there are experiences that are highly generalised and dispersed and that are shared – perhaps not by everybody, and certainly not experienced in precisely the same way by everyone – but generalised nonetheless.

Globalisation is experienced very differently in New York and Ballyhaunis, but if we want to speak meaningfully of the ways in which culture and forms of life in Ireland are asymmetrically interdependent with political economic and cultural processes in the United States, then notions of collective historical experiences of modernisation at a global level remain essential and indispensable. The effects of 'instrumental rationalisation' (the organising principle of discursive practices of individuation and totalisation now operating at a global level) in contemporary Ireland, for example, are experienced very differently if you are a 200-acre dairy farmer applying for a European Union milk quota, or a single mother from Ballyfermot applying for Supplementary Welfare Allowance, or a Romanian Gypsy applying for asylum. These experiences are starkly differentiated by class, gender, ethnicity, language, culture and so on – even the outcome of the cases may be completely different; one successful, one endlessly frustrated, one routinely rejected – or, indeed, perhaps not. But what collects them? On what basis could we say that they have something in common? They are all processed by an impersonal legal-rational, rule-governed administrative apparatus called modern bureaucracy. Despite the fragmentation of identity and the individuation of experience in contemporary Ireland, Weber gives us a bead on and an understanding of an experience that is common to the differentiated identities that constitute modern Irish society.

While recognising the fragmented identities and differentiated experiences of contemporary Irish life, we must retain the ability to perceive and potentially to recover the basis of unity in the diversity. Christians used to believe that the basis of unity in human diversity was the soul. Marxists used to believe that the basis of unity in diversity was our capacity to produce and our relations to the means of production. Liberals used to believe that the basis for unity was our capacity for reason. Irish and other nationalists used to believe that the basis for unity lay in our shared ethnicity, and so on, in the same vein for feminists and a host of others. And many continue to hold these beliefs as self-evident truths. Against this orthodoxy, and against the position of other contemporary theorists, including Chomsky and Habermas, who ground society in the deep structures of communication, the most advanced schools of philosophy today hold that there is no preordained or fundamental ground of social unity. But that is not to say that there is (or are) no unity (or unities). Rather, the point is that whatever unities exist in any society at a particular historical time are solidarities: social and political collective identities whose ideologies are linked together, articulated with one another in ways that are contingent and transitory.

> The absence of a ground of the social means that whatever form of social articulation exists is going to be the result of a laborious process of political construction which creates new habits, new forms of thought, new forms of relation between people. It means the creation of a political tradition.[37]

The painstaking work of bringing together different ideologies and discourses of identity from a great diversity of points on the social fabric of contemporary Ireland is called 'hegemony'. To engage in hegemonic articulatory practices, to attempt to constitute a solidarity that would formulate values, norms and principles to guide collective action in a time of hyper-individuation and the fragmentation of a political imaginary, to create a new political tradition in Ireland after 'the end of Irish history', is to presuppose the possibility of forming a 'we'. To invoke such a collective subject of contemporary Ireland rhetorically, before that subject has appeared on the historical stage, is to make such a strategic utopian political assumption. And to provide a critical hermeneutic analysis of the forms of Irish culture under conditions of accelerated modernisation is to contribute towards setting that stage.

Notes

1 M. Berman, *All That is Solid Melts into Air: The Experience of Modernity* (London: Verso, 1982), p. 15.
2 Z. Bauman, *Modernity and Ambivalence* (Cambridge: Polity, 1993).
3 F. Jameson, *Postmodernism, or the Cultural Logic of Late Capitalism* (Durham, NC: Durham University Press, 1991).
4 U. Beck, A. Giddens and S. Lash, *Reflexive Modernization* (London: Polity, 1994).
5 Z. Bauman, *Globalization: The Human Consequences* (London: Polity, 1998); U. Beck, *What is Globalization?* (Cambridge: Polity, 2000); A. Giddens, *Runaway World: How Globalization is Shaping Our Lives* (London: Routledge, 1999); F. Jameson, 'Globalization and political strategy', *New Left Review*, 4 (2000), pp. 49–68.
6 K. Marx and F. Engels, *The Communist Manifesto* (London: Penguin, 1985).
7 W. Benjamin, 'Theses on the philosophy of history', in *Illuminations* (London: Fontana, 1992), p. 249.
8 Marx and Engels, *The Communist Manifesto*, p. 86.
9 Berman, *All That is Solid*, p. 72.
10 E. Durkheim, *Suicide* (New York: Free Press, 1966).
11 S. Freud, *Civilization and its Discontents* (New York: Norton, 1961); Durkheim, *Suicide*.
12 T. Hobbes, *Leviathan* (London: J. M. Dent & Sons, 1914).
13 M. Weber *The Protestant Ethic and the Spirit of Capitalism* (London: Macmillan, 1976), p. 71.
14 Marx and Engels, *The Communist Manifesto*, p. 82.
15 P. Kavanagh, 'The Great Hunger', in *Patrick Kavanagh: The Complete Poems* (New York: Peter Kavanagh Hand Press, 1972), pp. 79–104.
16 The constitutive Lack is a central Lacanian concept, present throughout his oeuvre. For example see 'In you more than you', in J. Lacan, *The Four Fundamental Concepts of Psychoanalysis* (New York: Norton, 1977). For a thorough exposition of the ideological function of the Lack, see S. Zizek, *The Sublime Object of Ideology* (London: Verso, 1989).
17 A fundamental tenet of the Liberal parliamentary Home Rule movement in nineteenth-century Ireland was that British administration of Ireland from London was inefficient and irrational. The abject failure of the English government and its offices in Ireland to respond adequately to famine conditions in the 1840s was one of the main proofs of the argument for Home Rule.
18 Marx and Engels, *The Communist Manifesto*, p. 84.
19 'Real Ireland' is the leading range of commodified images on postcards, calendars, and coffee-table books – photographs of 'traditional Ireland' showing houses, landscapes, shopfronts, farm animals and country folk.
20 For a full account of Dublin's developer culture see F. McDonald, *The Construction of Dublin* (Dublin: Grandon, 2000).

21 Louis Walsh, 'The starmaker', interview, *RTE Guide*, 21 April 2001.
22 W. Benjamin, 'Paris: capital of the nineteenth century', in *Reflections: Essays, Aphorisms, Autobiographical Writing* (New York: Harcourt, Brace & Co., 1978).
23 W. Benjamin, 'The interior, the trace', in *The Arcades Project* (Cambridge, MA: Belknap/Harvard University Press, 1999).
24 J. Joyce, *Dubliners* (London: Penguin, 1976).
25 M. McDonagh, *The Leenane Trilogy* (London: Methuen Drama, 1999).
26 Although not part of McDonagh's original set directions, this has become a common feature of subsequent productions.
27 Illicit whiskey (moonshine).
28 In Carl von Clausewitz's famous formulation, war is the continuation of politics by other means.
29 McDonagh, *The Leenane Trilogy*.
30 The 'D'unbelievables' duo of Kenny and Short do surrealist and absurdist comedy, akin to *Father Ted*, in which they frequently played cameos.
31 The GAA is the Gaelic Athletic Association, the national body promoting the Gaelic games of hurling and football.
32 The gombeen man (from '*gambín*', interest on a loan; from Middle English '*cambie*', exchange, barter; from Latin '*cambium*') is a village usurer, usually a shopkeeper, publican, merchant or estate agent, a native Irish petty bourgeois.
33 Samuel Johnson, cited in R. Corrigan (ed.), *Comedy: Meaning and Form* (New York: Harper and Row, 1981).
34 S. Freud, *Jokes and Their Relation to the Unconscious* (London: Penguin, 1981), pp. 261–2.
35 K. Keohane, and D. Chambers, 'Understanding Irish suicides', in M. Peillon and M. Corcoran (eds), *Ireland Unbound* (Dublin: Institute of Public Administration, 2002).
36 Beck, Giddens and Lash, *Reflexive Modernisation*, p. 32.
37 E. Laclau, 'God only knows', *Marxism Today* (December 1991), p. 59.

8

Fear and loathing in lost ages: journeys through postmodern Dublin

DAVID SLATTERY

I met them at the half-built arrivals area in Dublin airport. I was delighted that they all arrived together, though coming from different parts of the world. My sense of good fortune, rarely attached to contemporary Dublin transport, quickly evaporated when we got outside to find that a lightning strike among the taxi drivers, caused by the liberalisation of licences, had made a quick escape from the airport seem impossible. However, I found a 'new plate' and bribed him to take us into the city to the General Post Office (GPO), where, allegedly, it all started in 1916.

In the back of a wheelchair-accessible van, recently acquired from a driver unable to face the rigours of the new free market of the Celtic Tiger, we sped towards the GPO accompanied by a narrative from our driver on how 'fucking fantastic' everything was since the Celtic Tiger arrived in Dublin. On enquiring after our business, I assured him that my guests and I were in earnest pursuit of the craic.

There was Doctor Gunther Brenner, formerly of the Institute for the Study of Folklore at Heidelberg University. He left the Institute suddenly some six years ago and no one has had the nerve to enquire why. I believe he has spent some time in an asylum near Cologne and now writes a weekly column for a local newspaper. He was concerned with anonymity, arguing that not just uninformed informers should have their identities preserved, so I agreed to call him Hans. Hans had been in Ireland in the 1970s, touring the west with a German céilí band, and considered himself to be well informed on traditional Irish culture. I had met Hans at a conference in Cambridge the previous summer and he had begged me for an excuse to visit the 'sexiest destination in Europe'. Hans's views can be regarded with suspicion, if at all representative, as he is now outside the academy.

There was Doctor Claude de Ville from the Department of Sociology outside Lyon. I will just call him Claude, as he had no patience with disguise. Claude is a distant relation of Durkheim and for that reason his opinions are given more credit than they deserve. He resisted visiting Ireland for many years and, on this occasion, believed that he was sacrificing himself to the cause of science or, indeed, nonsense. Claude had allowed himself to be talked into the visit and considered it something of a privilege to be entirely ignorant of Dublin.

For gender balance there was Claude's girlfriend, Doctor Sarah Breakweather, who was a temporary lecturer in cultural studies in a North American university. Sarah was writing a book on travel and gender and was a regular visitor to Ireland, strictly post Peace Process. She was looking for an academic post in Europe, to be nearer Claude, and was specifically using this trip to check out the intellectual potential of Dublin. I had explained to her before her arrival that Dublin was only 'a stone's throw' from Paris, with its Joyce, Beckett and cuisine de France.

As Barbara O'Connor[1] reminds us, we Irish cannot help but be nice to foreigners and go out of our way to help them. Therefore, I was compelled to provide a traveller by the name of Harvey Keitel from Bristol, no relation to the actor, I was assured, with a lift into the city in our taxi. Harvey, in character, had a cameo role to play in our drama and was in Dublin to join, in Bobs in Temple Bar, a group on a stag weekend which had left England two days before.

In the taxi, I informed my collaborators of my plans to document our collective experience of postmodern Dublin and outlined my considered approach. I explained that I wished to write on the effects of globalisation on the city in such a manner that I might avoid the usual attitudes and platitudes: a jaded irony; a disaffected nostalgia inversely related to the extent of the experience of modernity; a Marxist superiority. To achieve this I had to develop an entirely original theoretical approach. Having been interrupted by Hans to tell me that, after much experimentation on his part, no such novelty was available, I continued in the same vein. I told my guests that attempts to understand postmodern culture tend to be Marxist in some respect, in that they invoke some notion of false consciousness and inauthenticity. Furthermore, I link life in Dublin to transformations in forms of consciousness rather than transformations in capital, which is very different from other understandings of the Celtic Tiger. Postmodern renderings of Dublin invoke a nostalgia for the 'modern Dublin' reputedly best exemplified in Joyce's *Ulysses* and redeploy that nostalgia into the listless contemporary.

This phenomenon is best seen in the traditional pub, which invokes a lost home industry manifest in sewing machines, sewing tables, mangles and other mechanical instruments of dubious efficacy. The modern pub reputedly was a place of rest from the daily imposition of work or, indeed, during long epochs of repression and unemployment, a place to eek out a few pints against a backdrop of mandatory idleness. The contemporary pub deploys implements from a false historical industrious consciousness as the props of leisure to remind one of the industry of the past. While relaxing in the postmodern Dublin pub, we are made nostalgic for an allegedly simpler past. But this is to suppose that the postmodern pub is a site for relaxation. It does not facilitate relaxation. Instead, it promotes an anxiety about the present in the form of a constant engagement with the past. How can we coherently embrace postmodernity and live comfortably in the inalienable midst of globalisation?

If I am fashionably appalled by the fungal profligacy of modern McDonald's, with its rendering of the potato as reconstituted fried uniformity with globally guaranteed quality and consistency, I am perhaps more appalled by the traditional Irish rendering of the potato as flowery spud. Like most of my kind inhabiting the global city of Dublin, I am contemptuous of the potato-ridden past but unable coherently to situate myself in the pasta present. Towards the end of developing a methodology appropriate to the rendering of the globalised postmodern condition, I had invited these thinkers to the most profligate site of postmodern productions. Could we capture the meaning of postmodern Dublin that runs together the redundantly isolated categories of drink, drama, lies, stories, academic analysis, literature, history, exaggeration and much more? Thus I defined our mission: the pursuit of the postmodern conflation we call the craic.

Our now silent taxi driver dropped us on O'Connell Street, outside the Ann Summers lingerie shop opposite the GPO. Harvey begged us to allow him to tag along until such a time as he could, with good conscience as an Englishman, enter the pub and join his friends. It was 11.00 a.m. and he had nowhere to go. Unconsciously suspecting that he may have a structuring role in our day, we willingly allowed him to stay.

In response to expressions of surprise on the faces of my visitors gazing at the contents of the Ann Summers window in good Catholic Ireland, I quickly drew their attention to the building across the boulevard and explained that the GPO is the original site of pure Irish asexual consciousness, where, in 1916, Catholic Ireland rose up to throw off the yoke of the cosmopolitanism of colonial consciousness. Harvey wondered why Irish nationalism was involved with philately and we looked forward to his removal from the narrative.

I informed my audience that not since medieval times had sin been an object of such commercial focus in Dublin. Contemporary Dublin sees sex released from its necessary association with Catholicism and freed into a general regime of commodification. Irish sin, or sex, is transformed in postmodern Dublin and forms a new defining relationship to money. In modernity, sex was articulated through a series of necessary transgressions focused on marriage. Today, sex is articulated through a series of expenses focused on the deployment of the necessary equipment: Ann Summers provides that equipment opposite the site of pure celibate national consciousness, if our revisionist historians are to be ignored. I explained that postmodern Dublin was characterised by many examples of such historical transformations and oppositional disruptions in the tranquillity of our modern consciousness. We were overtaken by a tourist bus blasting historical trivia from its upper deck. The guide called the attention of his passengers to the Millennium Spike in front of the GPO. Perplexed, my guests looked around for this sign of the times until I explained that this was a tour of the idea of the Spike, as it had not yet been built.

With this kind of talk, my audience could immediately discern my Foucauldian influences. I wanted to approximate his kind of serial history that was neither traditionally hermeneutical nor teleological. Could we, I asked, waving my arms energetically above my head to encompass the streetscape, avoid analysing Dublin as just another monument to pleasure in postmodernity appropriate to the well documented anthropocentric thought of modernity? I wanted to strip Dublin of its ethnological content, resituate it as archaeology and embrace the much postponed confront-ation with the tangles of postmodernity. What kind of positivity could the discourses of contemporary Dublin reveal?

Hans interrupted my monologue to remind me that Gellner[2] believed that both orthodox Marxists and liberals predicted a transition from the form of nationalism evident in the GPO to a form of universalism manifest in Ann Summers, which he describes as a kind of international identification with one standard culture. Gellner imagined that this cultural homogenisation might yet happen but it conspicuously had not happened to date. This great mistake, he claimed, is the one thing that unites Marxists and liberals: cultural difference persists in the face of unifying discourses and aspirations. Would Gellner have changed his mind if he had the opportunity to visit contemporary Dublin with us? The question of whether the production of Dublin was one of different cultures seemed central to Hans. Specifically, the question of whether the European Union, as a form of globalisation, is a unifying or fractur-ing force in Dublin.

Claude's view on this was that while national culture was the product of the state, culture in general is the product of institutions such as the pub and sex industries. He argued that an analysis of institutions as sites for the invention of traditional culture needs to be made, to determine to what extent these institutions can fulfil roles such as those identified by Hobsbawm[3] as belonging to state traditions. The macroscopic processes of our social, political and economic development are essential in under-standing changes which take place in our perception of ourselves. Claude reminded Hans that we may not be straying too far from master narratives such as Marx's sense of the grammar of commodities. When discussing cultural sites as the loci for the production of tradition and national identity, I was put in mind of Georgian Dublin. In the Georgian street-scape we see the commandeering of old materials in the production of traditional narratives on identity that are novel for unique purposes. This is a feature in the invention of the traditional pub. Such inventions use the large storehouse of materials accumulated in our past, from folk-lore, industry, religion and archaeology. In the past, the state rallied these resources to create a nationalistic culture legitimising the links between the new state and a mist-shrouded past: thus we have the GPO, Kilmainham Hospital and Gaol, and Christchurch. Today, these materials are under the command of individual institutions like Temple Bar Properties, Ann Summers and the Guinnesses' Brewery.

At that point, I had planned a tour of Georgian Dublin along North Great George's Street into Parnell Square, taking in the Joyce and Writers Museums, along with the Hugh Lane Gallery, in order to test our hypothesis, but it began to rain so we retreated to the nearby Epicurian Foodhall, where our diverse culinary tastes could be satisfied. Here Claude enjoyed traditional French cuisine from Christophe's, Hans had a curry with free nan bread and Sarah opted for a vegetarian wrap. Harvey had a salami panini. As I could not remember whether the wrap had replaced the bagel as that month's fashion food, I settled for a kebab. We all had coffee despite my nostalgia for traditional tea. We returned to our dis-cussions of globalisation, tradition and the city while consuming our food.

I blithely remarked that the viral efficiency of the spread of ethnic menus in Dublin, as an example of globalisation, is generally welcomed by us locals, who maintain a healthy amnesia about the past in Irish cooking. Tourists struggle to find traditional Irish food, as if there had been such a phenomenon in history, and in the pursuit of this their searches end in such places as Johnny Fox's Irish Pub or Gallagher's in Temple Bar, where they feed on smoked salmon, cod in various sauces and lamb. The Great Famine of the 1840s was more than a humanit-arian disaster – it was embarrassing proof of the absence of a culinary tradition. In many other areas, however, outside of food, we are often uncomfortable with the eradication of what we view as our heritage. Like Lowenthal, we can see heritage as the very essence of society – the anthropological.[4] Fish now sustains established menus in Dublin. Globalised postmodern Dublin is allowing us to re-represent our identity, to ourselves, where the only inauthentic place is the hysterically imme-diate present.

Sarah informed us that academia had subjected the study of the pro-duction of new cuisines to a general neglect, because academics were too intellectually snobbish to study tourism, which she held as being mostly responsible for the development of contemporary heritage consciousness. Without tourism, there would be no restaurants in Dublin. She believed that tourism is one of the most promiscuous forms of contemporary behaviour. She wondered if this neglect is part of social science's in-security about all things regarded as politically incorrect, where correctness is identified with a view of authentic behaviour. She said that Denison Nash suggests that this neglect might be traced to the view that touristic encounters with the other are viewed as the antithesis of what researchers have sought to do in sustained participation/observa-tion: he suggests that we have feared contamination through association with the shallow concerns of the 'inauthentic' tourist.[5] In her book she wished to tackle the notion of authenticity as a processional feature of the mode of production of interpretations, rather than as a nature adher-ing to any behaviour itself.

Harvey, an accountant, who made a brave effort to appear interested, asked her what happens when researchers such as ourselves go on holiday, especially to Dublin? We all impressed on him that we were strictly researching and were not in pursuit of the shallow experiences of tourists like him. We concurred that, as a result of what might be a simple over-sight, a political prudishness, or more likely the constipations of modern-ity, or the anthropological neglect of contemporary society in favour of the exotic other at the margins of colonial consciousness, anyone pursu-ing a study of postmodern Dublin is confronted by something of a *tabula rasa* in content and, most especially, theoretical approach. In the liber-ating context of this neglect, we turned to Baudrillard, Foucault and Lowenthal, among others, between mouthfuls, to provide us with some framework within which we might make sense of Dublin: most especially to make sense of contemporary simulations which could define the Dublin of these intellectuals on holiday in Dublin. Nowadays, people come to Dublin because, after all, everyone has been here – it shares a remembered nature with Woodstock.

We opted for traditional scones and, over these, Hans took up the particular idea that perhaps the absence of mass industrialisation in Dublin places its inhabitants in a peculiarly advantaged position to exploit current cultural formations, where the postindustrial seems to have a relation-ship with the postmodern. It could be argued, he claimed, that there is a relationship of epistemological interdependence between tourism and heritage as they emerge in contemporary Dublin. They are epistemically related to each other in postmodern consciousness – in place of the rather banal functionalist conclusion that they are related economically through demand. The functionalist cannot account for the emergence of the past as a contemporary consumable at this precise historical point. This, he believed, was peculiarly the case in the example of food.

But Claude interrupted that for Baudrillard, contemporary experience of the world is part of the generalised postmodern simulacra, where all sense of reality escapes us. Gazing around the Epicurian Foodhall, he argued that contemporary Dublin seemed to fit this model of simulated reality quite well. But I argued that it remained to be determined whether the city is not just an inauthentic historical representation but rather simulated history in this sense: in other words, contemporary Dublin has a complex relation to history that is concerned with the simulation of the traditional narrative chronology. Simulation is not some arbitrary free-for-all but is constrained by its own logic. However, any argument for the limits of simulation seemed difficult to sustain in the unrestrained confines of the Epicurian Foodhall.

To test our ideas on simulation we determined, unlike Baudrillard, to check out Temple Bar via the nearby Halfpenny Bridge. This would allow us to achieve both a valuable research goal and the charitable act of delivering Harvey to his mates enjoying the craic. We chatted as we strolled along Abbey Street. Sarah held forth on MacCannell's concern with the inauthenticity of modern tourism. She told us that he believes that the Boorstin-type analysis of tourism as a pseudo-experience is the characteristically intellectual-snobbish view that other people, like Harvey, are tourists, while myself, Claude, Sarah and Hans are, indeed, travellers.[6] This snobbery appears as a constant in research into simulations, where those who do not participate are at a loss as to how anyone, like Harvey, could be 'conned' by the craic in the pubs of Temple Bar. But she argued that this attitude is to mistake simulation for pretending. Simulation is a technically precise mode of signification and not the free-play of the imagination.

Increasingly animated, pushing our way through the indifferent crowds on Liffey Street, past the 'Hags with the Bags', Claude argued the absurdity of treating authenticity as an end of a process, rather than as a strategy for producing cultural products, as revealed in the extreme relativism of Crick's argument that all cultures are 'staged' and thus inauthentic, since cultures are constantly invented, remade and re-organised.[7] This position, he contended, would result in the absurdity of denying reality. Postmodernists, he told an increasingly distracted Harvey, do not deny reality but simply claim that an appeal to reality has no explanatory force.

Thus preoccupied, Harvey failed to observe, or along with some fifty-seven other people ignored, a 'red man' signal for the crossing at the bridge and walked under the Viking Splash Ship that was at that moment driving by. Harvey was hit on the head by the prow and left for dead on the street by these Vikings, like thousands before him a millennium ago. An elderly local who was passing by this scene called the ambulance on her mobile phone. On asking what had happened, I informed her that our recent acquaintance from Bristol had been run over by the Vikings, to which she replied 'Jasus – ye must be really having the right craic'.

This encounter with a local brought to my mind Cronin's claims that dialogue has been the process of authentification in contemporary travel

writing in Ireland, where anecdote provides comic relief and we Irish
are portrayed as irrepressible in the face of misfortune and intrinsically
burlesque.[8] This is a device deployed by Joyce to authenticate Bloom's
experience of Dublin. I consoled my surviving colleagues that the principal
process of authentification in Dublin is provided by such street scenes,
bringing the drama of the burlesque in contact with the artificial experience of the visitor. Here, in the form of a boat that sailed the streets of
Dublin, we found a genuine example of the deployment of opposition.
Thus comforted, we agreed that, once the ambulance had arrived to take
Harvey away to some more prosaic reality inside the emergency ward,
we would temporarily adjourn to Mulligan's, spurning the tacky com-
merciality of the nearby Russian bar, Pravda. Relieved of our structuring
prop, we waited while the ambulance made its way to us through the
gridlock. I was reminded how, for Urry, tourism is generated through
difference and results from a basic binary division between the ordinary/
everyday and the extraordinary. For this reason, Urry[9] believes that any
account that suggests tourism is motivated by a search for the authentic
is incorrect. Feifer[10] has even suggested that many tourists, what he terms
post-tourists, delight in the inauthenticity of the normal tourist experience, exemplified in front of us on the street in the form of six Vikings
offering first aid to Harvey. From all this, we can see that the notion of
authenticity is a complex one.

We waited for the ambulance. While doing so, I fell into a reverie on
my experience of living in Dublin. I have come to think about authenticity in terms of bounded strategies and spaces: in moving through the
city we are moving through modern authentic representations and postmodern simulations, with no effort made to distinguish between them.
Borrowing from Lowenthal's analysis of factitious history, we might come
to think of this as a strategy to persuade both the tourist and the resident
that the entire city is presenting the same type of truth throughout, regardless of the differences between economic spaces: contemporary Dublin
disguises the differences between Merrion Square and Mountjoy Square
from the visitor. This reflects how Dublin is caught between modern modes
of representation and postmodern simulation.

We waited for the ambulance. Simulation is the postmodern mode of
signification that produces an economy of signs through which we think
ourselves in culture and through which we communicate. Obviously, the
meaning of simulations often escapes us at a conscious level, so there is
a need to unpack their cultural values: this is the heuristic strategy. I
realised that this is what Baudrillard attempts to do and what we were
attempting in our study of Dublin. I daydreamed about authentification
processes as an aspect of the production of images, rather than their
relation to a philosophically privileged reality. The image of Dublin precedes any notion of 'real Dublin'. This is why the Millennium Spike

featured on the Dublin bus tour prior to its being built. In post-modernity, simulation takes over from representation. But representation tries to absorb simulation by interpreting it as a false representation and produces a discourse on the real. This is the way daydreaming tries to absorb consciousness. Simulation can include representation as simula-tion, just as consciousness can accommodate a reverie or daydream. The idea of authenticity belongs to history at the level of history's relation to reality, but it belongs to postmodern experience in terms of authenti-cating procedures. So I realised that Dublin cannot be authentic in a naively realist way. The city, with its diversity of ethnic restaurants and food, in the absence of ethnic difference, does not work on the basis of imagining or pretending we are in a real place or epoch. It works through the precise processes of simulation. I decided to abandon the notion of authenticity as a burden from modernity. But could I really leave it go? What would happen if I did not cling to our well established modes of validation? Surely the result could only be disastrous?

The ambulance arrived! Harvey briefly regained consciousness and during that moment we assured him that we would find his mates in Bobs and let them know what had happened. Relieved of our inauthentic tourist we made our way to Mulligan's, the interior visible only through the invitingly open door. Here the visitor is confronted by a range of Dublinesque images that reinforce our literate past: the real home of James Joyce.

We changed to mass-produced lager after two pints of Guinness and, at this point, Claude could not resist invoking Baudrillard, who, he told us, characterises the contemporary experience of the world as being medi-ated by postmodern consciousness, which, he argued, has its conditions of possibility in simulation. He informed us that simulation has come to replace the anthropomorphism of modernism in an epistemological trans-formation that has radically altered both our experience of culture and our modes of cultural production. The presence of forms of simulation lends weight to the operation of postmodern consciousness, whether we like it or not. Contemporary pub behaviour, with what appears to be the fairly extensive deployment of simulacra, suggests itself as a fruitful place to test hypotheses on postmodern behaviour: in this context, we were informed, pub behaviour in Dublin is a metaphor for contemporary western behaviour in general. It provides an opportunity to make a theoretically informed analysis of the self – where we think ourselves through simu-lations – and of the other – where we come to think others through how they are simulated. 'Stimulated?' enquired an animated customer and we all laughed at this propitious pun in the pub.

To celebrate this methodological breakthrough, we had three more lagers each, just for the craic, and made our way back to Pravda, having lost some of our concern for its cultural dislocation along the boardwalk

overhanging the river. As we made our way above the river, we realised
that Dublin is to be understood from the point of view of both cultural
production and consumption and, towards this end, we realised that
Baudrillard is useful. The production of the boardwalk does not have a
use value, because it runs parallel to the footpath, but is primarily consumed
simply as a sign: it has a culture value in consumption. The boardwalk
is another means people have for relating themselves to the social order.
These kinds of architecture can be used to think within contemporary
social order. In this way, it is a semiotic order that precedes the individual,
like any language. Much of Dublin is about establishing the individual's
place in the social order rather than fulfilling needs and so has a use value.

We consumed the boardwalk, gingerly sidestepping the winos and,
once inside Pravda, we saw an example of how Dublin has been stripped
of all images of colonisation and emigration – these, if they exist at all,
are featured signs rather than historical evidence of conquest. The story
in Pravda is one of productive cooperation, where there are no embarrassing conflicts. Conflict is incongruous with the craic. The inability to
simulate political or ideological divisions that have marked modern
consciousness is a hallmark of simulation evident throughout the city.
This is no better manifestation than being surrounded by Cold War
iconography. Thus, the postmodern rendering of the craic avoids embarrassing conflict.

This seemed a good location to debate the merits of Marx, surrounded by the most incontrovertible evidence of his demise. However,
Claude would not have any of it. It seemed to Claude that Bourdieu's
notion of habitus[11] provides us with a means of analysing ordinary
practices such as 'having the craic'. Irishness is expressed in the craic –
having fun – which is exported through the globalisation of the Irish
pub, a fun divorced from emotion. We reflected on the ironic inversion
of drinking in a Russian pub in Dublin and wondered how we should
behave never having internalised such an experience. Claude argued that
the relationship between history and the craic in Pravda is not a necessary one: it is just one of many techniques of authentification, where the
notion of the craic has come to occupy the role of the most important
authentifier. I refused to go back to that idea. Claude continued that
simulation is different from pretending but has a real impact on our
mode of imagining the past in our contemporary experience and, therefore, necessitates serious consideration. Sarah informed us of attempts
that have been made to understand the nature of its operation rather
than simply dismissing ourselves as anachronistic modern snobs. She
told us that, as academics, we need to wake up and smell the vodka.
Now drunk, like every other drunk, Sarah decided to relocate to Dublin.

Claude, now slightly drunk, insisted on spelling out Bourdieu's rele-
vance to our present situation.[12] Cultural capital contains the symbolic

competence necessary to appreciate certain forms of culture: in our case, to be able to appreciate Pravda. Most of the customers in Pravda are made up of the much increased, in Dublin, service class, which Bourdieu terms the 'new petty bourgeoisie'. Bourdieu argues that this group demands 'to have fun'. There is a fear of not getting enough pleasure and this is combined with a search for self-expression and 'bodily expression' and for communication with others. This new class, then beginning to swarm Pravda, are to be found teeming at the counter, wearing labelled clothes and talking in loud voices to each other over the throb of music and general conversation and talking with their absent counterparts on mobile phones, where what can be overheard is more important than what can be communicated. They were having the craic. Thus we discovered that the craic, as an expression of postmodern entertainment, had taken all the danger out of history and redeployed it for consumption. There were no spies in Pravda and no members of the proletariat.

Claude, now shouting over the increasing din of background music and the cacophony of mobile phones, designed to eradicate the mainstay of the modern pub experience, conversation, screamed at us about the growing role of the media in minimising the importance of separate and distinct systems of information on which a social class or group would base its behaviour. Individuals from all social groupings are exposed to more generally available systems of information and each grouping can now see some representations of the private spaces of other social groupings on television. The media have provided a hugely increased circulation of the representations of other people's lives, including those of elite groups such as the royal family and the working classes depicted on the television soap opera *Fair City*. This kind of institutionalised voyeurism allows people to adopt the styles of other groups and to cross social boundaries between different social groupings. The media have also dissolved the distinction between private life and public behaviour. This is the same type of person as the one who, screaming into her mobile phone in virtual conversation with someone made interesting only by being absent, crashed into our tray of pints and made us resolve to leave immediately for a quieter place to exchange our important views. We found it noteworthy that the craic can be 'had' in all Irish pubs, even Russian ones.

Thus, with Pravda rapidly filling up, and becoming increasingly anxious that we might miss some worthwhile experience, we continued our journey to Temple Bar. However, I realised that if we hurried we could see the sun go down on Dublin harbour from the viewing tower in Smithfield. We left Pravda and hastily made our way across Capel Street, through the closing Fruit Market, past the restored traditional Distillery Buildings and into Smithfield Hotel. In the lobby of the hotel, we were just in time to collide with the arrival of a loud group of American tourists intent on taking traditional set-dancing lessons. We ascended the tower struggling with vertigo brought on by the alcohol rather than the height and took up our places on the viewing deck. We wondered about the nature of the panorama before our eyes. Boorstin,[13] anticipating Jean Baudrillard, argued that contemporary Americans cannot experience 'reality' directly but thrive on pseudo-events. These pseudo-events are the indirect experience of an unreality. We have inherited them through globalisation in the form of the Patrick's Day Parade, for example. Indigenous populations are induced to produce extravagant displays for the gullible observer, who, in turn, becomes further removed from reality. Sarah remarked on the lack of extravagance in the Smithfield display. When tourists come to Dublin they want to gaze on the splendour of the city – the real Irish experience – and not on inner-city poverty, which must be screened from their view. On this model, the real becomes invisible while the symbolised unreal is made real. Thus, down below, Dublin Corporation struggles with the removal of the view of the indigenous. The view now is purely postmodern, in that it tries to efface the distinction between the past and the present, a distinction that gives rise to history.

Back on the ground, we retired to the Cobblestone pub to listen to traditional music in the company of real travellers who act as travellers on RTÉ. We were in the Company of Professional Simulators, masters of the trade: those who simulated themselves but who, in the act of self-simulation, were thus removed from modernity. As the boundaries between the masses and ourselves blurred, travellers and those who play them on television blurred, live traditional music and that in the museum across the square blurred, we again took up the challenge of making sense of it all over a few pints of real Guinness; our vision was blurring. As we chatted, and drank and listened to the music and enjoyed the craic, we felt all the boundaries that had hitherto held us in place dissolve. This was surely the site of real Dublin culture in postmodernity. We witnessed the dissolving of boundaries between high and low culture and between different cultural forms such as art, education, photography, music, sport, shopping, drinking, acting and research. In the Cobblestone, postmodern culture affects the audience through its impact, through regimes of pleasure, and not through passive aesthetic contemplation. Under the influence of Guinness, the sign of postmodern Dublin, we experienced the dissolution of the bonds of modernity.

A real fight broke out in a corner of the pub, which quickly consumed the entire crowd and, to the sounds of sirens, we found ourselves back out on Smithfield Square with the sky on fire. But how were we to make sense of this scene when nothing in our experience had prepared us for it? Hans wondered if there was a gas-field beneath our feet. Here was incontrovertible evidence that the visual has come to dominate bourgeoisie society,[14] partly as a result of photographic culture, in the form of 'blazing dustbins at the top of poles'. The epistemic order – which functions as a historical *a priori* to structure both the field of knowledge and the content of the perceived in a specific period – broke down. Cronin reminds us that implicit in the Foucauldian gaze is the idea that seeing is culturally determined and politically coercive.[15] Cronin mentions ruins as examples of constructs rather than mere natural givens, selected for observation on the basis of political, social/cultural criteria that change with circumstances.[16] Edward Said claims that the western convention of writing about ruins was to reduce present-day societies to the remains of a once glorious past.[17] Here, in the embarrassing ruin that constitutes two sides of Smithfield Square, the blazing poles seem to distract us from the decidedly unromantic streetscape. Without knowing how to respond to these as pure spectacles, we made our way, by gaslight, to Zaytoon on Parliament Street, where we had resolved to take dinner in the form of real kebabs.

We were on Church Street before we realised that Claude was missing. Sarah said that she had seen him with a group from the pub who had retreated quickly down an alleyway. We decided to look for him after getting something to eat. However, we agreed to try the Porter House for Real Ale before Zaytoon. Equipped with Weiss Biers, we took up shouting at each other in the display of the window. Here, alcohol is to be consumed as a public spectacle, where the very processes of production are on display. Postmodern pubs have huge windows (or no windows at all) to facilitate the outside looking in, so that those inside can exercise their sign value as customers enjoying the craic and those outside can revel in their sign value. The craic, after all, is a disposition that needs to be made visible for its meaning. Inside the pub, we were bombarded with different levels of representation in a technique similar to the way factional documentaries function. The Porter House interior exteriorises the processes involved in the manufacture of beer. This visual confession creates an environment sympathetic to the production of beer predominantly as sign value rather than beer as intoxicant.

Our conversation turned to how we might deal with the decidedly unromantic nature of the streetscape around Smithfield and how we might reconcile this with an integrated experience of Dublin. I related my reading of Cronin, where he tells us that attention to the material fabric of Irish life invites aesthetic disappointment, so the attention of the traveller shifts to the landscape.[18] Trapped in the city, we turn to the people for romance, or at least the people as represented through the institutions for the production of people. The predominant such institution in Dublin is the pub. At that point, it seemed clear to Sarah that, unlike other European cities, Dublin is the place of drink, rather than, for example, sex, where identity is produced. Relationships are difficult to form in the craic of the super-pub, where individual communications surrender to regimes for the production of the collective. Cities are either ignored or condemned for their visual poverty. This outer, visual poverty is compensated for by the vision of the inner eye, which is informed by fiction, history and myth, which has its home inside the traditional pub. In this way, images of Ireland in the imagination are what excite the traveller and we, as increasingly excited images of Ireland in the pub, excited the gaze of those passing outside. This seems to push the contemporary experience of Ireland into the heart of simulacrum.

A concern with the spectacle of scenery has dropped out of contemporary Irish travelogues, perhaps because of competition with visual media, and has been replaced by a sense of dialogue and theatricality, often centred on the pub. Social theorists tour Dublin through their theories and then travel to Dublin to carry out their postmodern fieldwork, where fieldwork is the experience of what they already know.

We were left with the consideration of whether the major organising principle in this mode of cultural production is symbolic or economic. This seemed particularly relevant in the thriving business of the Porter House. Bourdieu rightly highlighted the relational dynamic that operates between these two structuring principles. The heritage industry appears to mark a shift in the sociology of knowledge from the relatively autonomous museum to the economic capital of entertainment. In the Porter House, living museum of beer production, site of cultural production and habituated display of bodies at ease with postmodernity, a living lesson in how to have the craic, these principles come together. This is the Irish habitus. Its grammar is globalised heritage, which is necessarily universally recognisable. There is a moving together of economic and symbolic capital in this very Irish German pub.

There in the pub, before eyes that would be astonished were they not bleary, I unveiled my brand new technique. I call my method decomposition, or more precisely pristine Aquinian decomposition, or, for short, pure tommyrot. Only this approach can reveal the complex nature of the postmodern global city. Decomposition is interdisciplinary, because it involves the collaborative efforts of scholars from cognate disciplines actively engaging themselves together in fieldwork. It is an active deconstruction of the sole egomaniacal ethnographer in the field: it is multi-egotistical as opposed to multi-sited. With its reference to Aquinas, it maintains the infallibility of that essentially Irish intellectual inheritance. Like Aquinas, I aimed to dominate the Irish intellectual scene for hundreds of years; like Bourdieu, I aimed to disconcert those who practised sociology without reflecting on it. After that, I remember very little.

At 5.00 a.m. I was interviewed by Sergeant McGuire in Store Street garda station. He was friendly enough and gave me two styrofoam coffees.

However, I had to make a statement and thus I tried to explain to his sceptical modernism what it was we had being trying to accomplish. I explained to him that Ireland is always portrayed to travellers as a place of friendly and quaint people, a place steeped in past traditions and ways of life, poetry and the craic. The Irish are seen as having a peculiar skill at enjoying themselves: Irish people are constantly portrayed talking, laughing, drinking, dancing and playing music and, indeed, theorising in pubs. Leisure is represented as the tourist joining in the craic. How was I supposed to resist this and disappoint my guests? I explained how thinkers like O'Connor[19] showed how these images had their origin in British-produced images of Ireland, which are stereotypes emerging from colonial rule. Just as landscape, work and leisure have been commodified in tourism and are the result of cultural construction, so also are we, the people. O'Connor[20] argues that the people of Ireland have featured centrally in images of Ireland because of its colonised, economically dependent and peripheral condition. Ireland shares with other 'peasant' societies the setting up of the 'peasant' as a tourist attraction. This has meant that Irish people's behaviour has become an element of the tourist's experience. What could I do in those circumstances but join in? He asked me how much we had had to drink but I told him that it was impossible for me to know with any certainty because part of our received Irish charm is to exaggerate everything.

I further defended myself by informing him that Lowenthal[21] argues that an awareness of the past has a relationship to our wellbeing. Despite my short-term memory lapse, I was aware of the past as a realm both coexistent with and distinct from the present. Historical interpretations are shaped by anachronisms and hindsight: history is necessarily anachronistic because we can only live in the contemporary world; history employs hindsight to shape our interpretations of past events. We constantly see historical events differently as new consequences emerge. Oral narratives telescope, expand and rearrange segments of the past in line with whatever significance is attributed to them, where perceived changes tend to cluster within discrete periods separated by long intervals where nothing happens. I asked Sergeant McGuire to tell me what impact academic narratives might have on the way I might apprehend what had happened. Combine these narratives with the traditions of storytelling in Ireland, with their humour, fictions, exaggerations, scatologies and iconoclasms and downright lies, and the constraints of academic narratives, and you would have a complex mixture.

I told the increasingly uninterested Sergeant that Lowenthal also argues that we illuminate the diversity of the past by presenting it in the present and this is what he was demanding of me. But I impressed on him the difficulties facing his interrogation because in such processes we anachronise the past by making it intelligible in the present. We shape the past to fit our present-day image of the past: we shape the past to make the past fulfil our present-day need for certain kinds of stories. He had a need for a story of misdoings; I had a need for a story for the academy. By combining this with the narrative styles of modern Ireland and postmodern narrative strategies, we could demolish the traditional genres of recounting. I suspect that I did not convince Sergeant McGuire but, in any event, he promptly let me go, with a warning to behave myself.

We never got to Temple Bar: we skirted its edges. We never arrived at the heart of the matter – Bobs. I never saw Claude again but I understand that he is living outside Galway in a dormer bungalow with members of a travelling family who have stopped travelling. Sarah now lives with Hans in Heidelberg and I meet her on occasion when she is in Dublin.

Notes

1 B. O'Connor and M. Cronin (eds), *Tourism in Ireland. A Critical Analysis* (Cork: Cork University Press, 1993).

2 E. Gellner, 'On nations and nationalism', *Mediterranean Ethnological Summer School*, 1 (1995).

3 E. Hobsbawm and T. Ranger (eds), *The Invention of Tradition* (Cambridge: Cambridge University Press, 1983).

4 *Sunday Times Review of Books*, 12 January 1997.

5 D. Nash, *Anthropology of Tourism* (Oxford: Pergamon, 1996).

6 D. MacCannell, *The Tourist: A New Theory of the Leisure Class* (London: Macmillan, 1976).

7 M. Crick, 'Sun, sex, sights, savings and servility', *Criticism, Heresy and Interpretation*, 1 (1988), pp. 37–76.

8 O'Connor and Cronin (eds), *Tourism in Ireland*.

9 J. Urry, *The Tourist Gaze. Leisure and Travel in Contemporary Societies* (London: Sage, 1990).

10 M. Feifer, *Going Places* (London: Macmillan, 1985).

11 P. Bourdieu, *Distinction* (London: Routledge and Kegan Paul, 1984).

12 *Ibid.*

13 D. Boorstin, *The Image: A Guide to Pseudo-Events in America* (New York: Harper, 1964).

14 D. Bell, 'Framing nature: first steps into the wilderness for a sociology of the landscape', *Irish Journal of Sociology*, 3 (1993), pp. 1–22.

15 O'Connor and Cronin, *Tourism in Ireland*, p. 53.

16 *Ibid.*, p. 60.

17 *Ibid.*, p. 59.

18 *Ibid.*

19 *Ibid.*

20 *Ibid.*, p. 73.

21 D. Lowenthal, 'How we know the past', in *The Past is a Foreign Country* (Cambridge: Cambridge University Press, 1995).

9

Contemporary discourses of working, earning and spending: acceptance, critique and the bigger picture

ANNE B. RYAN

It has become commonplace to assert that Irish people now have more choices and enjoy a higher standard of living than ever before. An assumption also exists that the role of the ordinary citizen is to be a member of the paid labour force and a consumer, in order to 'keep the economy going'. Many people consequently live in a work–earn–spend cycle, spending much of what they earn on possessions and services now considered essential for everyday life. Savings are at an all-time low and credit card debt at an all-time high, especially among people under thirty-five.[1] Everyday life is often experienced as harried and fraught. Media discussions often portray Irish society as increasingly similar to that in the United States, and often assume that ordinary people have little choice regarding the shape of their lives.[2]

However, significant numbers of Irish people have chosen not to engage to this extent with a work–earn–spend culture and are resisting the idea that life must be pressured. They are critical of the notion that work–earn–spend lifestyles are indicative of progress and a high standard of living. In this, they share conclusions with an estimated fifty million people in the United States and other 'developed' countries, who contest the dominant models of wellbeing put forward by growth economics.[3] The ideas and practices of this group receive little attention in the mainstream media, however.

This chapter reflects on two qualitative research projects, carried out between 1999 and 2001, with people experiencing both ways of life. The discussion that follows examines the discourses available to the participants which help them interpret their experiences and make life choices. It goes on to discuss the connections between individual choices and the ways that economic values affect society, and asserts that the public and private spheres cannot be considered in isolation from each other.

The research themes

Both research projects gathered data concerning work, money and related themes in contemporary life, by means of focus-group discussions and individual and pair interviews.

How Was It For You?

The first study, reported in *How Was It For You? Exploring Couples' Experiences of the First Year of Marriage*, was commissioned by a marriage and relationship education and counselling organisation, and the participants were all under forty, married and based in Dublin.[4]

From this study, two broad groups emerge. One group's themes concern the demands of jobs, coping with constant tiredness, a lack of time for family and friends, and a feeling of being constantly over-pressed. I call them the TINA ('there is no alternative') group. Most of this group have no children but would like them in the future and worry about how they will fit them into their lives. They tend to blame factors outside their control for the shape of their lives. Many of them look to buying things like furniture, holidays, cars or clothes in order to create a sense of identity and to compensate for the difficulties of everyday life. Most have no savings and worry about what might happen if they were made redundant. Several feel that they cannot continue with their lifestyles. They express awareness of contradictions, namely, that they have a high 'standard of living', in the sense that they have plenty of material goods, but they acknowledge that this is not the same as a good quality of life. However, they are so busy coping with work, commuting and simply surviving the rat race that they have no time to take a step back and think creatively about alternative ways of living. Their talk is dominated by reports of lack of choice and a lack of control over the shape of their lives.

The *How Was It For You?* study reveals another group of people, who report having a good quality of life, even if it means having fewer material possessions and living on smaller incomes than the first group. I call them the 'creative alternatives' group. They express responsibility for creating the kinds of lives they want, and satisfaction with modest houses, cars, furnishing and clothes. Many of them have savings, however small, which provide a cushion for emergencies. They are very reluctant to borrow money, except for a small mortgage. They speak of prioritising their happiness and wellbeing and those of their children. In short, they express criticism of consumerist values and support for the belief that the most important things in life are relationships and the time for friends, family and personal development. These couples are all very different from each other. Some are quite traditional in their approach to gender roles, the women staying at home to do childcare, while the man earns the income. In other cases, both partners have cut back on paid work, in order to look after a baby. One couple, who have no children, job share and devote time to voluntary work.

Balancing Your Life

The emergence of the creative alternatives group in the *How Was It For You?* study prompted me to find more people who had actively taken steps to prioritise quality of life and to pursue alternative routes to happiness, thereby challenging mainstream instrumental values. I collected data from people who are single, partnered, at different life stages, with and without children, rural, provincial and urban, for a book called *Balancing Your Life*.[5]

Some of the people who feature in *Balancing Your Life* have recently downshifted from pressurised jobs but several others chose their lifestyles well before the boom of the 1990s. The latter show that the search for quality of life and a critical attitude to a work–earn–spend culture are not necessarily short-lived phenomena. Some are living on very small incomes but they have also reduced outgoings and avoided debt. They all express a sense of responsibility for their own lives and a lack of reliance on institutions and leaders. They have experimented with the variables of paid work and unpaid work until they have found what is right for them. They speak of wanting enough money, and more of the things money cannot buy: health, happiness, love and peace of mind. They all express a sense of control of their lives, although they are not rigid in their expectations of how their lives should be. They mirror the assertion that, in most circumstances, believing that one is in control of one's fate is closely associated with happiness and satisfaction with one's life.[6]

The creative alternatives

The individual stories from both studies are all very different but those pursuing creative alternatives have some things in common: they have given time to deciding their priorities, questioned the consumerist orientation of contemporary Ireland, and challenged norms and taken-for-granted ways of living and doing things and understanding the world around them. They are sceptical but not cynical. While many of them possess little material capital, they do possess cultural and human capital, that is, a variety of options provided by education, experience or background. Many have ambitions, goals or strong passions concerning life work, rather than career, and they have their own measures of success in relation to them. They also have an ability to live with complexity, uncertainty and ambiguity. For many of the downshifters, some recent turning point inspired them to turn away from consumerist culture and working long hours at jobs. The long-timers have questioned the dominant wisdom concerning money, work and possessions since their young adulthood.

Discourses and subjectivities

The preceding overview of the research themes provides the context for discussing the discourses on which the participants draw. The TINA group draws largely on mainstream discourses of progress, economic growth and consumerism, which serve to construct self-regulating subjects who experience a lack of agency, that is, the ability to effect change in their lives and in society. The creative alternatives group draws on discourses critical of the mainstream, which promote the concepts of limits, priorities and *enough*. These critical discourses are often associated with agency, because they encourage people to take action, however small, to effect the changes they want to see.

A discourse is not a language or a text but a historically, socially and institutionally specific structure of statements, categories and beliefs, habits and practices.[7] Discourses are used to filter and interpret experience and the discourses available at a certain historical moment frame the ways that people can think or talk about, or respond to, phenomena. They 'invite' us to be human in certain ways, or to respond to others in certain ways. They produce certain assumptions (about, for example, women, men, economics, work, childcare or money) and they provide subjects with positions and emotional attachments from which people speak and act.[8]

Discourse, language and visual imagery do not simply reflect or describe reality. They play an integral role in constructing reality and experience, in the ways that we know and understand the world, and in what we assume to be natural or normal. Discourse analysis can tell us a great deal about how social forces influence what individuals do, say and think. Research that uses discourse as its analytical tool concentrates on the accounts, understandings and meaning repertoires of the participants, rather than on their individual psychologies. It examines how their interpretation of their experiences is affected, constrained or enabled by the discursive resources available to them. In this way, it avoids any tendency to judge individual participants and, at the same time, it concentrates on the social and historical content of subjectivity, that is, the sense of oneself, including ideas, beliefs and emotions. Subjectivity is 'the conscious and unconscious thoughts and emotions of the individual, her sense of herself and her ways of understanding her relation to the world'.[9] It is a three-way process concerning discourse, emotional responses and relations in the present moment, all existing in a dynamic, mutually productive relationship with each other.[10]

Both 'reality' and 'critical' discourses emerge in the accounts of every-day life offered by the research participants.[11] The reality discourses include discourses of reality versus quality, lack of choice, work as constraint, job equals life and a work/life split. Critical discourses include limits, mindful spending and life work. In the discussion of the discourses that follows, the following questions are addressed:

1 What is the central premise of each discourse?
2 With what themes is it associated?
3 How does it operate?
4 What conditions facilitate its operation?
5 What discourses does it complement, and what discourses does it oppose?

Reality discourses

Many TINA accounts employ a fatalistic discourse that generates assumptions such as 'that's progress' or 'that's reality, there's nothing that can be done about it' to explain experience, including work patterns and spending habits. In turn, these discourses allow participants to blame other people and outside forces for their dissatisfactions and distress.

The 'reality' discourses have the effect of making people feel trapped in a cycle of earning, working, spending, consuming and meeting financial commitments, including the servicing of debts. They include a discourse that emphasises lack of control, and that makes people feel they cannot get out of this cycle and have few options for challenging excessive spending or critically examining possessions. Because they foster the idea that people should borrow, and possibly stretch themselves to pay for the most they can afford in terms of house, car, wardrobe and other possessions, these discourses have the effect of making paid work the central feature of life, around which all other life considerations need to revolve. As people try to fit other aspects of life – such as relationships, children and personal development – around work, they often feel stretched to the limit all the time, an experience that has been described as 'overload syndrome'.[12]

New essentials and defensive spending

The discourse of 'new essentials' hinges on the premise that the costly trappings of contemporary living are necessary. Within this discourse, couples are assumed to need two full incomes simply to make ends meet. House prices and the need for a range of essentials, from the latest in mobile phones to bottled water, are cited as justification for living beyond one's means, or just breaking even each month. In turn, this discourse facilitates short-term financial thinking, borrowing and credit, and precludes the idea of doing without, living within one's means or building up savings. An emphasis on income rather than net worth or assets also facilitates a certain puzzlement about where all the money goes.

Some reality accounts also assert that, because one cannot avoid spending money in contemporary life, one must be organised, so that credit card and other debt does not get out of control. Significant by its absence in these discussions is any consideration of whether the purchases are themselves necessary. Reality discourses also facilitate the idea that women and men have naturally different consumer needs, especially the notion that women need more 'retail therapy' than men.[13] In this, they also draw on essentialist discourses that portray gender difference as normal and natural.

A discourse of 'defensive spending' complements the discourse of new essentials. It centres on the premise that people must spend in order to keep abreast of their contemporaries. Gift buying, especially at Christmas, is seen as a way of remaining on a par with friends and relations who buy expensive gifts. Resentment of this practice is common, but it is seen as inescapable, because of the expectations of others. Several participants give accounts of family cultures of buying expensive gifts. Anybody who resists this practice, even by questioning it, is considered petty. The discourse of coping – that is, of planning ahead for future spending, even to the extent of taking on extra paid work to 'cover Christmas', and being organised about paying off any credit card debt – is used as the best way to deal with this culture.

The discourse of defensive spending is particularly strong in relation to children and supports the idea that they need the 'right' clothes so that they will not be conspicuous at school and in social situations. It also supports assertions that without apparent essentials such as computers and fee-paying schools, young people will be left behind in the job and education markets. This discourse is also associated with a practice of parents buying things for their children in order to compensate for the fact that they spend long periods of time apart, while parents are at work.

New essentials discourses also support the creation of self-esteem and self-assertion by means of possessions. They have the effect of conflating self and possessions, which makes it difficult for people to distinguish between want and need. They preclude the possibility that self-esteem may be more durable if it is the product of self-reflection and a critical examination of one's needs, rather than consumption-oriented desires.

Work

In many accounts, work emerges as something that provides a sense of self-worth and importance, as a source of friends and social interaction, as helping individuals to develop their talents and aptitudes and as a provider of security. However, reality discourses portray work only as paid employment, or jobs, and do not recognise that unpaid work can also provide these satisfactions.

These discourses also support the idea that there is a hierarchy of types of work. There is the stimulating, high-status work associated with 'career', which provides identity and companionship and a good income. And there are the low-paid, low-status, dead-end jobs that nobody really wants to do, but for which money is seen to be some compensation.

On the other hand, because home life can be complicated, time consuming and unpredictable, and the relationships there often require a lot of attention, these discourses also support a reading of the world of paid work as a respite from home. Paid work becomes so closely identified with 'life work' or career, for many people, that the roles involved in it take precedence over all the other roles that people take on. Then, they find it difficult to fit all those other roles into their schedules.

The reality discourses concerning work also divide life itself into job and leisure, or work time and 'time off'. At the same time, accounts recognise that the emphasis placed on paid work has meant less time for interpersonal relationships outside the job and that, as a consequence, many social structures are weak, leisure is often lonely and boring, and social and personal health can suffer.

The reality discourses surrounding paid work also see jobs as the means by which people are socially included and good citizens, and so ignore the fact that many people in high-status, high-paid jobs do not have the time or inclination to do the caring work that builds a strong civil society. They are also inadequate for addressing the fact that the low paid or those in dead-end jobs are not necessarily genuinely socially included simply by virtue of being employed.

Blame, lack of control and gender

The discourses of 'blame' and 'lack of control' can have the effect of ruling out part-time working, taking career breaks or considering freelance work. A lifestyle where paid work is central leaves little time for personal reflection and development, or for family, relationship, community or voluntary work. The idea that couples need two full incomes precludes creative approaches to having and caring for children. The perceived need for two full incomes also makes childcare a consumer issue, because the only perceived option is for both partners to continue working full-time and to pay for childcare.

The assumptions surrounding these choices are further complicated by a discourse of gender difference, which operates on the assumption that having children is an issue more pertinent to women than to men.

This has several effects. It means that women are constrained by the idea that they must 'do' career and children in the correct order. That is, they believe that they need to make career progress before having children. It rules out the possibility of men being active parents and taking responsibility for childcare, thus possibly freeing women to concentrate on career for a while. It also precludes the most creative and potentially sustainable solution, which is for women and men to construct peer relationships, where both work fewer hours and both actively participate in childcare and other domestic work.[14]

A self-regulating subject

People experiencing the dilemmas of overload, consumerism, time poverty and essentialist conceptions of gender can reflect on these issues only according to the ideas that they already have. In more abstract terms, they can draw only on the discourses that are available to them. These tend to be the dominant or 'normal' discourses, which are taken for granted as 'the way things are', as common sense. Therefore, many people do not have access to discourses that could facilitate solutions beyond the obvious. The problem is also compounded by the fact that they are so busy working that they do not have time to think beyond the obvious and beyond what is considered normal.

Consumerist 'new essentials' discourses, the dominant discourses of work and the work–earn–spend culture, all help to blind the human subject to the possibilities for alternatives to how society is currently organised. The type of subjectivity that emerges tends to see money and technology as the solutions to life's challenges and dissatisfactions.

Normality

The mindfulness and conscious choice associated with the limits group of discourses are in direct contrast to the way people often unconsciously 'buy in' to consumerist discourses. They may become sucked into a cycle of borrowing and credit, which seems entirely normal, because it is what most people are doing, before they have had the opportunity to reflect critically on these issues.

'Normality' is both a useful and a dangerous discourse. It can be useful for people to know that their experience is similar to that of other people. But it can be dangerous if statistical normality – for example, in the idea that it is normal to need the new essentials, for couples to need two full incomes, or to experience overload syndrome – precludes questioning the situation or considering alternatives. The 'normality' of the work–earn–spend cycle can have the effect of making people believe that no alternatives exist. A discourse of normality can also be used as the justification for adhering to a belief in essential gender differences, for justifying separate spheres of responsibility for women and men, and for the assumption that women and men have fundamentally different communication styles and emotional needs. Then, if individuals experience contradictions or dissatisfaction with these divisions, they have the added problem of feeling that they are not normal.

Critical discourses

The second main group of discourses is critical in the sense that it questions the taken-for-granted assumptions of the dominant or mainstream culture of work–earn–spend. The central premises of the critical discourses revolve around a questioning attitude to money, credit, spending and possessions, and they depend to some extent on self-knowledge and a prioritising of needs.

Limits

A strong premise within the critical discourses is the idea that personal limits exist. Other critical concepts associated with the discourse of limits are frugality, thoughtful spending, responsibility and 'less is more'.

A discourse of limits emerges in research accounts of everyday life concerning material possessions, money, work, success, achievement, priorities and business. Its central assertion is that, if people understand what is enough, they can be fulfilled and happy, in control of their lives and not at the mercy of forces that tell them they must always have more and spend more in order to be more. This discourse distinguishes between wants and needs, and judges goods and services according to their functionality.

The effect of the discourses grouped under the discourse of limits is to give people a sense of responsibility and of the ability to shape their lives, whereby they avoid feeling buffeted by forces outside their control. In other words, individuals can achieve a measure of agency. Agency exists when people have resources for controlling their life choices, even to the extent that they feel able to cope with individual crises, such as redundancy, or more widespread difficulties, such as high house prices or an economic recession.

The discourses centred on the premise of limits cannot be considered in isolation from the reality discourses, because they often are developed in opposition to them. Furthermore, the reality discourses frequently provide resources for undermining the idea of limits, because they mesh powerfully with dominant ideas of what is normal, or common sense, or 'just the way things are'. Thus, the reality discourses have strong explanatory power when people reflect on their lives. Those who take up positions in oppositional discourses of any kind cannot ignore the dominant discourses. Oppositional discourses, such as a limits discourse, are constantly vying with the dominant discourses and trying to undermine them, but they but have less explanatory power.

Limits discourses are much more likely to be *consciously* adopted than are the reality discourses. For some, their adoption may result from a critical examination of their financial situation and a decision to get it under control. For others, it may result from the decision to prioritise family life and childcare by parents, ahead of income, promotion or career development. For yet others, it may arise from efforts to deal with role and work overload.

Whatever the motivation, the result is a challenge to some of the most basic mainstream assumptions. For example, limits discourses question the contemporary assumption that two full incomes are always necessary for couples to make ends meet. They question the need for the range of possessions that are portrayed as necessities in Irish society today. They are a direct challenge to a culture of credit and borrowing, because they promote the value of living below one's means, instead of just within them or beyond them, and of having a savings cushion in the event of a crisis.

Work

Work, in the accounts drawing on critical discourses, is more than a job. Within this group of discourses, work is anything that gives satisfaction, recognition or personal growth, or that contributes to the wellbeing of others, or to the welfare of the planet. Critical discourses do not support the mainstream discourses' distinction between 'work' and 'life'. They introduce the idea of life work, which can include paid work, but not as a given. Some of the types of life work encountered among these discourses are learning, activism, art, spirituality, friendship, family, parenting, caring and entrepreneurial and community work.

Accounts drawing on critical discourses of work emphasise the ways that time poverty, stress and the centrality of paid work or lack of it do not sustain human happiness. They are critical of the single-mindedness that is encouraged in pursuit of career success, especially of the ways that such single-mindedness can lead people to compartmentalise their lives and deny the ways that the different sections are connected to the whole, and to other people.

A discourse of visible versus invisible work also emerges. It asserts that the predominant economic model portrays paid work as the only work that contributes to wellbeing. Accounts drawing on critical discourses of work emphasise the importance of work traditionally considered not to contribute to the economy. They emphasise how many activities essential for human happiness are not officially counted as part of the economy.

People who do not have jobs, do not participate in business or do not accumulate money, including children, retired people, old people, the unemployed, carers in the home and volunteer workers, are economically invisible. In this sense, these discourses are critical of conventional economic indices of wellbeing. They also contribute to the feminist assertion that housework and caring work are important and relevant to both sexes.

Critical subjectivities

Discourses represent political interests and, in consequence, are constantly vying for status and power in the subjectivity of the individual. In themselves, they are a component of subjectivity and affect the choices that individuals make and, ultimately, affect their relationships and the communities that they live in. This is not to suggest that it is always easy to resist social pressures and dominant discourses. One may have an emotional investment in a discourse because it gives meaning to one's world and oneself. But it is to suggest that people often have more options than they think they have. Nor is it to suggest that discourse is the sole route to social change, but rather to assert that the discursive and the subjective are often overlooked in discussions of social change.

Living with a consciously chosen discourse of limits can result in the assertion that less is more. It can also have the outcome of critical reflection on the self and on unacknowledged emotional attachments to consumerism, success or the creation of identity by means of job or possessions. This process, if adequately supported and given access to radical discourses of the self, has the potential to support the construction of critical and politicised subjectivities.[15]

The process of constructing a critical self, at variance with mainstream regulatory discourses, also necessitates communication with one's intimates. Decisions based on quality-of-life priorities have to be negotiated and constantly revisited. The individual lives in interdependent systems with other people. Therefore, beliefs, attitudes and priorities, and the emotional responses that accompany a questioning approach to life, need to be constant topics for discussion. Adults in a household or community (and children, when they are old enough to participate in discussions) have to know themselves and each other, and constantly reflect and negotiate. Thus the potential exists for a limits discourse to create the conditions whereby the whole system, or the community, can be taken into account, along with the individual.

Gender

Both reality and critical discourses are prey to gender-difference discourses. This demonstrates the all-pervasiveness of gender as a factor shaping contemporary social relations. The potential for women and men to be radical about gender roles can be lost if discourses of limits, adopted in the search for quality of life, are assumed to mean a return to a traditional past, where women looked after the home and men worked in the formal paid economy. This may be the case if individuals draw on discourses of essential gender difference and equity, as distinct from equality. The assumption that there are separate spheres of skill and responsibility for women and men rules out men's involvement in childcare, and the associated pleasures and satisfactions, as well as difficulties. It also precludes women's self-development by means of participation in the paid workforce. Further, it means that each sex may have little appreciation of the difficulties of the work of the other. Since most women have been part of the paid workforce at some time, it is more likely that a 'separate spheres' arrangement will mean that men have little appreciation of the work of running a home. Ultimately, both women and men are disadvantaged by assumptions of gender differences and have more to gain from questioning them.[16]

The bigger picture

As people seek quality of life, it becomes clear that none of their problems or choices exists in isolation. Global politics and economics are connected to harried lifestyles, difficulties with money and debt, a deteriorating environment, the growth of conspicuous and competitive spending, and the lack of control over their lives that many Irish citizens experience today.

The mainstream view of politics is narrow, seeing it as a pursuit of power, centred on political parties and pressure groups. But there are other ways of looking at politics, which see that both individuals and society are connected at a deep level, and that economic decisions and social relations exist together in a dynamic relationship. Economics is a key aspect of politics – to have people economically unaware is to undermine democracy, participation, human connectedness, happiness and citizenship. The way that an economy is organised is a political decision.

The conventional economic thinking that dominates in the Republic of Ireland and in most western countries understands the economy as the visible economy – businesses, buying and selling of goods and services, paid work and money making. This visible economy is seen as the primary source of society's wealth and wellbeing, and depends on the concept of economic growth. Growth is concerned with raising productivity, increasing competitiveness, developing new markets, increasing employment, stimulating investment and encouraging consumer confidence so that people spend more. Barbara Brandt[17] says that this thinking promotes a very narrow view of the economy, as purely the activities of the investment community. It also promotes the idea that economic growth should take precedence over all other considerations and that the rest of life – people in their homes, families, communities, unpaid work, government, education, art, culture, religion and spirituality – is dependent on the visible economy. It is assumed that economic growth will bring about progress for everybody, usually understood as individual betterment and material enrichment, without taking into account other systems, such as family, social cohesion, the environment, or fragile ecosystems.

Many alternative economists and systems thinkers, such as Hazel Henderson, Herman Daly, Richard Douthwaite and Barbara Brandt,[18] argue that growth may actually make us poorer, because environmental and social costs mount faster than production benefits. Most conventional economists acknowledge the existence of ecological/environmental costs but assume that they will be sorted out by technology. In practice, they ignore social costs, because they are not easily measured. Robert E. Lane's research[19] shows that, after a certain point, increasing wealth does not bring increasing happiness. In fact, living in an age of wealth and in a high-tech economy is the cause of extreme stress. People may become rich in material possessions but poor in time. High earnings and consumption serve purposes that go way beyond meeting needs – they bestow self-esteem, status and identity. In the past, this effect was often confined to men, but now it is available to women also, and this is often portrayed as gender equality.

The world's high- and middle-income groups are those caught up to the greatest extent in the work–earn–spend cycle. They have the most consumer power but exist in a world where half the population has never made a telephone call. The consumer class is concentrated in the highly industrialised regions and its way of life is depleting the world's raw materials, yet its affluence exists in the midst of poverty. And this consumer class is also setting a standard to which many less affluent people aspire.

Consumption patterns like these are also responsible for class inequalities. With increasing consumption, lower-income children and adults are left behind in the market, and the gap between the affluent and the poor becomes unbridgeable. This results in gated communities trying to protect themselves from the poor outside. And as the pressures on private spending grow, support for taxes and public spending goes down. Public goods and facilities get little support, which causes them to deteriorate or even to cease to be available, and this adds to the pressures to spend privately.[20]

In one sense, it is a highly elitist suggestion that already privileged people give up high-powered jobs, and the high-consumption lifestyles that go with them, in order to create a better life for themselves. But in another sense, it would be an enormous change if the consumer class developed awareness of these issues and began living with purpose, clarifying their priorities, consuming only what they need, avoiding meaningless jobs, and devoting time to their families, relationships and communities.[21] Such a change could create the conditions for understanding that economics is relevant to everybody and that the ways that the economy is organised is a political decision.

Citizens worry about the over-materialistic values being transmitted to children, the downsizing of companies in the name of efficiency, the destruction of the natural environment, the long working and commuting times often demanded to keep the economy growing, and the consequent lack of time for self and relationships. The dominant reality discourses tell them there is no alternative if we are to survive in the competitive global economy. Indeed, Richard Douthwaite points out[22] that that is largely true. Because of the ways that many countries, including Ireland, are locked into trade agreements, governments have little choice about how the economy is run. Because of global trade agreements, governments are required to run their countries in very specific ways. If they do not, international investors will cause a financial crisis by shifting their funds elsewhere.

Within the present political and economic system, then, there is little choice. Democracy in growth economies, which include Ireland, has been undermined by the extreme wealth owned by global corporations. But the system cannot continue indefinitely, because it depends on and is depleting natural and finite resources, such as oil and gas. It also has personal, psychological and social consequences which many people consider unacceptable.

Effects on spiritual and intellectual development

Many – especially older – people often wonder why some people are unhappy in their lifestyles and paid work. They are not prepared to shed too many tears for a high-earning younger generation whose main problems seem to be time poverty and job stress. However, growth economics has had considerable effects on society and the world of paid work has changed in recent years. Brian Thorne points out that we are being taught that life means 'endless toil and competition, the pursuit of ever-greater achievement, the race for material affluence'.[23] Policies directed at achieving greater efficiency and competition at ever lower costs have created a 'culture of contempt' that permeates the way we treat each other in the marketplace. Many people lack time to stop and think, to question the dominant discourses and to engage in intellectual debate and educational activities that develop alternatives. And while some suffer from time poverty, others suffer from involuntary material poverty, which is degrading to the human spirit because of the helplessness, despair and passivity it generates.

The World Health Organisation predicts that by 2010 depression will be the second most common disease in the developed world.[24] Mild chronic depression is often caused by a lack of meaning or a sense of purpose in life. Time poverty, stress and lives dominated by paid work or the lack of it do not sustain human character, spirit or happiness. Richard Sennett defines character as the part of the person that concerns long-term emotional experience, loyalty and commitment to others. The short-term nature of our economic life and the consequent demands of much paid work today can set inner, emotional lives adrift, he says, and with them the sense of self that supports us over time.[25] This growth-oriented way of thinking and being has seeped into our minds and damaged our ability to experience pleasure in simple things, to prioritise health and happiness. It has also 'dumbed down' discussions in the mainstream media about the problems we face.

The growth economics of late modern capitalism needs human subjects who do not question the dominant discourses, but who compartmentalise their lives and deny the ways that the different sections are connected to the whole, and to other people. We are encouraged to ask the question 'Who needs me?' only in relation to our paid work, points out Sennett. In addition, home and the relationships centred on the home are messy and uncontrollable, but work relationships are frequently ordered and predictable. As a result, many people prefer to spend their time at their job and to pay other people to do the messy caring and domestic work. Employment also offers subjects a structure for their time. Many fear the reality of what they would do with their time if they did not have a job to go to for five or six days a week.

One does not have to believe in gods or religions to accept the importance of spirituality. It is also connected to the concept of soul, which Charles Handy, an atheist, defines as that which is best in oneself.[26] It is impossible to be truly human on one's own. Spirituality can be seen as a consciousness of the collective and of the connections between humans and the natural environment. Brian Thorne describes it thus:

> The individual's spirit or spiritual dimension is his or her creative source of energy, which reflects the moving force within the universe itself. In other words, it is because I am essentially a spiritual being that I am, whether I know it or not or whether I like it or not, indissolubly linked to all that is or has been or will be. I am not an isolated entity but rather a unique part of the whole created order.[27]

Dominant economic discourses, which demand compartmentalisation and short-term thinking, have serious detrimental effects on the human spirit and on the capacity to engage in critical thinking. Such thinking is based on the questioning of received wisdom and assumptions and on a quest for alternative kinds of knowledge about how to live.

Promoting discourses of limits: creating the conditions for critical thinking

Limits discourses, at the very least, create the conditions for critical thinking about the bigger picture and the longer term. If we slow the treadmill of paid work and promote a discourse of 'enough' concerning money and possessions, we can create conditions where the 'public dialogue' is questioning and critical.[28] Reality or 'no alternative' discourses, and the consumerist practices associated with them, are inherently short term, and over-immersion in them precludes critical thinking. They support simplistic media discussions about economics, human experience and social life, and foster a politically illiterate and self-regulating citizenry. People experiencing overload have little time to think critically. They may (and most do) experience contradictions, because the discourses available are inadequate to explain all of their experiences. But they have few resources for acting on the insights that contradictions can initiate. Below, I outline some of the possibilities created by a discourse of limits.[29]

Shopping as an expression of knowledge

Through our spending, we vote, in effect, for the continuation of the dominant economic discourses. If we want alternatives, consuming less and consuming critically are part of what is required.

By consuming less, we use fewer resources. And the good news is that if we consume less, we need less money, we need to do less paid work, we have more time and we can balance our personal lives. We can also be more active citizens when we have more time. We can become involved in voluntary work and other projects that contribute to human relations. We have the time to consume wisely, by seeking out local sources for goods and services, rather than buying from large corporations. Shopping (or not) is an expression of political and economic knowledge and commitment.

We can also support other local economic initiatives, such as those described by Richard Douthwaite.[30] Many of these initiatives have the characteristics of mindful markets, as outlined by David Korten. Korten argues that alternative economics is not against markets, but it is opposed to the free movement of capital around the globe and to the constant pressure to produce more, without regard for the social and environmental consequences. Mindful markets, he writes, use life rather than money as the standard for evaluating economic choices and performance.

The full costs – environmental, human and social – of business decisions are met by those who make the decisions. Such markets favour human-scale, local-ownership businesses; they strive for full disclosure of information and are regulated to avoid extremes of wealth and poverty, since a viable democratic society needs a ceiling and a floor with regard to the distribution of wealth and assets. They also encourage the sharing of knowledge and technology, and are self-reliant and diverse. Communities have the ability to manage their borders so that cross-border trade and capital flows are not all in one direction. Finally, mindful markets are ethical, with clear and enforceable rules, subject to due legal process.[31]

Challenging economic invisibility

We need to recognise that the work that is done for free is an important contribution to society and the economy. We need to challenge the split between paid and unpaid work, to value the contribution of volunteers, carers, retired people and children.

As part of the initiative to challenge economic invisibility, women and men need to develop egalitarian relationships, where both contribute to the visible and the invisible economy. Both in the workplace and in the home, men need to identify more as fathers, carers and performers of domestic work, and to recognise that their interests coincide with those of women. Studies of couples who have actively and successfully sought to create equality in their relationships indicate that both women and men need to examine their understanding of work, career and success and personal limits.[32]

Pursuing a sense of connection along with personal development

Both individuality and connectedness are important in challenging the dominant economic and social paradigm. The physicist and philosopher Fritjof Capra has observed that, through self-assertion, the individual maintains diversity and energy, which are essential to the creative potential of the whole. Combining individuality with integration into a group or collectivity makes for a healthy system.[33] Modern ways of living emphasise individualism and compartmentalisation. Individuality is different from individualism, and a sense of connectedness is not the same as being bound by cultural norms. In broadening the sense of our connection to other people and to the world, and by developing our self-reflective consciousness, we can become happier individuals, as well as agents of change in our worlds, local and global.

Conclusions

Discourses and the practices associated with them are not static. They constantly shift and change according to circumstances of time and place. Central to critical thinking is the question of who benefits from a particular discourse and who is disadvantaged by it. Some discourses are so dominant that they appear natural and normal but they are not simply authored by people and forces 'out there'. Everybody participates in constructing, maintaining, challenging and changing them. People can be agents of change. The first step in becoming an agent of change in one's own life can be a questioning of the discourses that are dominant within contemporary society, and an examination of the benefits and disadvantages associated with them. When people take responsibility for their life choices, and acknowledge the contradictions, frustrations and complex emotions that they may feel, they are better placed to contribute productively to creative social change.

Notes

1 Europay International, survey, August 2001, cited in the *Irish Times*, 28 September 2001.
2 *The Sunday Show*, RTÉ Radio One, 1 September 2002, was the most recent example at the time of writing.
3 P. H. Ray and S. R. Anderson, *The Cultural Creatives* (New York: Harmony Books, 2000).
4 A. B. Ryan, *How Was It For You? Exploring Couples' Experiences of the First Year of Marriage* (Dublin: ACCORD and Department of Social, Community and Family Affairs, 2001).
5 A. B. Ryan, *Balancing Your Life: A Guide to Work, Time, Money and Happiness* (Dublin: Liffey Press, 2002).
6 R. E. Lane, *The Loss of Happiness in Market Democracies* (New Haven: Yale University Press, 2000).
7 M. Foucault, *The Archaeology of Knowledge* (New York: Pantheon, 1972), *Histoire de la folie* (Paris: Gallimard, 1972), *Birth of the Clinic* (London: Tavistock, 1973), *Power/Knowledge: Selected Interviews and Other Writings 1972–1977* (New York: Pantheon, 1980).
8 E. Burman, *Deconstructing Developmental Psychology* (London: Routledge, 1994).
9 C. Weedon, *Feminist Practice and Poststructuralist Theory* (Oxford: Blackwell, 1997), p. 32.
10 A. B. Ryan, *Feminist Ways of Knowing: Towards Theorising the Person for Radical Adult Education* (Leicester: NIACE, 2001).
11 The process of discourse analysis involves detailed examination of large chunks of text, in this case the transcripts from interviews and focus groups, and the presentation of textual evidence for every comment and conclusion made by the researcher. To present the textual evidence for the various discourses discussed in this chapter would take up many pages. Short extracts from accounts do not demonstrate the complexity of discourse,

and the ways that several different discourses (possibly contradictory) can be drawn on by one person in the course of a single conversation or discussion. Added to this, many of the participants in the *How Was It For You?* study took part on condition that their accounts were made available to personnel from the commissioning organisation only. For these reasons, I have decided to use no quotes from participants and to concentrate on commenting on the discourses that emerged from both studies, having first described them briefly. In my book *Balancing Your Life*, several participants in the second study are quoted at length. However, discourse analysis of their accounts is not included there, as the book is for a general readership.

12 R. A. Swenson, *The Overload Syndrome: Learning to Live Within Your Limits* (Colorado Springs: Navpress, 1998).

13 'Retail therapy' refers to the idea that shopping can help people feel better, if, for example, work is taxing or boring.

14 B. Purcell, *For Our Own Good: Childcare Issues in Ireland* (Cork: Collins Press, 2001).

15 Ryan, *Feminist Ways of Knowing*.

16 J. H. Bray and E. N. Jouriles, 'Treatment of marital conflict and prevention of divorce', *Journal of Marital and Family Therapy*, 12:4 (1995), pp. 461–73; M. S. Kimmel and M. A. Messner, *Men's Lives* (Boston: Allyn and Bacon, 2001); J. Van Every, *Heterosexual Women Changing the Family: Refusing to be a 'Wife'!* (London: Taylor and Francis, 1995).

17 B. Brandt, *Whole Life Economics: Revaluing Daily Life* (Philadelphia: New Society Publishers, 1995).

18 B. Brandt, *Whole Life Economics*; R. Douthwaite, *The Growth Illusion: How Economic Growth Has Enriched the Few, Impoverished the Many, and Endangered the Planet* (2nd edn) (Dublin: Lilliput Press, in association with New Society Publishers and Green Books, 2000); H. Daly, *Steady-State Economics* (2nd edn) (London: Earthscan, 1991); H. Henderson, *Beyond Globalization: Shaping a Sustainable Global Economy* (West Hartford, CT: Kumarian Press, 1999).

19 R. E. Lane, *The Loss of Happiness in Market Democracies* (New Haven: Yale University Press, 2000).

20 N. Schor, *The Overspent American: Upscaling, Downshifting and the New Consumer* (New York: Basic Books, 1998).

21 D. Korten, *The Post-corporate World: Life After Capitalism* (San Francisco: Berrett-Koehler, 1998), p. 222.

22 R. Douthwaite, 'The growth illusion', in H. Bohan and G. Kennedy (eds), *Working Towards Balance: Our Society in the New Millennium* (Dublin: Veritas, 2000).

23 B. Thorne, *The Secular and the Holy: Person Centered Counselling and Christian Spirituality* (London: Whurr Publishers, 1998).

24 R. Sennett, *The Corrosion of Character: The Personal Consequences of Work in the New Capitalism* (New York: W. W. Norton, 1999).

25 *Ibid.*

26 C. Handy, *The Hungry Spirit* (London: Arrow, 1997).

27 Thorne, *The Secular and the Holy*, p. 78.

28 'Bryony L. Hoskins in conversation with Susan Brownmiller', *Feminism and Psychology*, 11:4 (2002), p. 550.

29 In the following paragraphs, I deliberately use the word 'we', described as 'the dangerous pronoun' by Richard Sennett, in *The Corrosion of Character*. I use it to reinforce my assertion that these are issues of concern to everybody, not just abstract ideas.

30 R. Douthwaite, *Short Circuit: Strengthening Local Economies for Security in an Unstable World* (Dublin: Lilliput Press, 1996, second edition forthcoming on Feasta website, www.feasta.org).

31 Korten, *The Post-corporate World*.

32 A. R. Hochschild, *The Second Shift* (London: Piatkus, 1990); B. Purcell, *For Our Own Good: Childcare Issues in Ireland* (Cork: Collins Press, 2001).

33 F. Capra, *The Web of Life: A New Scientific Understanding of Living Systems* (New York: Anchor Books, 1996), p. 4.

10

The centralised government of liquidity: community, language and culture under the Celtic Tiger

STEVE COLEMAN

The privatisation of Telecom Éireann in June 1999 came at the high-water mark of Ireland's 'Celtic Tiger' phase. About 600,000 Irish citizens bought shares in the state-owned company, which promptly changed its name to Eircom. For most buyers, it was their first experience of stock ownership.[1]

In the television advertisement campaign for the share offer, we saw singers in locations all over Ireland sing verses from the traditional Irish-language song *Dúlamán*. This was followed by shots of people dancing in costumes in the style of Macnas – the Galway-based group which specialises in spectacular street theatre, originally inspired by the Catalan radical theatre company Els Comediants. Then, some fine print appeared about the terms of the share offer and, at the very end, we saw a shot of people approaching a bonfire somewhere in the mountains, carrying burning torches. Other bonfires were visible in the distance. This last image carried an oddly inverted echo of the traditional customs of St John's Eve, *Oíche Shin Sheáin* (23 July), in which bonfires would be lit on heights. Children would ignite wads of paraffin-soaked rags in the fire and throw them like flaming missiles into the air. *Fóid choise* or 'travelling sods' of turf were taken from the fires and hurled at animals and into fields, and placed in family hearths – using 'other world' power to ensure the fertility of individual hearths in the coming harvest.[2] The advertisement, though, ran this ritual backwards – people brought fire *to* the central fire. It was as if this Telecom flotation ritual siphoned off goodness from individual hearths, creating an all too worldly power – a multinational corporation.

Here, the state was selling back to its people something that already belonged to them – a semi-state company – but it was also selling back to them a particular sense of their own 'traditions'. Throughout Irish history, relatively localised cultural forms have been appropriated as emblems of wider collectivities. In the process of Irish nation building, forms

175

of popular expression which originated in the relatively autochthonous culture of local rural communities following the breakup of the Gaelic feudal order were translated to the national sphere as emblems of the ethnic nation state.[3] Symbols of what is typically imagined as a rural, 'traditional', egalitarian past were presented as the common essence of what was an increasingly urban, industrialised and class-stratified populace. The Telecom advertisement gave this process a 1990s twist by including urban scenes, such as the ruins of the gasworks in Ringsend, as back-drops for the traditional singers – a reflection of the new-found visibility of Irish in 'Celtic Tiger' Dublin.

This use of the Irish language and 'traditional' culture in a sophisti-cated media campaign[4] for an event of historic sociopolitical significance seemed to highlight the new enhanced position and prestige of language and tradition in the Ireland of the 1990s. The advertisement's style was reminiscent of cultural extravaganzas like the Irish-themed dance show *Riverdance*, or festive theatre companies like Macnas, and new loci of culture, such as the Galway Arts Festival and Dublin's Temple Bar. Media pundits proclaimed in the 1990s that 'we're not ashamed to be [or to speak?] Irish anymore'. They could point to the new fashionableness of Irish-medium education (Gaelscoileanna), clubs like Dublin's Club Sult, and the new Irish-language television channel, Teilifís na Gaeilge (T. na G., later renamed TG4). Many of these new forms and channels of expression displayed a cultural and linguistic hybridity which seemed to transcend the narrow confines of an obsessively purist nationalist culture. There were suggestions that, having reached an Irish version of Fukuyama's 'end of history',[5] material affluence would enable the recovery of the Irish language and traditions and the overcoming of the dichotomies between past and present, rural and urban culture, and between Irish and world culture. Was the curse of the Famine finally over?

I would like to propose a more complex interpretation of these events, grounded in what Hardt and Negri identify as 'a dynamic within modernity', between the sociocultural expression of immanent community and its reappropriation on a transcendent plane:

> *Modernity itself is defined by crisis*, a crisis that is born of the un-interrupted conflict between the immanent, constructive, creative forces and the transcendent power aimed at restoring order.[6]

Hardt and Negri suggest that all cultural forms in modernity have this dual aspect, a duality that is especially evident in Irish-language culture. Since the seventeenth century,[7] the Irish language has stood for, and has been variously celebrated or reviled as, the expression of the (real or imagined) Irish 'multitude'. At the same time, it has served as a powerful symbol of the potential 'imagined community' of the nation state. Irish-language culture thus embodies all the tensions and contradictions historically pertaining to relationships between community, nation and state.

The Irish state has followed patterns typical of nineteenth- and twentieth-century nation building, in that it has sought to establish a unity of geographic space, language and ethnic culture. But Ireland has been caught in the webs of colonial and neo-colonial domination, first by Britain and latterly by processes of global capital. These regimes have enforced cultural and ethnic hybridity (through conquest and the movement of labour power) as well as extreme social and economic inequality. In reaction to this, the Irish state has made periodic attempts to impose (and, if necessary, to invent) a homogeneously 'indigenous' Irish language and culture, in part to legitimate itself as the true expression of the Irish people. But the perceived symbolic power of English has been enduringly attractive to Irish elites. In fact, only the lower echelons of the state civil service embraced Irish.[8] The Irish state has not been able to achieve the political unification, economic independence or linguistic revival felt to be the nation state's due. Ireland's consolidation as an imagined community[9] – through 'print capitalism', broadcast media and the growth of the modern state – has occurred almost exclusively through English. At the same time, this consolidation has been dependent on an ideological valorisation of the Irish language and the continuing (narrowly) 'symbolic' role of Irish-speaking communities. The logic of the Irish state has led it to take a stance which conceptualises 'tradition' as the preserved cultural remnant of 'progress' (see below). From this perspective, the Irish language and its speakers embody a 'tradition' which is, at best, eccentric to Irish 'modernity'.

The Telecom advertisement shows that the modern Irish state still needs indigenous culture to legitimise itself, even while fully embracing the new regime of transnational capital. According to an advertising trade journal:

> The brief handed down to [the advertising agency] Irish International was straight forward – design a campaign to generate awareness about the flotation and to inform the public that the shares are available to everyone. Irish International operated in accordance with European law which limits the content of any campaign for a public flotation to purely factual information without any persuasive elements.... *The decision to use traditional Irish vocalists rather than mainstream singers is intended to reinforce the message that everybody is eligible to buy shares.* The commercial is supported by press, outdoor posters and local and national radio, all of which run with the strapline 'whoever you are'.[10]

Disappointed Eircom investors later complained that the advertising campaign 'skilfully managed to convey the message that it would be almost unpatriotic to buy shares'.[11] The advertisement's use of Irish-language song ('rather than mainstream singers') is an example of Bourdieu's 'strategy of condescension':

> which consists in deriving profit from the objective relation of power between the languages that confront one another in practice ... in the very act of symbolically negating that relation, namely, the hierarchy of languages and those who speak them.[12]

There was more than profit at stake, however. In Negri's terms,[13] 'to say state is only another way to say capital' – as capitalism develops, the state acts more and more as both the embodiment and representative of capital. The Telecom campaign involved more than an attempt to boost share prices: it also represented the state's attempt to relegitimise itself, in its new 'Celtic Tiger' form, as a 'shareholder democracy'.

The Irish language and political economy

By the nineteenth century, Irish was well on its way to becoming a minority language.[14] Following the loss of native sovereignty and the colonisation of Ireland, English had become increasingly identified with the domains of religion, government and commerce. Even before the Great Famine, Irish was being rapidly abandoned in Gaeltacht (Irish-speaking) areas. The nineteenth century saw the penetration of the colonial market economy to the poorest and most remote areas of Ireland. Rural Irish-speakers encountered colonial power relations, the ideologies and practices of political economy and the English language as one package. Additionally, both the major nationalist social movements and the modernising Catholic Church operated through English. The Famine hit the poorer, Irish-speaking areas the hardest; emigration and migratory labour practices made knowledge of English a necessity in these areas, and supported an ideology which saw Irish as pertaining only to the past. Irish became more and more the peripheral language of the home, of older people and of the inchoate expressions of resistance embodied in popular culture. English was seen by virtually everyone as the only vehicle for class mobility and for progress more generally, that is, for the creation and reproduction of modern social relationships.

This dynamic has continued to the present day. Thus, a 1971 study group found it 'quite striking' that the use of Irish as an everyday vernacular was confined to the most marginal parts of the officially designated Gaeltacht areas, which were themselves geographically and economically marginal to Ireland as a whole. Individual pockets of Irish-speakers tended to be 'more closely related to an English-speaking village' than to each other.[15] This fractal pattern of linguistic geography illustrates the degree

to which Irish was marginalised, while English was the language of communication, commerce and the middle classes. For the writer and activist
Máirtín Ó Cadhain, born in the Connemara Gaeltacht in 1905:

> thar áit ar bith in Éirinn tá an tidirdhealú aicmeach, an class distinction,
> suntasach sa nGaeltacht. Gheobhadh Marx, Engels, agus Lenin cruthú
> breá ann ar a ndeimhne gurb iad an ardaicme agus lucht an rachmais, na
> capitalists, is túisce a thréigeas saíúlacht nó cultúr na muintire. B'ionann
> na boicht agus lucht na Gaeilge. Bhí an fuath aicmeach seo gríosta ionam
> i bhfad sul ar léigh mé an chéad focal den Chonaolach ná de Das Kapital.
> Agus nuair a léigh thuig me ar an bpointe céard é. Agus tá seo amhala sa
> nGaeltacht fós. Cé an fáth nach mbeadh? Ní call do dhuine a dhéanamh
> ach breathnú ar an anbhás atá aicme an rachmais á imirt ar chultúr na
> muintire.[16]

> class distinctions are more prominent in the Gaeltacht than anywhere
> else in Ireland. Marx, Engels, and Lenin would get a fine proof [there] of
> their theory that it is the upper classes and the merchant classes – the
> capitalists – who are the first to abandon the wisdom or culture of the
> people. [To them] the poor and Irish-speakers were one and the same.
> This class hatred was ingrained in me long before I ever read a word of
> James Connolly or of *Das Kapital*. And when I read them I immediately
> understood what it was. And the same condition still prevails in the
> Gaeltacht. Why wouldn't it? One only has to look at the havoc that the
> capitalist class is wreaking on the people's culture.

Conradh na Gaeilge (the Gaelic League), founded in 1893, was an
extremely broad-based social movement which not only advocated the
revival of Irish but also used it in the creation of new forms of culture
and sociality. Although putatively apolitical and 'cultural' in its aims,
Conradh na Gaeilge offered a radical challenge to the ideology which
identified 'progress' with the English language and the British state. Thus,
it offered exactly what poor rural Irish-speakers were lacking – the hope
of making a future through Irish. Unfortunately, in Conradh na Gaeilge's
vision, this progress was largely of a non-utilitarian nature. Chatterjee
notes that postcolonial and decolonising nationalism features a pervasive
dualism between the 'spiritual' and 'material' realms:

> By my reading, anticolonial nationalism creates its own domain of sover-
> eignty within colonial society well before it begins its political battle with
> the imperial power. It does this by dividing the world of social institutions
> and practices into two domains – the material and the spiritual. The material
> is the domain of the 'outside',' of the economy and of statecraft, of science
> and technology, a domain where the West had proved its superiority and
> the East had succumbed. In this domain, then, Western superiority had
> to be acknowledged and its accomplishments carefully studied and repli-
> cated. The spiritual, on the other hand, is an 'inner' domain bearing the

'essential' marks of cultural identity. The greater one's success in imitating Western skills in the material domain, therefore, the greater the need to preserve the distinctiveness of one's spiritual culture.[17]

Although it was a predominantly urban, middle-class organisation, Conradh na Gaeilge did direct much of its efforts towards native Irish-speakers; it won the right to Irish-language instruction in Gaeltacht schools and opened a teacher training college in the Gaeltacht. But here, as else-where, it created only the conditions for the possibility of an Irish-speaking middle class. It failed to attack the class system itself – the main force behind the abandonment of Irish.[18]

Conradh na Gaeilge directly inspired the 1916 rebellion; it was the egg out of which the new Irish state was hatched. But this state did little to change the class foundations of Irish society and the decline of Irish in the Gaeltacht continued or actually increased after independence. Although it made Irish mandatory for admission to the National University and for entry to the lower grades of the civil service, the state did not generally change its own linguistic behaviour, and it functioned mainly through English, both internally and in many of its dealings with Irish-speakers in the Gaeltacht.[19]

The Gaeltacht and the state

Poor, rural and predominantly Irish-speaking regions in the west were the first areas of Ireland to undergo systematic state-sponsored 'development' under the auspices of the Congested Districts Board (CDB), founded in 1891. The CDB concentrated on building up basic infrastructure and ignored broader questions of community, language or culture. Under the newly independent Irish Free State, the Gaeltacht Commission of 1926 surveyed the country and drew what became the geographic boundaries of the official Gaeltacht. Although ostensibly aimed at pre-serving the Irish language in these areas, Irish state policy concentrated on developing a system of grants to individual families, rather than policies aimed at strengthening community *per se*. Through their developmental interventions, the colonial and postcolonial states have increasingly reified the Gaeltacht as an administrative zone. The general tendency has been towards an increase in state centralisation, the reduction or elimination of local government powers, and the suppression of any form of local autonomy.[20] The Irish state portrayed the Gaeltacht as the 'storehouse' or 'treasure' of identity in a nation state that was constitutionally defined as Irish-speaking. In reality, Irish functioned as a minority language but without any legal recognition or protection of its minority status. In what Ó Ciosáin calls 'the geographic fallacy',[21] the bureaucratic logic of the state and the romantic ideology of the nation worked hand in hand to define the Gaeltacht in terms of physical space, rather than in terms of community structure or language use. Official ideology reified the Gaeltacht as a geographic entity, while denying the Irish language a public role as a marker of a distinct ethnic or cultural identity within the Irish nation.[22]

The state's own efforts at language preservation have often worked against the local autonomy that is essential to the maintenance of a minority language. That this pattern has changed at all is largely the result of successive waves of Gaeltacht-based social activism, with significant support from urban Irish-speakers. In the 1930s, Muintir na Gaeltachta (People of the Gaeltacht) demanded civil rights for Irish-speakers and access to the means of production (arable land, fishing rights, industry) for the rural Irish-speaking poor. Their agitations received national attention, in part through publicity in *An t-Éireannach*, an Irish-language weekly socialist newspaper published in Dublin.[23] The state's response included the resettlement scheme in which Irish-speakers were relocated to County Meath; after a fight for recognition from the state, Ráth Cairn and Baile Ghib, in County Meath, remain as Irish-speaking communities to the present day.[24]

In the late 1960s, Gluaiseacht Cearta Sibhialta na Gaeltachta (the Gaeltacht Civil Rights Movement) made very similar demands, with the addition of the demand for an Irish-language radio service.[25] Members of the organisation set up a pirate radio transmitter in Connemara in 1970, the success of which embarrassed the state into setting up Raidió na Gaeltachta,[26] a Gaeltacht-based radio station which broadcasts nationally. Raidió na Gaeltachta was the first national institution to function through Irish only and the first to be largely controlled by Gaeltacht people.

A third wave of activism occurred in the 1980s and 1990s, centred on the demand for an Irish-language television service. Illegal television broadcasts were made from Connemara in 1987 and 1988.[27] Eventually, Teilifís na Gaeilge (later TG4) was set up by the state and began broadcasting in 1996.

These social movements sought local autonomy in Gaeltacht regions, and concentrated on building and maintaining community rather than focusing on language issues *per se*. This maximally contrasted with national language policy, which almost always failed to connect reverence for the 'spiritual' values of Irish (its non-utilitarian value as a vehicle of identity) with effective practical concern for maintaining communities of Irish-speakers. For the Irish state, 'the separation of the economic and the cultural, the symbolic and the material led to a contradiction between theory and practice in the maintenance of the defined cultural heartland of the country'.[28] Already in the 1930s, Muintir na Gaeltachta had opposed direct grants and 'handouts' to Gaeltacht people and the treatment of the Gaeltacht as a separate ghetto within an English-speaking nation state, arguing instead for a social revolution that handed control of production over to the people themselves.[29]

Gaeltacht social movements were part of larger milieux which featured the growth of new social networks and forms of community – in addition to Raidió na Gaeltachta, the last thirty-five years have seen the growth of Irish-language print media such as the independently minded news weekly *Amárach*, in Connemara,[30] as well as the creation of community development cooperatives. This period also saw the establishment of Irish-language publishers of books and local music, such as Cló Iar-Chonnachta, also in Connemara, founded in 1985. In the 1930s as well as the 1970s and 1980s, song composition flourished in the Gaeltacht. Local poets, taking full advantage of the new print and broadcast media, continued and adapted their long-held role as social critics articulating local responses to national and international forces.[31]

Social movements like Gluaiseacht Cearta Sibhialta na Gaeltachta follow a pattern typical of the relationship between Irish-speakers and the state.[32] The state makes 'symbolic' gestures to the language (e.g. constitutionally recognising Irish as the 'first official language' of the state) which it has to be forced into upholding. Protest consists of embarrassing the state with adverse publicity through the threat or actual practice of autonomous action. The state then attempts to co-opt social activism by creating or assuming control of institutions such as Raidió na Gaeltachta or TG4 (both are administered under the auspices of Raidió Teilifís Éireann, RTÉ, the state broadcasting authority). '[S]ince the 1920s Ireland had taken most action in favour of Irish out of the hands of the campaigners and enthusiasts and embedded it in the actions of the state.'[33]

In Akutagawa's and Hourigan's analyses,[34] these outcomes represent the 'failure' of popular political movements. They see the main results of local activism as the extension of state control within the Gaeltacht, and the creation of a new Gaeltacht middle class centred around local cooperatives and the broadcasting and film industries. These indigenous elites are treated by locals 'as an extension of national elites to be lobbied rather than [as] their local representatives operating at local level'.[35] Likewise, local cooperatives become 'merely structures through which government aid may be channelled into the Gaeltacht regions'.[36]

It might be more accurate, however, to say that Gaeltacht activism, while failing to achieve its overt goals, has transformed the relationship of local people with translocal forces and processes in a manner which prefigures what Hardt and Negri term 'postmodernisation'.[37] By opening up closed networks of both community and governance, Gaeltacht activism has, in effect, pointed the way for the reduced role of the postmodern Irish state in its Celtic Tiger phase. As 'the crucible of Irish postmodernity', the Gaeltacht has become the state's testing ground for decentralisation and local governance, as well as for the progressive recognition of linguistic and cultural minority rights.[38]

The 'local and universal' Gaeltacht

These developments present both opportunities for and threats to the construction of community. As Ó hIfearnáin argues,[39] the Irish state has progressively withdrawn from direct action:

> following a policy of disengaging with direct sponsorship not simply of language restoration policies, but delegation of responsibility for those areas where language support structures do exist to the voluntary, private and semi-state sector. This represents a shift in the way the state regards the language.... [T]he state has now hatched a new understanding that Irish speakers are a cultural and linguistic minority, while the majority must still be able to learn the language as it is part of their heritage and carries sentimental value.

Withdrawal from the ideology of Irish as 'everybody's language' has seen the progressive reduction of language requirements for access to the state sphere, including education, and increased toleration or even encouragement of locally based initiatives. These developments have opened the way for the creation of new forms of community but also for the complete dissolution of community into a spectacular simulacrum thereof. To illustrate what is at stake here, I would like briefly to contrast the formal organisation of Raidió na Gaeltachta with that of TG4.

Although local activists ended up with little representation on the staff or governing bodies of Raidió na Gaeltachta, the station still evolved in a fairly radical way, at least initially. Control of day-to-day operations remained largely in the hands of local staff, who influenced the station's development in several ways. Staff refused to develop a spoken version of Standard Irish and instead broadcast in their own local dialects.[40] The station developed as a network of local studios in the far-flung Gaeltacht regions. Local programming in local dialects was broadcast nationally (and now internationally, via satellite and the Internet). The station's news department has built up an international network of Irish-speakers for use as correspondents,[41] is well known for its ability to cover national news, especially political news, and has forced politicians to be able to account for themselves through the medium of Irish.[42] More subtly, the station has embraced not just local dialectal forms but also local modes of discourse. Types of knowledge and discourse which in the national sphere tend to be deprived of their functionality and received as 'folklore' – as emblems of the national past – retain their role as vehicles for community discussion on Raidió na Gaeltachta.[43] Since medieval times, poetry and song, in both literary and oral genres, have been a favoured medium for topical discussion and political debate among all social strata of Irish-speakers. These discursive forms have still functioned, to a certain extent, in modern Irish-language media. The station thus often functions as a seamless extension and radicalisation of 'traditional' modes of local discourse, while projecting them into a non-geographically based, open-ended communication community.

Raidió na Gaeltachta has helped build translocal community in exactly the opposite way to that theorised by Anderson, Gellner, Habermas and others. For these theorists, the creation of wider community requires the transformation of language through standardising media such as newspapers and commercial publishing. They see standardised language as, ideally, a maximally transparent medium for rational discourse that enables speakers to transcend their pettily 'local' points of view and become fully educated citizens of a geographically contained 'national' community.[44] The case of Raidió na Gaeltachta – a 'local' station with national and international reach – shows that, perhaps, the 'local' is not merely a geographic entity; locality is not a physical container for people but a wider set of concrete social relationships.[45]

This wider set of relationships is constituted by the tension between immanent 'democratic' impulses and their appropriation by structures of power. Thus, there has been constant tension within Raidió na Gaeltachta, and between the station and its listeners, over who controls the station (the state or local people) and over the station's mission or target audience – Gaeltacht people or a national audience.[46] The station was set up under the auspices of RTÉ, which directly appoints top management. There is also an *appointed* advisory committee of representatives of the different Gaeltacht communities. The first committee did not include any of the activists who had campaigned for the establishment of the station; most of its members were also members of Fianna Fáil, the party then in power.[47]

Paradoxically, it has been the national organisation (RTÉ) which has occasionally attempted to impose a 'local' definition of Raidió na Gaeltachta's news coverage, while 'local' Gaeltacht-based staff wanted the station to cover national and international news. At other times, RTÉ has sought to redefine the station as a 'national' entity by de-emphasising 'Gaeltacht' programming.[48] Both tendencies work to diminish the importance of local (as opposed to national) points of view. The question is one of autonomy for Irish and Irish-speaking communities, an autonomy which is outward-looking, versus a protected status as an inward-looking reserve.

In contrast, TG4 perfectly embodies the role of a Celtic Tiger state institution. The 'cash-starved youth rich channel'[49] acts as a commissioner and broadcaster of programming, significant amounts of which it buys from small independent producers. The station's advanced technology allows it to function with a minimal permanent staff. But although TG4 has headquarters in the Gaeltacht, it defines itself as a 'national' service and is much more firmly under the control of RTÉ than Raidió na Gaeltachta. Thus the original name of the station, Teilifís na Gaeilge, meant Television 'of Irish', that is, of 'Irish' as the heritage language of all Irish people, as opposed to Teilifís na Gaeltachta, Television 'of the Gaeltacht', the voice and point of view of the habitually Irish-speaking community (however that community is defined). This shows in the station's programming, most of which features simple, standardised (and English-subtitled) Irish comprehensible to learners and non-native Irish-speakers. Little of its programming seems to present a Gaeltacht point of view; it has a quality of placelessness that Raidió na Gaeltachta's lacks, while the recent change of the station's name to 'TG4' – an acronym without a referent – bears an uncanny resemblance to the transformation of 'Telecom Éireann' into 'Eircom'. The telephone company's new name reflected its new international provenance as a multinational corporation and presaged a withdrawal from its earlier commitment to Irish-language policies. Would the same be true of TG4?

As with other institutions, the point of view projected by TG4 closely reflects its own power structure. In contrast, the broadcasting service envisioned by many activists would project the points of view of local communities and, in so doing, would change the relationship between localities and the wider world, much as Raidió na Gaeltachta has. Seosamh Ó Cuaig, a member of Gluaiseacht Cearta Sibhialta na Gaeltachta who is now a journalist with Raidió na Gaeltachta, put the matter like this:

Tá [TG4] ar an gcaoi sin mar gheall gur ón taobh amuigh atá an rud ag tíocht. 'Gabhfaidh muid siar agus slánóidh muid na Sioux Indians', sin é an meon atá ann. Ní fhéadfá Sioux Indian a chur i gceannas ar na Sioux Indians. Níl sé sin ann le Raidió na Gaeltachta, fós. Is é Raidió na Gaeltachta t-aon institiúid Gaeltachta dá raibh againn. Tá RTÉ i gceannas air, ach is é meon na Gaeltachta a bhí ann. Tá an-léigear air sin agus go leor daoine ag iarraidh deireadh a chur leis. Tá brú ar Raidió na Gaeltachta béim a chur ar an ngné Náisiúnta. Ach céard is brí leis sin? Ní áitiúil agus náisiúnta ach áitiúil agus uilíoch. Sin é a deirimse.[50]

[TG4] is that way because it is coming from the outside. 'We'll go West and save the Sioux Indians', that's the mentality there. You couldn't put a Sioux Indian in charge of the Sioux Indians. It isn't that way with Raidió na Gaeltachta, yet. Raidió na Gaeltachta is the only Gaeltacht institution we ever had. RTÉ is in charge of it, but it is the mentality of the Gaeltacht that was in it [from the beginning]. This is under severe siege with a lot of people trying to put an end to it. There is pressure on

Raidió na Gaeltachta to emphasise the national aspect. But what does
that mean? It isn't [a case of] local and national but local and universal.
That's what I say.

The 'mentality of the Gaeltacht', in its particularity as a locally grounded
perspective, not only can speak for itself but has something to say to the
world. As with the Sioux Indians, only autonomy can safeguard such
perspectives. A 1993 flyer issued by Ráth Cairn's production company
to present proposals for the Irish-language television channel makes this
point very clearly:

> Is iad na réigiúin Gaeltachta sin na lárionaid óna mbreathnófar ar an
> saol. Caithfidh an tseirbhís a bheith lonnaithe sa nGaeltacht agus a bheith
> i lámha mhuintir na Gaeltachta agus lucht na Gaeilge.[51]

> The Gaeltacht regions are the centres from which one will see the world.
> The service must be located in the Gaeltacht and in the hands of Gaeltacht
> people and Irish-speakers.

Although 'locally' grounded, such a radically decentralised approach
could paradoxically transform the nature of the Gaeltacht, identifying it
less with geographically bounded administrative zones than with the
unbounded, expansive community of Irish-speakers. This was, in fact,
the original meaning of the term 'Gaeltacht'. Such a transformation would
be the political expression of a concept of community immanent to Irish-
speaking culture.[52]

Conclusions

For the last few hundred years, the Gaeltacht has exemplified the crisis
of Irish modernity. Originally among the poorest and most class-ridden
areas of the state, Gaeltacht areas are now much more prosperous. A
series of struggles has forced the Irish state to cede a certain amount of
control and grant some degree of autonomy to Irish-speaking communities. Activists have successfully lobbied both the Irish state and the
European Union for infrastructure and community development funds.
In accordance with a shift in state language policy, local development is
now, to some extent, under local control. Ironically, these changes have
made the Gaeltacht an attractive place to live for non-Irish-speaking
families as well. Rising property values and an influx of non-Irish-speakers
have threatened to dissolve local communities. This is the negative side
of an otherwise necessary and positive development, the globalisation
of the Gaeltacht – its breakout from what Máirtín Ó Cadhain termed
'Claidhe na Muice Duibhe' (the Black Pig's Dyke) of geographical

segregation and second-class citizenship to which it had been relegated by traditional state policy.[53]

What is still very much at stake is the relationship between language and community. The Irish state's language policy has relied almost exclusively on primary and secondary school education to promote the language in non-Irish-speaking communities. Irish was, in effect, a vehicle of what Gellner terms children's 'exo-socialisation' into an official culture that was not the culture of the home.[54] Ironically, this pattern is now being followed within the Gaeltacht itself, as parents often see the language as pertaining to institutions and not necessarily to the home. These parents then speak English to their children, leaving it to schools and other community institutions to provide them with Irish.[55] Such behaviour could be seen as 'hard-headed realism' in a world where a knowledge of English is economically essential, while the benefits accruing to competence in Irish are still largely 'symbolic'. But it is grounded in a point of view which takes state intervention in support of the Irish language for granted. And yet, as the state increasingly withdraws from direct action on behalf of linguistic and cultural matters, the fate of the language will depend more and more on its profitability.

Much of what I have termed the 'postmodernisation' of the Gaeltacht is the result of advances in information technology, which have enabled easier local access to modern means of communication. Better communications networks mean that production can be increasingly decentralised – a knitting factory on Inis Meáin in the Aran Islands can be in continuous and instantaneous contact with both its designers and its markets in Japan, Europe and the United States. This is beginning to provide opportunities for people to stay in remote locales rather than emigrating to centres of production. Both Raidió na Gaeltachta and TG4 rely on technological advances that make possible radically decentralised communication networks and a greater variety of choice in both the production and consumption of mediated culture. Privately owned media, such as the Irish-language weekly *Foinse* and the Breton-language television channel TV-Breizh,[56] show that linguistic 'niche markets' are becoming profitably exploitable by the corporate sector.

Hardt and Negri maintain that:

> In the postmodernization of the global economy, the creation of wealth tends ever more toward what we will call biopolitical production, the production of social life itself, in which the economic, the political, and the cultural increasingly overlap and invest one another.[57]

Culture becomes capital, and vice versa, while political action increasingly consists of the struggle to maintain democratic autonomy in the face of global market forces. Yet what they term the 'informatisation' of production amounts mostly to the transition to a service-based economy,[58] a process in which Ireland is quite advanced. The typical service sector worker, whether he or she lives in Dublin, in Ros Muc, County Galway or even in Keokuk, Iowa, is now freer than ever to participate in a global community of Irish-speakers. As a cultural producer, he or she may find his or her products accruing market value because of their rootedness in a minority linguistic culture and tradition.

This could all be seen as a revolution but, as such, it is a far cry from that envisaged by Máirtín Ó Cadhain or the members of Muintir na Gaeltachta. Ó Cadhain wrote in 1969 that:

> Sí an Ghaeilge Athghabháil na hÉireann agus is í Athghabháil na hÉireann slánú na Gaeilge. Sí teanga na muintire a shlánós an mhuintir.[59]

> Irish is the Reconquest of Ireland and the Reconquest of Ireland is the salvation of Irish. The people's own language is what will save them.

By 'the Reconquest of Ireland' he meant James Connolly's call for a socialist revolution in Ireland which would overthrow colonial rule and put the means of production in the hands of the Irish people.[60] Ó Cadhain saw this as the only hope for saving the Irish language. He saw Irish as the means of expression and cultural medium of the most downtrodden social group in Ireland. In the second sentence of his statement, he expresses his belief that revolution should be a development immanent to the life and culture of the community, and vice versa. This seems to prefigure Hardt and Negri's call for revolution on what they term the 'plane of immanence'. Hardt and Negri see the development of capital itself, as well as popular resistance to it, as sufficient to constitute such a revolution, an assertion which might seem doubtful to even the most optimistic observer of 'Celtic Tiger' Ireland.

In the advertisement offering shares in Telecom Éireann, singers sang *Dúlamán*, a traditional song from Gaoth Dobhair, County Donegal, that represents the voice of a person selling seaweed. Investors who answered the advertisement's call could be forgiven for thinking that seaweed is exactly what they got for their money. As its share prices precipitously declined after its flotation, rumours abounded that Eircom would be dissolved at the behest of the transnational telecommunications corporations that held a majority interest in the new company. Concern over share prices dominated the grievances brought forward at Eircom's stormy annual general meeting on 13 September 2000. In votes at this meeting, small Irish investors found themselves up against the company's chairman, Ray MacSharry, who controlled 1.15 billion proxy votes from large corporate investors.[61] The voices of Irish-language activists, objecting to the new corporation's apparent withdrawal from its commitments to the language, were lost in the fray.

Notes

1 See www.rte.ie/news/archive/review1999/technologybymonth.html, accessed 18 July 2002.
2 K. Danaher, *The Year in Ireland* (Cork: Mercier Press, 1972), pp. 134–53.
3 D. Ó Giolláin, *Locating Irish Folklore: Tradition, Modernity, Identity* (Cork: Cork University Press, 2000).
4 'An estimated £4 million was spent [on the advertisement campaign], most of it in just over six weeks', *Irish Times*, 25 September 2000. In comparison, the annual operating budget of TG4 at its inception was £10 million; M. Kavanagh, 'Irish-language TV spurs cultural debate', *Electronic Media*, 15:43 (21 October 1996).
5 F. Fukuyama, 'The end of history?', *National Interest* (summer 1989).
6 M. Hardt and A. Negri, *Empire* (Cambridge, MA: Harvard University Press, 2000), p. 76; their emphasis.
7 J. Leerssen, *Mere Irish and Fíor-Ghael* (Cork: Cork University Press, 1996); B. Ó Buachalla, *Aisling Ghéar: na Stíobhartaigh agus an t-Aos Léinn, 1603–1788* (Baile Átha Cliath: Clóchomhar Tta, 1996).
8 T. Ó hIfearnáin, 'Irish language broadcast media: the interaction of state language policy, broadcasters, and their audiences', *Current Issues in Language and Society*, 7:2 (2000), pp. 100–1.
9 B. Anderson, *Imagined Communities* (London: Verso, 1983).
10 See www.adworld.ie/news_desk/march99/news133.html, accessed 9 August 1999; my emphasis.
11 B. Harrison, 'Marketing of Aer Lingus flotation gets underway', *Irish Times*, 25 September 2000.
12 P. Bourdieu, *Language and Symbolic Power* (Cambridge: Polity Press, 1991), p. 68.
13 A. Negri, *Marx Beyond Marx: Lessons on the Grundrisse* (New York: Autonomedia, 1991), p. 188.
14 G. FitzGerald, 'Estimates for baronies of minimum level of Irish-speaking amongst successive decennial cohorts: 1771–1781 to 1861–1871', *Proceedings of the Royal Irish Academy*, 84 (1984); B. Ó Cuív, 'Irish language and literature, 1845–1921', in W. E. Vaughan (ed.), *A New History of Ireland, Vol. IV: Ireland Under the Union, II* (Oxford: Clarendon Press, 1996), pp. 385–435.
15 An Foras Forbartha, *Staidéir na Gaeltachta: The Gaeltacht Studies. Vol. I, A Development Plan for the Gaeltacht (Dun na nGall, Maigh Eo, Ciarraí, Corcaigh, Port Láirge agus An Mhí). Imleabhar I* (Dublin: Foras Forbartha, 1971), pp. 58–9.
16 M. Ó Cadhain, 'Gluaiseacht na Gaeilge gluaiseacht ar strae', in An tSr. B. Costigan and S. Ó Curraoin (eds), *De Ghlaschloich an Oileáin: Beatha agus Saothar Mháirtín Uí Cadhain* (Indreabhán: Cló Iar-Chonnachta, 1987 [1970]), p. 327.
17 P. Chatterjee, *The Nation and Its Fragments: Colonial and Postcolonial Histories* (Princeton: Princeton University Press, 1993), p. 6.
18 Breandán S. MacAodha, 'Was this a social revolution?', in S. Ó Tuama (ed.), *The Gaelic League Idea* (Cork: Mercier Press, 1972), p. 29.
19 J. Walsh, *Díchoimisiúnú Teanga: Coimisiún na Gaeltachta 1926* (Dublin: Cois Life, 2002); Coimisiún na Gaeltachta 2002, *Tuarascáil* (Dublin: Rialtas na hÉireann, 2002).
20 M. Akutagawa, 'A linguistic minority under the protection of its own ethnic state: a case study in an Irish Gaeltacht', in G. MacEoin, A. Ahlqvist and

D. Ó hAodha (eds), *Third International Conference on Minority Languages: Celtic Papers* (Clevedon: Multilingual Matters, 1987), p. 130.

21 É. Ó Ciosáin, *Buried Alive: A Reply to 'The Death of the Irish Language'* (Baile Átha Cliath: Dáil Uí Chadhain, 1991), p. 7.

22 Akutagawa, 'A linguistic minority under the protection of its own ethnic state', p. 141.

23 É. Ó Ciosáin, *An t-Éireannach 1934–1937: Páipéar Sóisialach Gaeltachta* (Baile Átha Cliath: An Clóchomhar, 1993).

24 M. Ó Conghaile (ed.), *Gaeltacht Rath Cairn: Léachtaí Comórtha* (Indreabhán: Cló Iar-Chonnachta, 1986).

25 N. Hourigan, *Comparison of the Campaigns for Raidió na Gaeltachta and TnaG*, Irish Sociological Research Monographs 1, J. Gray, M. Peillon and É. Slater (eds) (Maynooth: Department of Sociology, National University of Ireland Maynooth, 2001).

26 R. Ó Glaisne, *Raidió na Gaeltachta* (Indreabhán: Cló Chois Fharraige, 1982).

27 Hourigan, *Comparison of the Campaigns for Raidió na Gaeltachta and TnaG*, p. 60.

28 N. C. Johnson, 'Building a nation: an examination of the Irish Gaeltacht Commission Report of 1926', *Journal of Historical Geography*, 19:2 (1993), p. 158.

29 M. Ó Cadhain, 'Claidhe na Muice Duibhe ar Mhuinntir na Gaedhealtachta', *An t-Éireannach*, 1 September 1934. Cf. Ó Ciosáin, *An t-Éireannach 1934–1937*.

30 É. Ó Ciosáin, 'Scéalta i mBarr Bata agus Pictiúir as an Spéir', *Léachtaí Cholm Cille*, 28 (1998), p. 14.

31 G. Denvir, *Litríocht agus Pobal: Cnuasach Aistí* (Indreabhán, Conamara: Cló Iar-Chonnachta, 1997); Ó Ciosáin, *An t-Éireannach 1934–1937*.

32 S. Coleman, 'Return from the west: a poetics of voice in Irish', PhD dissertation, Department of Anthropology, University of Chicago, 1999.

33 Ó hIfearnáin, 'Irish language broadcast media', p. 97.

34 Akutagawa, 'A linguistic minority under the protection of its own ethnic state'; Hourigan, *Comparison of the Campaigns for Raidió na Gaeltachta and TnaG*, p. 60.

35 Hourigan, *Comparison of the Campaigns for Raidió na Gaeltachta and TnaG*, p. 78, citing Akutagawa.

36 M. Johnson, 'The cooperative movement in the Gaeltacht', *Irish Geography*, 12 (1979), p. 71.

37 M. Hardt and A. Negri, *Empire* (Cambridge, MA: Harvard University Press, 2000), pp. 280–303.

38 D. Kiberd, 'Gael force', *Irish Times Magazine*, 24 March 2001.

39 Ó hIfearnáin, 'Irish language broadcast media', p. 110.

40 M. Ó Murchú, 'Smaointe faoi Chaighdeánú na Nua-Ghaeilge', *Teangeolas*, 18 (1984), p. 18.

41 I. Watson, 'A history of Irish language broadcasting: national ideology, commercial interest and minority rights', in M. J. Kelly and B. O'Connor (eds), *Media Audiences in Ireland: Power and Cultural Identity* (Dublin: University College Dublin Press, 1997), p. 218.

42 Ó Ciosáin, 'Scéalta i mBarr Bata agus Pictiúir as an Spéir', p. 20.

43 See Liam Ó Muirthile's discussions of Raidió na Gaeltachta and TG4 in his weekly column in the *Irish Times*, for example on 12 March 1998 or 7 October 1998.

44 M. Silverstein, 'Monoglot "Standard" in America', *Working Papers and Proceedings of the Center for Psychosocial Studies*, 13 (1987); M. Silverstein,

'Whorfianism and the linguistic imagination of nationality', in P. V. Kroskrity (ed.), *Regimes of Language: Ideologies, Polities, and Identities*, School of American Research Advanced Seminar Series (Santa Fe, NM: School of American Research Press, 2000), pp. 85–138; J. Errington, *Shifting Languages: Interaction and Identity in Javanese Indonesia*, Studies in the Social and Cultural Foundations of Language 19 (Cambridge: Cambridge University Press, 1998).

45 A. Appadurai, 'The production of locality', in *Modernity at Large: Cultural Dimensions of Globalization* (Minneapolis, MN: University of Minnesota Press, 1996), pp. 178–99.

46 F. Ó Drisceoil, 'Idir Radachas agus Coimeádachas: Fealsúnacht agus Féiniúlacht Raidió na Gaeltachta', *Oghma*, 8 (1996), pp. 97–105.

47 Ó Glaisne, *Raidió na Gaeltachta*, pp. 73–7.

48 Ó Glaisne, *Raidió na Gaeltachta*; Ó Drisceoil, 'Idir Radachas agus Coimeádachas: Fealsúnacht agus Féiniúlacht Raidió na Gaeltachta'; Watson, 'A history of Irish language broadcasting'.

49 Ó hIfearnáin, 'Irish language broadcast media', p. 111.

50 Seosamh Ó Cuaig, interviewed in *Foinse*, 5 March 1998.

51 Scun Scan, *Teilifís na Gaeilge: Moltaí Scun Scan Ráth Cairn* (Ráth Cairn: Scun Scan, 1993), p. 6.

52 M. Ó Murchú, 'An Ghaeltacht: Pobal i mBaol a Leáite', *Scríobh*, 6 (1984), pp. 63–9.

53 Ó Cadhain, 'Claidhe na Muice Duibhe ar Mhuinntir na Gaedhealtachta'.

54 E. Gellner, *Nations and Nationalism* (Ithaca: Cornell University Press, 1983), p. 38.

55 C. Ó Giollagáin, 'Scagadh ar rannú chainteoirí comhaimseartha Gaeltachta: gnéithe d'antraipeolaíocht teangeolaíochta phobal Ráth Cairn', presentation to the National Institute for Regional and Spatial Analysis, National University of Ireland Maynooth, 24 April 2002.

56 S. Moal, 'Broadcast media in Breton: dawn at last?', *Current Issues in Language and Society*, 7:2 (2000), pp. 117–34.

57 Hardt and Negri, *Empire*, p. xii.

58 *Ibid.*, pp. 284–9.

59 Ó Cadhain, 'Gluaiseacht na Gaeilge gluaiseacht ar strae', p. 327.

60 J. Connolly, 'The re-conquest of Ireland', in D. Ryan (ed.), *James Connolly, Collected Works* (Dublin: New Books Publications, 1987 [1917]).

61 J. McManus, 'Small investors have loud voices but lose the vote', *Irish Times*, 14 September 2000.

Northern Ireland:
a reminder from the present

PETE SHIRLOW

Social and cultural shifts on the island of Ireland are held to have diluted the authority of nationalisms that were tied to unidimensional and archaic notions of Irishness and Britishness.[1] It is contended that there is an ongoing and positive transition towards new modes and definitions of cultural belonging that in themselves reject the logic and validity of ethnocentrism. The Europeanisation of political and financial power, the influx of foreign capital, political morphology in Northern Ireland and the growth in consumption have all been identified as sociopolitical forces that have advanced more heterogeneous senses of identity and belonging.

The 'death' of an Ireland tied to the narratives of idyllic rurality, Gaelic custom, unionist triumphalism and devotion to the champions of ideological confrontation is interpreted as being paralleled by the customisation of new discourses of progress and postmodernity. Postnationalist readings maintain that identities in Ireland have and will continue to become less nation centred and more contingent upon choice, place, sexuality and other individually defined imaginings of self-value. This argument asserts that as the 'Irish' and 'British-Irish' become more 'cosmopolitan', they will ditch the rhetorical narratives of Irish- and British-based ethnicity. Such optimistic accounts aim to distil the contemporary from a 'redundant' past.

Dominant bourgeois readings retain the argument that the complex sociohistorical forces that shaped contemporary Ireland, such as the link between Catholicism and Irish nationalism, have been left behind in the rush towards more dispassionate and benign cultural reasonings. Ireland as a place is thus held to have been liberated from the bondage of nationalism and ethnicity. This view emphasises the idea that such a transition is based upon a shift from 'primitive' to modern conceptions of identity. What we are offered is an essentially ahistorical account which aims to hide the negative nature of present realities under the quilt of historical revision. A simplistic and binary argument seeks to suggest that the past was so appalling that the future must obviously be bright.

Social mobility and the growth in consumption may have partly undermined both the vocalisation and visibility of state-sponsored discourses of Irishness and unionism/Britishness. However, the debility of 'official' Irishness and the growth in self-selected identities in the Republic of Ireland do not mean that salient tensions between Irishness and Britishness have evaporated or will evaporate. There is, despite the reverie of postnationalist interpretation, the potential for ethnocentric tension to re-emerge.

This chapter aims to establish how the ideological divisions between Irishness and Britishness continue to be reproduced, despite the supposed evaporation of such discursive constructions. In pinpointing the divisions that remain and those that may reappear, this chapter argues that the capacity exists for sectarian consciousness to spread throughout the Irish body politic. The Irish 'problem' remains one of territory, given the existence of a border that acts as a social, constitutional, political and cultural divide. However, the northern problem may become a southern reality. A fundamental dilemma facing the Republic of Ireland is that the removal of the border – an abiding aspiration for most people in the twenty-six counties – holds the danger of unleashing cultural and political antagonisms not seen since partition. Unification would ultimately mean that Northern Ireland would no longer remain a 'place apart'. In becoming a place 'within', the north of Ireland could bring with it the multiple afflictions of ideological division and territorial disputation.

Postnationalist interpretation – northern style

In recent years, political change in Northern Ireland has been heralded as the beginning of the end of sectarian asperity. The creation of a power-sharing executive and the endorsement of a pluralist accord has been upheld as an 'exemplary constitutional design for an ethnonationally divided territory'.[2]

There have, of course, been positive political developments. David Trimble, the Ulster Unionist leader, has publicly accepted that 'it is legitimate for nationalists to pursue their political objectives of a united Ireland'. Trimble has also stated that his party endorsed 'the principles of inclusivity, equality and mutual respect'.[3] Sinn Féin have also worked hard to create some form of political change by taking seats in a Northern Ireland Assembly, which is located in Stormont, one of the most obvious icons of past unionist authority. Sinn Féin, in dropping its insistence that the British state must withdraw from Northern Ireland prior to the beginning of a negotiated settlement, indicated that it was prepared to adopt a different political course than hitherto. These shifts in discourse and direction would suggest that devolution in Northern Ireland and the formation of a power-sharing executive will help usher in a more inclusive political culture that will dilute ethnonationalist forces.[4]

The aim of the Belfast Agreement (BA) is to draw together atavistic political groups in order to promote a consociational accord, which would endorse Northern Ireland's place in the United Kingdom but at the same time uphold minority rights and cultural demands.[5] It is evident, however, that the return of a devolved administration has not resolved the long-term political future of Northern Ireland. Devolution is the first step along a path that leads ultimately to a range of possible constitutional arrangements.[6]

Commentators such as McGarry and O'Leary are correct in their analysis that the BA was intended to be a binational compromise dedicated to challenging the reproduction of sectarianism by conjoining disparate political ideologies.[7] Positive readings of the BA have highlighted how the negotiation of Northern Ireland's constitutional future was based upon the endorsement of both Irish national self-determination and the British constitutional convention. The political maturity of the BA is also saluted because it makes clear that the constitutional status of Northern Ireland can be altered only if the majority of people in Ireland, north and south, wish to effect such a change. This provides a sense that Northern Ireland is maintained by majoritarianism as opposed to 'colonial' administration.

The 'wisdom' of political change, it is argued, is also underlined by the fact that the Irish Republic now recognises Northern Ireland as a legitimate political and constitutional entity.[8] The BA has thus aimed to interweave symbolic recognitions of Irishness and Britishness. The replacement of the claim to Northern Ireland contained in Articles 2 and 3 of the Irish Republic's constitution with a more benign aspiration to unification is understood as a positive acceptance of the need for political renegotiation and understanding. The hosting of dual referenda clearly recognised and permitted a theoretical form of joint sovereignty, a North–South ministerial council and limited forms of cross-border cooperation. The compromises made by the Irish state were also reflected in the concerns of London to stress that the BA is not about maintaining the 'British' constitutional system. Compromise, it is argued, is based upon the creation of a new and renewable constitutional settlement.[9] In reality, however, the ability of the BA to dilute the rationale of ethnosectarianism is over-emphasised.[10]

In economic and cultural terms, the endorsement of equalisation, as outlined in the BA, is represented as being capable of diluting the logic for ethnically defined labour markets and claims of cultural disaffection. In terms of 'conflict resolution', the aim of the BA is to democratise a society in which discord over sovereignty has undermined the appearance of cross-community compromise. Furthermore, the pursuit of seemingly incompatible objectives such as the attenuation of British sovereignty – via the involvement of the Irish state in Northern Ireland's affairs – and safeguarding the union – via the principle of consent – bears witness to a constitutional stratagem aimed at encouraging issues of sovereignty to become gradually more ambiguous.

The BA is thus regarded as a mature political settlement which contains the capacity to delegitimise history and wider structures of territorial disputation. The argument is made that the BA can provide the political normality needed to create a northern version of the 'Celtic Tiger'. It is, thus, understood that the type of economic and social forces which aided the decline of ethnocentric imagining in the Republic of Ireland can be duplicated north of the border. Within this postnationalist interpretation lies the belief that rising economic tides can and will sink sectarian boats. Growth in consumption and personal prosperity is held to have the power and capacity to dilute the rationale of ethnic belonging. An argument is advanced that suggests that growing incomes and self-interest can divorce people from political dogma and their need to source identities through ideological confrontation. Within the postnationalist imagination is the belief that states can fashion democracies that are both inclusive and capable of moving beyond fear and prejudice.[11]

John McGarry[12] indicates what is probably the most desired outcome of political consensus building when he suggests that the BA will 'bring out the benign characteristics of rival identities and [will] marginalize chauvinists more effectively'. If anything, such a positive prognosis fails to square with the reality that the BA has, in fact, nurtured the conditions that have enabled the ethnic chauvinists to thrive.

In a broader sense, the BA is, in fact, part of a programme of promoting a postnationalist interpretation of places of identity on the island of Ireland.[13] The Irish and British states are convinced that the genius of 'conflict resolution' lies in the ability of both states to create institutions that reconcile order with personal, spatial and communal liberties. On the down side, the recognition of mutual consent, cross-border cooperation and the totemic institutionalisation of communal rights is problematic for certain groups whose political culture is tied to an unwavering obligation to an ethnically defined formation of territorial sovereignty.

A flawed process

One of the central problems with the BA is that it is concerned more with conflict management than with conflict resolution. This in itself provides the very political vacuum within which sectarian asperity can and does thrive. The BA institutionalised sectarianism. The facts that members of the Northern Ireland Assembly must designate themselves as nationalist, unionist or other and that all decisions taken must have majority support from both the nationalist and unionist blocs means that the capacity of alternative political interpretations is hindered. All decisions are effectively based upon ethnocentric majorities. In a climate of perpetual controversy, as demonstrated by the successive standoffs at Drumcree and the loyalist blockade of the Holy Cross girls' school, there is no place within the new administrative order within which an accommodationist middle ground can develop. It is not surprising, given the existence of a political system which undermines the power of appeals to cross-community sentiment, that parties such as the Women's Coalition and Alliance have seen their fortunes slump in recent elections.

Devolution and the delivery of the BA have not aided the development of a centrist political culture but rather have fortified the power of those committed to the strongest and most vociferous notions of cultural identity and political victory. If anything, the middle ground has been diminished further in a period of political transformation which was intended to facilitate its growth. This would suggest that political change is based around ethnosectarian power brokerage as opposed to meaningful cross-community dialogue and commitment.

If anything, the Northern Ireland Assembly has provided an arena within which ideological confrontation can be played out via the most public of media. A central problem in the political life of the region is that the strength of the communal blocs is now fairly similar. This, combined with a growing nationalist/republican electorate and the debacles over decommissioning, rioting and policing, provides the context in which the quest for accommodation can be overwhelmed by the desire for victory and revenge.

In a sense, the BA seeks to maintain a kind of political illusion. The deal struck at Stormont strives to make the border seem more fixed for unionists – through the endorsement of the principle of consent – and more permeable for nationalists – through the endorsement of an 'Irish dimension' in Northern Irish affairs. There is, nevertheless, a crucial problem in the idea of creeping porosity of 'the border', since it imagines a shared loss of memory regarding the significance of a cultural and political construct which has and continues to be the foundation of conflict. In reality, the fact that the consent needed for a united Ireland is slowly emerging due to demographic shifts, in Northern Ireland, means that unionism is further placed on the defensive while republicanism moves onward and upward.

For most unionists, it matters not one jot that the Republic of Ireland has come so far from the conservative and exclusive society associated with the De Valera era. The decline in the authority of the Catholic

Church and the move away from what are conventionally termed 'traditional' social mores among the wider population do not dilute the belief system which upholds the 'values' of Britishness. It is not unusual to hear politically conservative unionists using similar radical denunciations of the Celtic Tiger that would be common among the left in the Republic of Ireland. Unionists passionately believe that they would be politically invisible within a united Ireland. For many unionists, the argument remains that they cannot trust the ideological 'other' to treat them fairly. The border is no longer a metaphor for unionist integrity but is seen as a blanket that protects them from cultural and political dissipation. The recent growth in Sinn Féin's political base in the Republic 'proves' to unionists that their most obvious opponents are everywhere. The problem is that such fears and hostilities cannot be removed by a postnationalist interpretation that the Republic has somehow changed.

Unionists constantly seek the body of Irish nationalism within the Republic of Ireland. The failure of the Gaelic Athletic Association (GAA) to allow soccer to be played at Croke Park,[14] the remaining sectarian nature of the Irish constitution and the 'history' of decline among southern Protestants aids the belief that the Republic of Ireland remains, in spite of the ways in which it has changed, a place within which unionists do not feel welcome. Unionist resistance to a united Ireland is partly sectarian but is increasingly based upon a self-understanding of past, present and future victimhood.

The creation of the Northern Ireland Assembly also sought to persuade those who favour the unification of Ireland to be less impetuous in their demands for radical political change. The Social Democratic and Labour Party, which aims to play the postnationalist card in Northern Irish politics, has seen its fortunes degenerate as the more vociferous nationalist politics of Sinn Féin emerge as the dominant voice for Irish unity. Given the extent to which its mandate has grown, it would be naive to expect other than that Sinn Féin will push strongly for the dissolution of Northern Ireland.

It is evident that the BA endeavours to create the chimera whereby 'each side' will realise some of its critical goals and political objectives without being seen to 'lose face'. This attempt to foster some kind of political equilibrium has been undermined, however, by the growth in support for the Democratic Unionist Party (DUP) and Sinn Féin. In the eyes of the DUP, the Ulster Unionists are party to a 'process of surrender and duplicity'. For Sinn Féin, the 'refusal' of unionists to treat them 'equally' simply strengthens the argument that unionism can be reformed only when the British state removes itself from Ireland. In such a politically unstable process, the capacity to eliminate the causes of conflict is underwhelmed by ethnocentric power and its legitimisation by the BA.

It was not unexpected that the growing size and political influence of
Northern Ireland's nationalist community have continued to be accompanied by a violent loyalist backlash. The depth of sectarianism within
social life in the six counties means that the BA cannot overturn perceptions of religious discrimination and the belief that communities are being
socially and culturally marginalised, due to either intransigent unionism
or belligerent Irish nationalism. A significant section of the unionist community has already lost faith in a political process which has not delivered
the demise of militant republicanism. It is true that sectarianism plays a
part in the unwillingness of many unionists to accept Sinn Féin in
government and other political changes. However, there is also, within
unionism, a coherent sense of being in political and cultural decline. For
republicans, the recent growth in loyalist violence and the inability of
the Police Service of Northern Ireland to protect Catholic communities
are also primary concerns. It would seem that Northern Irish society has
shifted from intense violence to a version of warfare by proxy.

This latter form of war is based upon the conviction that ideological
confrontation must be maintained via the medium of ethnocentric
resource competition and cultural contestation. It is undeniable that a
significant section of the electorate in Northern Ireland wish to promote
ethnic chauvinism despite the good intentions spelt out in the BA. In a
society driven by the memory of a violent and not so distant past, the
building of trust can be destroyed by the reality of continual and
meaningful discord. The problem that remains is that what is determined
as ethnic chauvinism is understood by its promoters as rational and
valid. There is still a need to understand that the perpetual realities of
political intransigence and cultural contestation, which surround job
allocation, marching, decommissioning, flag bearing and policing, are
ever present.[15]

In recent years, both Sinn Féin and the Ulster Unionists have become
involved in the practice of stimulating ethnosectarian rivalries. Republicans have, of course, had to find ways to camouflage the concessions
that they have made. Determining ways in which to tolerate unionist
intransigence has been a central problem in terms of selling political
morphology to the republican 'heartlands'. It is evident, during the recent
upsurge in loyalist violence, that dissident republicans aim to usurp the
Provisional IRA's mantle as defenders of the republican people. Thus
far, the Provisionals and Sinn Féin have not taken the bait of a loyalist
violence which is dedicated to enticing them back to war. But, as a result
of such violence, they must still play political hardball if they are to
remain ideologically dominant.

However, the reality of unionist intransigence and the failure of an
'acceptable' policing agenda to emerge provide Sinn Féin with the opportunity to remobilise resistance to unionism and the British state. It is

one of the many ironies of Northern Irish politics that Sinn Féin can champion the cause of the oppressed and culturally marginalised even though they themselves are a central part of the political system.

Unionism's central problem is that it has not come to terms with the collapse of its authority. Political decline, demographic change and the loss of generations of those who graduated in British universities have all added to the sense of sociocultural fatalism among a significant section of the unionist people. The negativity of a unionist politics tied to the demonisation of Irishness remains pronounced and unmistakable. Within the more fundamentalist strands of unionist consciousness, the Republic of Ireland remains a place that must remain apart. Within such a discourse of unionist purity lies the inability to detach the politics of militant republicanism from those of other, rather different versions of nationalism.

The fact that Northern Ireland's constitutional future will be dictated by 'plebiscite politics' is potentially troublesome. Given the recent actions of loyalist paramilitaries and rejectionist unionists, it is evident that they interpret political change as favouring the cultural, political, economic and social ascendancy of the Catholic population. Unlike the Ulster Unionists, who argue that there is no guarantee that demographic shifts will bring about unification, other unionists argue that the unionist community is being sold out because of the desire within official circles to 'appease' the republican cause. This 'appeasement' of republicanism is heralded as an example of how the unionist community will be treated in a united Ireland. The conclusion at which the more militant elements of Ulster loyalism have arrived is that it has become necessary to make Northern Ireland ungovernable, in order to dilute the desire of the citizens of the Republic of Ireland to accept unification.

The growth in protests against Orange marches, the 'rumble in the Colombian jungle',[16] the emergence of Sinn Féin as the dominant voice of northern nationalism, the disbandment of the Royal Ulster Constabulary, gun running from Florida and the fact that decommissioning has been less than conclusive have each eaten away at unionist resolve to engage in civic politics. It is also the case that most unionists now speak of their 'alienation' within the northern state in a manner that was until recently the preserve of republicans.

A more positive political outcome was expected, given that devolution, regionalisation and the evolution of 'postmodern' politics are often understood as having the capacity to unravel the complexities and force of ethnic affiliation and social class. The very forces of political belonging which are supposed to be moderated by globalisation, social mobility and wider patterns of Europeanisation[17] continue to prove remarkably resilient in the context of the six counties. The realities of power sharing in Northern Ireland clearly indicate how the politics of modification and consensus building can run up against the bulwark and intricacies of ethnic belonging. Evidently, the power of cultural memory, perceptions of victimhood and notions of cultural dissipation still influence the politics of constitutional change in places as diverse as Belfast, Bilbao and Belgrade. As argued here, it is important to understand that the establishment of positive and inclusive state forms demands more than simply the creation of better economic conditions and tokenistic political change. Within the Northern Irish context, it is evident that the BA cannot, in the short term, resolve political antagonisms which are rooted in the perpetuation of partition, armed paramilitary groups and the territorialisation of cultural and economic claims.[18]

The past in the present

The impasse over decommissioning and policing, and hostility to the BA, illustrate how wider issues of social exclusion and subordination are often easily marginalised by political machination. In this sense, decommissioning and police reform have become obstacles to concrete social and economic change in the different and diverse communities of Northern Ireland. The recent growth in community violence and the re-engagement of the Ulster Freedom Fighters in random sectarian violence indicate how supposed political settlement is paralleled by actual sectarian discord. Contemporary history is still being forged by the reproduction of sectarian labelling and habituation.

Despite political morphology, sectarianism is being redefined via new forms of community expression. In a zero-sum logic of sectarian acknowledgement, the growth in Sinn Féin's vote indicates to many unionists that the 'other' community increasingly favours a more belligerent form of nationalism. In the eyes of republicans, the unwillingness of unionists to distinguish between Sinn Féin and the IRA and to accept the participation of the former in government articulates an aversion to having 'a Taig about the place'. The inability to stop or even adequately denounce the activities of militant loyalists is also seen as a refusal of unionism to drag itself away from established sectarian constructs. All are signs that both communities are seeking things that remain politically divergent.

One conclusion from the foregoing discussion is that the BA does not adequately challenge the populace to distance themselves from sectarianised belongings. The desire to dilute political hostilities is meaningless, given that to do so would be to accept some form of political defeat. However, the most fundamental problem is that sectarianism is reproduced via a range of institutionalised forms and lived experiences.

Crucial to any understanding of ethnosectarianism in Northern Ireland is an interpretation of how the spatialisation of fear, threat and attack has created an extensive sequence of sectarian enclaves. Modes of religious segregation have striven to create and promote ethnic homogeneity via complex modes of territorial separation.[19] Darby[20] notes:

> Just as one cannot hope to understand the Northern Ireland conflict without an acquaintance with its history, it is impossible to appreciate its pervasiveness without some knowledge of the background, extent and effect of residential segregation between Catholics and Protestants. This is both the cause and consequence of the province's history of turbulence.

The perpetual search for spatial enclosure and socio-spatial demarcation is clearly tied to Sack's notion[21] that the creation of illusionary spaces produces '[b]oundaries which are virtually impermeable [and which] isolate communities, create fear and hate of others, and push in the directions of equality and justice'.

A central part in the construction of identity in contexts of conflict is not merely to use space to promote ontological togetherness but to compact time and space through the generation of a sense of connection to place. The spatialisation of ethnic affiliation is understood as both a directive of community space and a classification of ethnosectarian belonging.[22] Religious segregation is held to actualise constructs of identity via the mediation of inclusion and exclusion and the subjective geographies of necessary separation.

Continuously being remade, the construction of territorial division encapsulates distinct, eulogised and communally devoted places, circumscribed by their very difference from the territorial 'other'. An understanding of the mechanisms through which the ethnic other is excluded and the 'home territory' cast as pure and uncontaminated are essential to comprehending conflict and conflict resolution.[23] A devotion to community underpins the casting of the 'other' community as treacherous, dangerous and untrustworthy. Parallel to this is the compulsion to construct the 'communal self' as trusted, safe, culturally homogeneous and morally superior. Therefore, the demonisation of the 'other' community as violent and repressive is conditioned by a celebration of one's own community as sacred, politically resistant, honourable, dependable and culturally wholesome. A central aspect of the reproduction of religious segregation has been to celebrate the loyalty and devotion afforded to the 'communal self' and the cultural and political spirit that has emerged within 'interfaced' areas.

Interfaces had historically operated as arenas within which the performance of ethnosectarian violence was both assembled and conspicuous. This work was also crucial in that it verified how interfaces rendered communities as victims of petrified parameters. The prominence of interfaces in the late 1960s and 1970s, and the influx of refugees into ethnic enclaves, due to the resurgence of violent conflict, created sanctuary spaces that mapped 'safe' and 'unsafe' areas for local people.[24] The physical process of ethnicising space led to the subjective coding of the 'other' side of the interface as sources of deviance, transgression and marginality.[25] The imagined symbolic purity of the 'communal enclave' and the symbolic impurity of the 'collective other' were further reinforced when the ethnic refuge was threatened and abused via violence, intimidation and paramilitary or state targeting.

As a result of ethnic enclaving and the growth in violence from the late 1960s, communities tended to face in on themselves. Those who wished to promote cross-community contact and conflict resolution were, in many instances, deemed to be betrayers of the enclave. Evidently, the potential for conflict resolution was destroyed by the same spatial devices that enacted violence.[26] As Downey notes:[27]

> Within ten years of violence most forms of pan-cultural contact had been dissolved. Safe places for Protestants and Catholics to meet had all but evaporated. Friendships that had spanned decades could no longer be upheld. Children of those who had once had friendships on 'the other side' knew nothing of what had been. Fear, mistrust, and hatred made pluralism a dirty word.

Furthermore, violence ensured that communities looked inwards as the 'collective self' became a victim of a 'ravaging' 'collective other'. In order to rationalise reactive violence, communities needed to create a communicative dimension which not only supported conflict but which mobilised fear as an instrument for survival. Fear of being attacked and the existence of a complex mosaic of ethnic enclaves meant that those living in districts where the conflict was most pronounced needed to develop a comprehensive understanding of implied threat and menace.[28] The evolution of complex modes of segregation and habituation not only created safety consciousness but also stimulated the reading of the 'other' community as transgressive, deviant and marginal.

Although incidents such as the infamous dispute at the Holy Cross girls' school are presented simply as acts of mindless thuggery, it is evident that fear and a sense of cultural dissipation drive the use of violence. More importantly, a new generation of young men who see their role as defenders of their community has emerged as a result of tit for tat violence. In a sense, new forms of violence are encouraging new and robust modes of sectarian deployment.

Table 11.1 provides evidence of the growth of sectarian attitudes among 800 respondents who live in the most segregated areas of Belfast.[29] These areas constitute over sixty per cent of the city's population. In 1999, there was evidently confidence among both communities that positive political change was taking place. Around thirty per cent of both sections

Table 11.1 Community attitudes to peace building and reconciliation, 1999 and 2002: percentage of respondents affirming the survey statements

	Catholics		Protestants	
	1999	*2002*	*1999*	*2002*
Relationships with the 'other' community have improved since 1994	34	18	28	11
The 'other' community has become less sectarian since 1994	28	21	22	18
The 'other' community wishes to cause my community harm	19	38	27	49
I am less afraid to enter areas dominated by the 'other' religion since 1994	32	22	31	18
Both communities are committed to peace building in equal measure	38	18	29	14

of the population believed that intercommunal relations had improved since the ceasefires of 1994. By 2002, the proportion of respondents who believed that such relationships had been enhanced had significantly declined. This decline was mirrored in the falling proportion of respondents who believed that the 'other' community was less sectarian, or that crossing territorial barriers had become less difficult. In 1999, a mere nineteen per cent of Catholics and twenty-seven per cent of Protestants believed that the 'other' community wished to harm their community. By 2002, these shares had grown to thirty-eight per cent and forty-nine per cent, respectively. In addition, the share of Catholics and Protestants who believed that both communities were committed to peace building halved during the same period. Table 11.1 indicates that sectarian prejudice and fears that were already manifest in 1999 have grown since.

Given the realities of ethnopolitical separation, it is perturbing that the BA does not mention the term 'sectarianism'. Instead, the BA talks of bringing together the 'two traditions' via endorsing the principle of 'party of esteem'. The term 'sectarianism' was not invoked because it is highly subjective and loaded with political meaning. Yet it is the most significant political discourse within Northern Irish society. A fundamental problem is that the power of memory and the reappearance of violence continue to shape the reproduction of sectarian atavism. The prospect of benign developments in the future have little meaning for communities that have ample reasons for distrusting each other in the here and now.

Conclusions: a nation once again?

Commentators such as Ruth Dudley Edwards see the ability to 'progress' in a 'new world' as symptomatic of an ability to shift away from outdated nationalist values and political dogmas.[30] The logic of this and other such arguments is that ideological 'backwardness' is contingent upon significant flaws in collective psyches.

There is no doubting that a nationalism premised upon an intimacy between the Irish state and the Catholic Church has become rather less evident. However, in spite of important recent changes in the nature of Irish nationalism, the Republic of Ireland falls a good deal short of being a postnationalist utopia.

Incidents such as the booing at Lansdowne Road of an international footballer who happened to play for Glasgow Rangers would suggest that a sectarian consciousness persists among the Republic's supporters. The appearance of the Angelus on the national television station intimates that Catholicism continues to exert a certain influence in the affairs of the twenty-six counties. The continuing ban on abortion and clerical control of teaching indicate that the Catholic Church retains consider-able authority. Recent Church pronouncements that all children who attend their schools must be christened and that their parents must be 'good' Catholics provide echoes of the De Valera era. The fact that such prescriptions failed to create greater political controversy suggests that many citizens of the supposedly modern and pluralist Republic still have some sympathy for the view of the Catholic Church as a moral arbiter.

Bertie Ahern, the leader of this supposedly new and postnationalising society, appears to be working towards a more explicitly nationalist agenda. His attack upon revisionism at Bodenstown[31] and his desire to orches-trate the reinterment of Kevin Barry and nine other IRA men executed during the war for independence are episodes which suggest that he is engaged in an ideological conflict with Sinn Féin over who is a 'true' republican. The growth in Sinn Féin's vote south of the border will con-tinue as it develops and extends support from within the nationalist hardcore. Lest we all forget, two IRA hunger strikers were elected to the Dáil in 1981, compared with one in the supposedly more belligerent North.[32] The election of these hunger strikers put Fianna Fáil out of power and reminded them of the need to keep a closer eye on the chang-ing tides of nationalist opinion.

Most people in the Republic of Ireland engaged in an understated nationalism during the conflict in Northern Ireland. Most citizens switched off from the scenes of death and mayhem. Few openly discussed northern affairs, as to do so could lead to being condemned as a fellow traveller with the IRA. However, the decline in violence and the shift of Sinn Féin into civil politics means that the opportunity to express serious opinions about Northern Ireland is now rather greater than before. Anecdotal and personal experiences suggest that there has, in recent years, been a growth in anti-unionist prejudice in the Republic. The recent rehabilitation of Michael Collins, an individual who had previously virtually disappeared from Irish history, and the controversy that attended the proposal that the Orange Order should march in the centre of Dublin both suggest that nationalism continues to exercise an appeal within the twenty-six counties. Each of these events merely provides rejectionist unionists with the ammunition they need to preach that the Republic of Ireland remains a monocultural and sectarian state.

The desire for unification may not be the most visible part of public discourse in the Irish Republic but it is, nonetheless, an important emotional demand. However, if unification ever becomes a serious proposition, then it is possible that nationalist agendas would come to the fore.

There is a strong possibility that the prospect of a united Ireland would be accompanied by a loyalist backlash. Attacks south of the border would, in all likelihood, form part of loyalist militants' campaign to prevent unification. A bombing campaign in Dublin would provide the conditions under which ethnosectarianism might grow. As the drift towards a united Ireland accelerated, unionists would seek to highlight the sectarianism perceived within the twenty-six counties. The political agenda of unionists prior to a united Ireland would be to demolish the arguments of those seeking to dissolve the border. Such an approach would, within the Republic of Ireland, draw Irish nationalism out. It is, perhaps, only when nationalism in the Republic is challenged that its true depth and nature will emerge.

Within a united Ireland, unionists would have significant political power. They would undoubtedly work to gain as many resources as they could for the north of Ireland. A central allegation that might gain ground within the twenty-six counties would be that the unionist community was being treated with undue generosity. Such accusations might be levelled in the context of tax rises introduced to support the northern economy. The potential for anti-unionism to emerge before and during the early phases of a united Ireland could be substantial.

The fundamental problem for the Irish Republic is that a united Ireland will bring with it the forms and issues of political engagement that have been hitherto associated solely with the six counties. Over a million politically motivated citizens would suddenly become part of a society in which social fractures have been carefully stage-managed. Unionists would strongly advocate equality for their community and, in so doing, could serve to foment socioreligious tensions unseen since partition. Loyalists are shrewd enough to know that violence and the threat of destabilising the Irish economy through ensuring that foreign investors were dissuaded from locating in the Republic are potential trump cards.

Either way, it is clear that unionism would seek concessions that could cause social disharmony. The obvious impact of unification would be that the north would become not only a place which was no longer apart but a place that was more politically important than any other region outside Dublin. People in the Republic may pretend to be benign about Northern Ireland but that will all change if and when a united Ireland is realised and brings with it new forms of territorial division and political dispute. The only thing that can, perhaps, be said with any certainty about Irish history, then, is that it is rather far from being at an end.

Notes

1 R. Kearney, *Postnationalist Ireland: Politics, Culture, Philosophy* (London: Routledge, 1997).
2 B. O'Leary, 'Comparative political science and the British–Irish Agreement', in J. McGarry (ed.), *Northern Ireland and the Divided World: Post-Agreement Northern Ireland in Comparative Perspective* (Oxford: Oxford University Press, 2001), p. 53.
3 Cited by J. McGarry, 'Northern Ireland, civic nationalism and the Good Friday Agreement', in McGarry (ed.), *Northern Ireland and the Divided World*, p. 106.
4 At the time of writing, the Assembly had just been suspended due to allegations concerning spying within the Northern Ireland Office by members of Sinn Féin and the Provisional Irish Republican Army.
5 A. Lijphart, *Patterns of Democracy: Government Forms and Performances in Thirty Six Countries* (New Haven, CT: Yale University Press, 1999); S. Keenan, 'Force of habit', *Red Pepper*, 86 (August 2001), p. 6.
6 T. Nairn, 'Farewell Britannia', *New Left Review*, 2:7 (2001), pp. 55–74.
7 McGarry, 'Northern Ireland, civic nationalism and the Good Friday Agreement'; B. O'Leary, 'The nature of the British–Irish Agreement', *New Left Review*, 233 (1999), pp. 66–96.
8 O'Leary, 'The nature of the British–Irish Agreement'.
9 Nairn, 'Farewell Britannia'.
10 P. Stewart and P. Shirlow, 'Northern Ireland: between war and peace?', *Capital and Class*, 69 (1999), pp. vi–xiv.
11 J. Michie and M. Sheehan, 'The political economy of a divided island', *Cambridge Journal of Economics*, 22 (1998), pp. 243–59.
12 McGarry, 'Northern Ireland, civic nationalism and the Good Friday Agreement'.
13 T. Eagleton, 'Nationalism and the case of Ireland', *New Left Review*, 234 (1999), pp. 67–82.
14 Croke Park is the principal venue and home of the Gaelic Athletic Association. Rule 4 of that organisation bans the playing of 'foreign' games on grounds owned by the GAA. Despite this rule, American football and boxing have been hosted at Croke Park.
15 D. O'Hearn and C. Fischer, *Jobs or Just Promises? The IDB and West Belfast* (Belfast: West Belfast Economic Forum, 1999); D. O'Hearn, S. Porter and A. Harpur, 'Turning agreement to process: republicanism and change in Ireland', *Capital and Class*, 69 (1999), pp. 7–26.

16 Three members of the Provisional Irish Republican Army (Niall Connolly, Martin McCauley and Jim Monaghan) were arrested on 11 August 2001 by the Colombian authorities, which charged them with aiding the Marxist-inspired FARC paramilitary group.

17 Kearney, *Postnationalist Ireland*.

18 Stewart and Shirlow, 'Northern Ireland: between war and peace?'

19 J. Anderson and I. Shuttleworth, 'Sectarian demography, territoriality and political development in Northern Ireland', *Political Geography*, 17 (1999), pp. 187–208; F. Boal and N. Douglas, 'The Northern Ireland problem', in F. Boal and N. Douglas (eds), *Integration and Division: Geographical Perspectives on the Northern Ireland Problem* (London: Academic Press, 1982); J. Bradley and D. Hamilton, 'Strategy 2010: planning economic development in Northern Ireland', *Regional Studies*, 33 (1999), pp. 885–90.

20 J. Darby, *Intimidation and the Control of Conflict in Northern Ireland* (New York: Syracuse University Press, 1987), p. 25.

21 D. Sack, *Homo Geographicus: A Framework for Action, Awareness and Moral Concern* (Baltimore: Johns Hopkins University Press, 1998), p. 254.

22 N. Jarman, *Material Conflicts: Parades and Visual Displays in Northern Ireland* (London: Berg, 1977).

23 Anderson and Shuttleworth, 'Sectarian demography, territoriality and political development in Northern Ireland'; P. Shirlow and M. McGovern, 'Language, discourse and dialogue: Sinn Féin and the Irish peace process', *Political Geography*, 17 (1998), pp. 171–86; P. Shirlow and I. Shuttleworth, 'Who is going to toss the burgers? Social class and the reconstruction of the Northern Irish economy', *Capital and Class*, 69 (1999), pp. 27–46.

24 O. Downey, *A Meaningful Society* (Barchester: Young's Press, 2001).

25 D. Morrow, 'Suffering for righteousness sake? Fundamentalist Protestantism and Ulster politics', in P. Shirlow and M. McGovern (eds), *Who Are the People? Unionism, Protestantism and Loyalism in Northern Ireland* (London: Pluto, 1997).

26 Boal and Douglas, 'The Northern Ireland problem'.

27 Downey, *A Meaningful Society*, p. 19.

28 F. Burton, *The Politics of Legitimacy: Struggles in a Belfast Community* (London: Routledge, 1978).

29 These data are taken from ongoing research conducted by the author in interface areas in Belfast. A full account of the findings will appear in a forthcoming text.

30 Ruth Dudley Edwards, 'We must not take our eyes off the IRA', *Daily Mail*, 24 October 2001, p. 18.

31 Bodenstown graveyard contains the remains of Wolfe Tone, a founding member of the United Irishmen and icon of the Irish republican movement. The graveyard forms an important part of the Irish republican landscape.

32 Bobby Sands was elected to the Westminster constituency of Fermanagh and South Tyrone.

Index

abortion, 99–103, 204
accounting procedures, 19–20
Aer Lingus, 56, 117
age dependency ratio, 60–1
Ahern, Bertie, 204
Akutagawa, M., 182
Allen, Kieran, 102–3
Amnesty International, 86, 88
Ansbacher accounts, 69, 71
Aquinas, St Thomas, 152
Association of Secondary Teachers Ireland, 67
asylum seekers, 75–9, 82–5, 88, 118
authenticity, 146–7

Barrett, A., 47
Barry, Kevin, 204
Baudrillard, Jean, 144–50 *passim*
Beauty Queen of Leenane, The 132–3
Beck, U., 122, 135
Belfast Agreement, 194–7, 200, 203
Benjamin, Walter, 123, 130–1
Berman, Marshall, 122–5, 135
Binchey, Meave, 126
Blair, Tony, 9
Boorstin, D., 150
Bourdieu, Pierre, 77, 83, 148–9, 152, 177–8
Boyzone, 130
Bradley, J., 57
Brandt, Barbara, 166–7
Breakweather, Sarah, 140

Brenner, Gunther, 139–40
Brittan, Leon, 64
budget deficits, 65
budget surpluses, 50
Burke, Ray, 69–70

capitalism, 7, 63–4, 90, 107, 178
Capra, Fritjof, 171
Cassells, Peter, 62
Catholic Church, 14, 83, 101, 103, 125, 178, 196–7, 204
'Celtic Tiger' metaphor, 3–4, 38, 74, 95, 115
Cement Roadstone Holdings, 69
Chatterjee, P., 179–80
Cherish, 98
child custody cases, 105
childcare, 97–8, 105–7, 161–2
Chomsky, N., 136
class divisions, 98–9, 179
Clinton, Bill, 56
Cobblestone, The (Dublin pub), 150
Coca Cola (company), 19
Collins, Michael, 205
colonial legacy, 112–13
comedy, 133–4
commodification, 25
Conference of Religious in Ireland, 68, 98
Conlon, C., 99
Connolly, James, 188
Conradh na Gaeilge, 179–80
Co-operation North, 129

corporatism, 11–12, 21–2
  competitive, 62–9 *passim*
Costello, Declan, 102
Crick, M., 145
Cronin, M., 145–6, 151
cultural capital, 148–9
cultural political economy, 113–19
  passim
culture, 110–11, 176–7, 186–8
  globalisation of, 129–30, 135, 143,
    148, 150, 152

Daly, Herman, 167
Darby, J., 201
De Valera, Eamon, 114, 117, 196,
  204
de Ville, Claude, 139–40
'defensive spending', 160
Democratic Unionist Party, 197
demographic change, 60
dependency, economic, 20–1, 59
  see also age dependency ratio
depression, 169
Dillon, L., 99
discourse analysis, 158–72
domestic violence, 104–5
Doolin, 127–8
Douthwaite, Richard, 167–8, 170
Downey, O., 202
downshifting, 157–8
Doyle, Roddy, 119
dual labour markets, 81
Dublin, 2, 140–52
Dubliners, 131
Dudley Edwards, Ruth, 204
D'unbelievables, the, 133–4
Dunkerely, James, 112
Durkheim, E., 124–5, 131, 139

Eagleton, Terry, 118
Economic and Social Research Institute (ESRI), 50, 59, 61
economic growth, 3, 13, 15, 18–21,
  26–9, 34–41, 47, 51, 56, 166–9
  and employment, 41–3,
economic migration, 79–84
Economist, The, 59
Eircom, 175–8, 188

employment, 22–4
  and growth, 41–3
  of women, 95–8, 107
'end of history' metaphor, 6–7, 10, 16,
  29, 176
European single market, 37, 52
European Union, 62–5, 95–6, 115

Faust, 123–7
Feifer, M., 146
feminist analysis, 95
Fianna Fáil, 83, 100
Flatly, Michael, 127
Foras Áiseanna Saothair, 80
foreign investment, 37–41
Foreign Policy (magazine), 110
Foucault, Michel, 142, 151
Freud, Sigmund, 133
Friel, Brian, 126
Fukuyama, Francis, 6–8, 10, 176

Gardiner, Kevin, 3
Gateway (company), 56
Gellner, E., 142, 187
gender roles, 165–6, 171
Gibbons, Luke, 116
Giddens, Anthony, 7–10, 14, 122, 135
global studies, 113
globalisation, 7, 29, 43–4, 52, 64,
  110–20, 122, 124, 141
  index of, 110
  of Irish culture, 129–30, 135, 143,
    148–52
Gluaiseacht Cearta Sibhialta na Gaeltachta, 181–2
Goethe, Johann Wolfgang von, 123–
  4, 127
Gramsci, Antonio, 114
Great Hunger, the, 125–6, 143
gross national product and gross domestic product, 40, 53
  components of, 45–6

Habermas, Jurgen, 65, 136
habitus, 134, 148, 152
Hall, S., 88–9
Handy, Charles, 169
Hardt, M., 176, 182, 187–8

Harney, Mary, 79–80
Haughey, Charles, 69, 124
health care, 49, 69, 81
hegemony, 136
Heise, Lori, 105
Henderson, Hazel, 167
Hobsbawm, E., 142
Hourigan, N., 182
housing, 49
How Was It For You? study, 156–7
Hughes, G., 47
Hussey, Gemma, 116, 118

imagined communities, 83, 89, 114, 176–7
immigration, 27–8, 74–6, 84, 90, 118
    see also asylum seekers; economic migration
income, distribution of, 47
Industrial Development Authority, 57
inequality, 22, 47–52, 66–9, 74, 98
information technology (IT) sector, 36–9, 56–7
Intel Corporation, 21, 38, 115
International Monetary Fund, 29, 36
investment, 37–43, 47
Ireland on Sunday, 101
Irish Congress of Trade Unions, 96
Irish Development Authority, 116
Irish language, 176–88
Irish National Organisation of the Unemployed, 99
Irish Refugee Council, 78, 88
Irish Times, The, 103
Irish Tourist Board, 74
Irishness, 2, 25–6, 83–4, 89, 117–19, 148, 192–4, 199

Jameson, Fredric, 29
Joyce, James, 126, 131, 140, 146–7

Kavanagh, Patrick, 125–7
Keitel, Harvey, 140
Keller, B., 63–4
Kenny, John, 133–4
Kiberd, Declan, 114, 117
Korten, David, 170

Labour Force Survey, 98
labour market flexibility, 22–3, 42, 57–8, 64, 81, 97
labour market segmentation, 47
    see also dual labour markets
labour shortages, 79–81
Lane, Robert E., 167
Lash, S., 122, 135
Lees, Sue, 106
Lemass, Sean, 128–9
liberalisation, 48, 64, 70, 95
lifestyle, 155–7, 168
Living in Ireland Survey, 97
Lonesome West, The, 131–2
Lowenthal, D., 143, 146, 153
Lowry, Michael, 69–70, 124

McAleese, Mary, 118
MacCannell, D., 145
McDonagh, Martin, 131, 134
McDonald's, 141
McGarry, John, 194–5
Macnas, 175–6
macroeconomic stability, 36–7, 45, 48
MacSharry, Ray, 11, 13
McVeigh, Robbie, 112
Mahon, E., 99
Marx, Karl, 124–7, 131, 135, 148, 179
Microsoft, 44
Miles, R., 87
'mindful markets', 170–1
modernisation theory, 4–9, 12–14, 17–18, 26
Monbiot, George, 9
Morgan Stanley (investment bank), 115
Muintir na Gaeltachta, 181
multinational corporations, 18–21, 35–46 *passim*, 51–2, 115

Nash, Denison, 144
National City Brokers, 60
National Competitiveness Council, 70, 80
national identity, 83, 90, 117, 119, 142–3
nationalism, 15–16, 26–7, 75, 83–4, 89–90, 120, 179, 192, 204–5

Negri, A., 176, 178, 182, 187–8
neo-liberalism, 8–10, 35, 43, 48, 51, 57, 61, 64, 70–1
New Labour, 9
Nice Treaty (2001), 62, 65
Nolan, B., 47, 98
Northern Ireland
   Assembly, 196–7
   peace process, 26–7, 132
   power sharing, 194, 199

O'Brien, Flan, 126
Ó Cadhain, Máirtín, 179, 186–8
O'Connell, Maurice, 56
O'Connell, Michael, 14–15
O'Connor, Barbara, 140, 153
O'Connor, Gussie, 127
O'Donohue, John, 84
O'Flynn, Noel, 85
O'Hearn, Denis, 112, 115–16
Ó hIfearnáin, T., 183
O'Leary, B., 194
O'Leary, Michael, 117
O'Malley, E., 43
O'Regan, Brendan, 128–9
Orange Order, 205
Organisation for Economic Cooperation and Development (OECD), 36, 70
Ó Riain, S., 43–4
O'Toole, Fintan, 62, 118

Pfizer (company), 39
Police Service of Northern Ireland, 198
politics, attitudes to, 166
Porter House (Dublin pub), 151–2
postmodernism, 5–6, 88, 122, 140–52 *passim*
poverty, 23, 47–50, 68, 74, 98–9, 168–9
Pravda (Dublin bar), 146–9
Private Finance Initiative, 9, 70
privatisation, 64–5, 70
productivity, 44–5, 67
profit-shifting, 21, 37–8, 40, 44
Provisional IRA, 198
pub culture, 141, 147, 151–2
public ownership, 64

public services, 23, 48–9, 69
public spending, 65

quality of life, 156–7, 165–6

racism, 27–8, 74–6, 81–90, 118
   institutional, 76–8, 88
Raidió na Gaeltachta, 181–5, 187
Raidió Teilifís Éireann (RTE), 182, 184–5
Rattansi, A., 88
reflexive modernisation, 122
refugee status, 76, 78, 84, 89–90, 118
Riverdance, 127
Roach, Stephen, 58
Robinson, Mary, 118, 126
Ronan, Johnny, 129
Ryanair, 117

Sack, D., 201
Said, Edward, 151
Sayad, A., 85
sectarianism, 193–204 *passim*
Sennett, Richard, 169
Seosamh Ó Cuaig, 185–6
September 11th, 2001, 6, 29, 59, 71, 117
Sexual Abuse and Violence in Ireland (report), 106
sexual morality, 14, 103
sexual violence, 104–6
Share, P., 16
Short, Pat, 133–4
simulation, 146–7, 150
single European currency, 64
single European market, 64
Sinn Féin, 193–4, 197–200, 204
Small Firms Association, 79
social change, 16–18, 28, 134, 165, 172
Social Democratic and Labour Party of Northern Ireland, 197
social exclusion, 87
social partnership, 11–12, 21–2, 37, 42, 62–71
   myth of, 66–70
social security, 68
social services, 49

social unity, 136
software industry, 44
Spencer Dock, 129
Storries, B., 63–4
Sum, Ngai-Ling, 113
Supermacs, 130
Sweden, 65
Sweeney, Paul, 11–12, 59

taxation, 49–51, 68–71, 87, 97–8
  corporate, 19, 35, 37–8, 49, 52,
    110
Teilifís na Gaelige, 181–7
Telecom Éireann, 175–8, 188
TG4 *see* Teilifís na Gaelige
Thatcher, Margaret, 135
'third way' politics, 9
Thorne, Brian, 168–9
Thrift, Nigel, 113
tourism, 143–6
Tovey, H., 16
trade unions, 70, 97
traditional practices and beliefs, 17,
    26–7, 116–19, 125, 142–3, 176
transfer prices, 38, 53
transnational corporations *see* multi-
    national corporations
Travers, John, 12
Trimble, David, 193

U2, 119, 126
Ulysses, 140
unification of Ireland, 16, 193–7,
    205–6

unionism, 196–200, 205–6
United Nations, 75, 89–90
  High Commissioner for Refugees,
    78
United States, 4–6, 23, 29, 34–40
    passim, 51, 61–3, 115, 119
  1990s boom in, 57–9, 70–1
Urry, John, 119, 146

Viagra, 39
visa controls, 79–80

wage restraint, 58, 67–9, 87
Walsh, Louis, 130
Waters, John, 103–5
Waters, Malcolm, 113
Weber, Max, 8, 125, 131, 136
welfare, measurement of, 52
welfare state provision, 65
Westlife, 126, 130
Whelehan, Harry, 102
Whitaker, T. K., 115
White, Padraic, 11, 13
Wilde, Oscar, 130
Wittgenstein, Ludwig, 89
women in Irish society, 95–107
Women on Waves Project, 100
work
  attitudes to, 160–1, 164–5
  hierarchy of, 161
work permits, 79–81, 89
World Health Organisation, 169

X case, 100–2